HNC HND BUSINESS

Core Unit 4:

Organisations, Competition and Environment

Course Book

New in this August 2002 edition

- **Updated for recent developments**

- **New examples**

PUBLISHING

EDEXCEL HNC & HND BUSINESS

First edition 2000
Second edition August 2002

ISBN 07517 7061 2 (previous edition 7517 7034 5)

British Library Cataloguing-in Publication Data
A catalogue record for this book is available from the British Library

Printed in Great Britain by Ashford Colour Press, Gosport, Hants

Published by

BPP Publishing Limited

Aldine House, Aldine Place

London W12 8AW

www.bpp.com

We are grateful to Edexcel for permission to reproduce the Guidelines in
this text.

CONTENTS

INTRODUCTION

The HNC and HND qualifications in Business are very demanding. The suggested content, set out by Edexcel in guidelines for each unit, includes topics which are normally covered at degree level. Students therefore need books which get straight to the core of these topics, and which build upon their existing knowledge and experience. BPP's series of Course Books have been designed to meet that need.

This book has been written specifically for Unit 4: *Organisations, Competition and Environment*. It covers the Edexcel guidelines and suggested content in full, and includes the following features.

- The Edexcel guidelines

- A study guide explaining the key features of the book and how to get the most from your studies

- A glossary and index

Each chapter contains:

- An introduction and study objectives

- Summary diagrams and signposts, to guide you through the chapter

- Numerous activities, topics for discussion, definitions and examples

- A chapter roundup, a quick quiz with answers, answers to activities and an assignment (with answer guidelines at the end of the book)

BPP Publishing are the leading providers of targeted texts for professional qualifications. Our customers need to study effectively. They cannot afford to waste time. They expect clear, concise and highly-focused study material. This series of Course Books for HNC and HND Business has been designed and produced to fulfil those needs.

BPP Publishing
August 2002

Titles in this series:

Core Unit 1	Marketing (8/00)
Core Unit 2	Managing Financial Resources (8/02)
Core Unit 3	Organisations and Behaviour (8/00)
Core Unit 4	Organisations, Competition and Environment (8/02)
Core Unit 5	Quantitative Techniques for Business (8/02)
Core Unit 6	Legal and Regulatory Framework (8/02)
Core Unit 7	Management Information Systems (8/02)
Core Unit 8	Business Strategy (8/00)
Option Units 9-12	Business & Finance (8/02)
Option Units 13-16	Business & Management (1/01)
Option Units 17-20	Business & Marketing (1/01)
Option Units 21-24	Business & Personnel (1/01)

For more information, or to place an order, please call 020 8740 2211, or fill in the order form at the back of this book.

If you would like to send in your comments on this book, please turn to the review form on the last page.

EDEXCEL GUIDELINES FOR CORE UNIT 4: ORGANISATIONS, COMPETITION AND ENVIRONMENT

Description of the Unit

The aim of this unit is to encourage students to investigate issues concerning the interaction of organisations and the environment they face, in particular directing focus on the environment in a national and European context. The unit also equips students with an understanding of the context in which organisations function. Additionally, it provides for the development of a solid base of understnading of the parameters within which organisations act that can be built upon in further untis.

Summary of outcomes

To achieve this unit a student must:

1 Identify the **objectives and purpose of organisations**

2 Investigate the key features of the **local and national economy** in which organisations operate

3 Investigate the main **external market factors** which may influence the organisation

4 Explore the significance of the **European dimension** for UK-based organisations

Outcomes and assessment criteria

The learning outcomes and the criteria used to assess them are shown in the table below.

Outcomes	Assessment criteria
	To achieve each outcome a student must demonstrate the ability to:
1 Identify the **objectives and purposes of organisations**	• Identify a range of objectives appropriate to an organisation • Identify three stakeholder objectives in an organisation and evaluate the extent to which they are achieved • Explain the responsibilities of an organisation and the strategies used to meet them

Outcomes	Assessment criteria
2 Investigate the key features of the **local and national economy** in which organisations operate	• Explain the major features of an economic system • Analyse differing views of the role of the state and their implications • Discuss the impact of two policies on an organisation • Investigate the significance of a regional or local development issue and the impact on an organisation
3 Investigate the main **external market factors** which may influence the organisation	• Explain the different market structures • Use three different examples to illustrate the relationship between market forces and organisational responses • Explain the possible ways that an organisation may gain competitive advantage
4 Explore the significance of the **European dimension** for UK-based organisations	• Explain the features of the European Union • Identify two policies of the European Union and analyse the impact on a UK-based organisation • Analyse the arguments for and against UK entry into the European Monetary Union • Analyse the challenges and opportunities to UK businesses of enlargement of EU member states

Generating evidence

Evidence of outcomes may be in the form of written or oral assignments/test.

Evidence is likely to be produced at outcome level although opportunities exist for covering more than one outcome in an assignment. Evidence could include individual or group assignments based around investigations into actual business organisations or case study material. Time-constrained assignments based on case study material could also be included.

Students must demonstrate their understanding of organisational aims and objectives and stakeholder input into the development of these, and also the local, national and European economies and their impact on the organisation. Students must investigate how organisations interact with the external environment.

Content

1 Objectives and purposes of organisations

Types of organisations: private, public, voluntary, charitable

Aims of organisations: profit, market share, ROCE, sales, growth, levels of service, customer/user perceptions

Stakeholders: identification of stakeholders, satisfying stakeholder objectives, the concept of corporate mission

Responsibilities of organisations: physical performance, measuring efficiency, health and safety, equal opportunities, responsibilities relating to consumer and employment law, responsibilities of organisations vis-à-vis the outside world, the national environment, ethical practice

2 Local and national economy

Types of economic system: command, free enterprise, mixed

The role of the state: the spectrum of political philosophy, government social interventions

Government policy: fiscal policy in the UK, monetary policy in the UK, industrial policy in the UK, social welfare policy in the UK, regional and local development issues in the UK, regulatory bodies in the UK (eg Offer, Ofgas, Oftel, Ofwat)

3 External market factors

Market types: perfect competition, monopoly and oligopoly

Market forces and organisational responses: supply and demand, elasticity, customer perceptions and actions, issues relating to supply, cost structures, economies of scale, growth of organisations, the labour market, the impact of technology on organisations, the cultural environment, the concept of competitive advantage

4 European dimension

Organisations: the European Commission, Council of Ministers, Directorates General, the European Council, the European Parliament, decision-making process and the reform of community institutions

The economies of Europe: European Monetary Union (EMU), European Monetary System (EMS), EU budget – import duties and levies, agricultural import levies, VAT, social policy, the Social Chapter, tax harmonisation, Common Agricultural Policy (CAP), regional policy

Links

This unit provides for the development of a solid base of understanding of the parameters within which organisations act, which can be built upon in further units and particularly 'Business Strategy' (Unit 8) and 'European Business' (Unit 29).

This unit offers opportunities for demonstrating Common Skills in Communicating and Managing Tasks and Solving Problems.

Resources

The European Commission Office in London has a Web site which students can access. Also *The European* newspaper, *Euromonitor* and *The Economist Intelligence Unit* are sources of information which will be useful for the EU aspects of this unit.

World Wide Web sites can be useful in providing information and case studies (eg www.bized.bris.ac.uk which provides business case studies appropriate for educational purposes).

Delivery

This unit will probably be delivered as a stand-alone unit, but there are opportunities for some integration of assignments with the units identified above. The extent to which this can be achieved will depend on whether students are completing an HND or HNC and if European Business forms part of the programme.

In the case of the latter unit, Outcome 4 of 'Organisations, Competition and Environment' (Unit 4) clearly provides a basis for linkage. In making decisions about linked assignments, consideration will need to be given to the order in which units are delivered.

STUDY GUIDE

This Course Book gives full coverage of the Edexcel guidelines. It also includes features designed specifically to make learning effective and efficient.

(a) Each chapter begins with a summary diagram which maps out the areas covered by the chapter. There are detailed summary diagrams at the start of each main section of the chapter. You can use the diagrams during revision as a basis for your notes.

(b) After the main summary diagram there is an introduction, which sets the chapter in context. This is followed by learning objectives, which show you what you will learn as you work through the chapter.

(c) Throughout the book, there are special aids to learning. These are indicated by the following symbols.

Signposts guide you through the text, showing how each section connects with the next.

Definitions give the meanings of key terms. The *glossary* at the end of the book summarises these.

Activities help you to test how much you have learnt. An indication of the time you should take on each is given. Answers are given at the end of each chapter.

Topics for discussion are for use in seminars. They give you a chance to share you views with your fellow students. They allow you to highlight holes in your knowledge and to see how others understand concepts. If you have time, try 'teaching' someone the concepts you have learnt in a session. This helps you to remember key points and answering their questions will consolidate your knowledge.

Examples relate what you have learnt to the outside world. Try to think up your own examples as you work through the text.

Chapter roundups present the key information from the chapter in a concise format. Useful for revision.

(d)   The wide **margin** on each page is for your notes. You will get the best out of this book if you interact with it. Write down your thoughts and ideas. Record examples, question theories, add references to other pages in the text and rephrase key points in your own words.

(e)   At the end of each chapter, there is a **chapter roundup**, a **quick quiz** with answers and an **assignment**. Use these to revise and consolidate your knowledge. The chapter roundup summarises the chapter. The quick quiz tests what you have learnt (the answers often refer you back to the chapter so you can look over subjects again). The assignment (with a time guide) allows you to put your knowledge into practice. Answer guidelines for the assignments are at the end of the book.

(f)   At the end of the book, there is a glossary of key terms and an index.

CORE UNIT 4

ORGANISATIONS, COMPETITION AND ENVIRONMENT

Chapter 1:
ORGANISATIONS AND THEIR OBJECTIVES

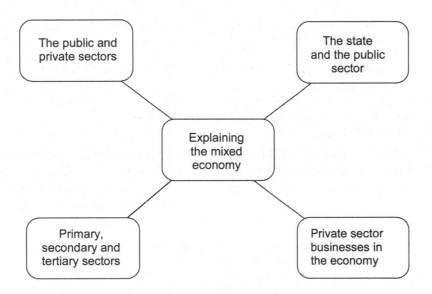

Introduction

This chapter presents an overview of the nature of the UK economy and the sectors of industry within it.

It starts with an introduction to the *mixed economy*. The management of the mixed economy is a function of government, which the government fulfils through its overall economic policy and through legislation to regulate business activities.

Businesses operate in an environment that is subject to constant change. The volatility of this environment means that businesses have to be both reactive and proactive. Economic change influences the objectives of firms as they seek to spot both opportunities for expansion and threats to their existing products or services.

In this chapter we identify differences between the public and private sectors, explain the functions of primary, secondary and tertiary industries and explore the changing balance of power between them.

Your objectives

In this chapter you will learn about:

(a)   The role of the state

(b)   The nature of the public and private sectors

(c)   The nature of the primary, secondary and tertiary sectors

(d)   Business objectives

1 THE PUBLIC AND PRIVATE SECTORS

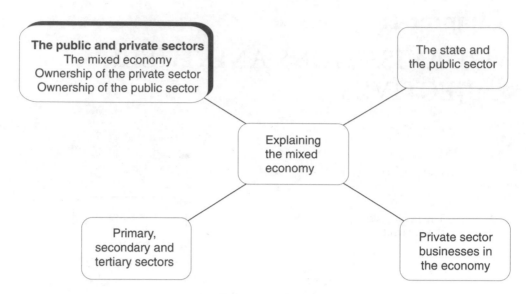

1.1 The mixed economy

All states have to deal with the problem of *scarcity*. There are never enough resources to satisfy all the needs of society. The factors of production - *land, labour, capital and entrepreneurship* - are limited; every country has to make decisions about how to make the best use of the resources it has. This dilemma is known as the economic problem: finite resources and infinite wants.

In order to resolve the dilemma, each state has to decide (a) what it needs to produce, (b) how to produce it and then (c) who will benefit from this production.

In advanced economies there are various ways to deal with these questions of scarcity. Different countries use different approaches or types of economic system.

Definitions

1   *Free enterprise economy* - sometimes called *capitalism*. In this type of economy most decisions are taken through the operation of the market mechanism. Supply and demand and the ability to pay influence decision making. There is very little government intervention in business decision making.

2   *Command economy* - sometimes referred to as state controlled. In this type of economy decisions are taken collectively, usually by central planning committees. The government controls what is produced, how much is produced, the price and who the goods are available to. Decisions are intended to benefit all members of society. Citizens all contribute to the common good of the state. There is a lot of state intervention in this type of economic system.

3   The *mixed economy*. In this type of economy there is a balance between market forces and state intervention. The view is taken that certain activities need to be regulated by the state whilst others can be left to the influence of the market. A mixed economy usually comprises:

(a)   A free enterprise sector, where economic decisions are based on market forces

> (b)   Public ownership and control of key central industries
>
> (c)   Welfare sector to provide a minimum level of medical, social and educational services for all citizens regardless of wealth

In advanced economies there are various ways to deal with these questions of scarcity. Different countries use different approaches or types of economic system.

(a)   *What goods and services will be produced?* In a market economy, this will depend on what consumers want to buy, and what they will pay for each product or service. The decisions about what will be produced relate to demand and supply. (Satisfied demand is *consumption*; the actual supply of goods and services is referred to as *production*.)

(b)   *How will these goods and services be produced?* The producers or suppliers of goods and services might be small companies, large companies, monopolies, state-owned enterprises or the government itself. The choice about who will produce the goods and services, and what mix of resources the producers will use, will depend on the costs of resources and the efficiencies of resource utilisation.

(c)   *To whom will the goods and services be distributed?* Some goods and services are provided free by the state (for example, in the UK, some health care and education) but others have to be paid for. The distribution of goods and services will depend on the *distribution* of income and wealth in society. This in turn will depend on what individuals and organisations earn. (The theory of distribution in economics is concerned with what rewards are earned by the owner of scare economic resources or factors of production: land, labour, capital and entrepreneurship.)

Within the mixed economy, public and private sector organisations differ primarily in terms of their ownership. We look first at private sector ownership.

1.2   Ownership of the private sector

Private sector organisations are not owned by the state or run by the state. Private-sector organisations provide a huge variety of goods and services.

EXAMPLES: PRIVATE SECTOR ORGANISATIONS

Organisations that seek profit for their proprietors by satisfying customers' requirements at a suitable price include:

(a)   Sole trader businesses (eg a local greengrocer)

(b)   Partnerships (eg a local firm of solicitors)

(c)   Private companies (not quoted on the stock market)

(d)   Public companies ('plcs', mostly quoted on the stock market)

Organisations with objectives other than purely profit include various types of mutual amd voluntary organisations.

(a)   Co-operatives and other mutual organisations such as building societies

(b)   Charities, which have specific charitable objectives

(c)   Trade Unions, Employers' Associations, Professional Associations

(d)   Various other voluntary societies, clubs and associations

We now look at the ownership of the public sector.

1.3   Ownership of the public sector

Public sector organisations are owned by the state. Some provide services paid for by taxation. Others levy charges on users directly, although such charges may be reduced by subsidy. The *public sector* refers to *all* publicly funded or publicly owned bodies, even though they may not form part of the obvious apparatus of government.

EXAMPLES: PUBLIC SECTOR ORGANISATIONS

Service organisations owned by central government and/or local government include the following:

(a)   Civil Service agencies

(b)   The Crown Prosecution Service

(c)   Local authorities

(d)   Schools

(e)   Environmental protection agencies such as the National Rivers Authority

(f)   The Employment Service (which runs Job Centres)

(g)   The Diplomatic Service

(h)   The Armed Forces

(i)   Public libraries

(j)   The Fire Service

State-owned ('nationalised') industries in the UK include the Royal Mail, London Transport and the British Broadcasting Corporation.

In theory, public sector organisations are run on behalf of the public and are accountable to Parliament. Since 1979, it has been government policy to turn public-sector organisations into private-sector ones. In other words, the state or the public no longer own many formerly public-sector organisations, such as British Gas or the main water companies. We discuss this process of *privatisation* and the reasons for it later in this chapter.

We now go on to discuss the extent to which the state should assume responsibility for economic behaviour and control over firms.

2   THE STATE AND THE PUBLIC SECTOR

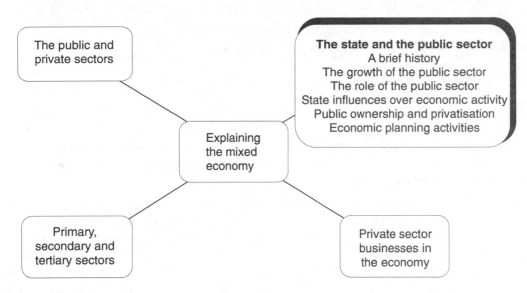

2.1   A brief history

Four key features of the modern state are as follows.

(a)   It has complete sovereignty in a defined territory, unless it cedes some of this sovereignty (for example through treaties such as the UK membership of the European Union).

(b)   It has legislative and coercive powers. In other words, it can lay down the law and enforce it.

(c)   It can raise taxation and distribute the proceeds.

(d)   In theory, the government is neutral in its approach to all sectors of society.

Note the following points.

(a)   These features have not always existed in government. In Stuart England the Monarch was encouraged to pay for foreign wars out of his or her private income. Asking Parliament for money was the exception.

(b)   The state is not necessarily synonymous with a particular ethnic or linguistic group. For example, Belgium includes Flemish and French speakers as its major groups. However, the fact that the state has so much power in a particular territory means that nationalistic conflicts may arise over which group controls it (as in the former Yugoslavia).

(c)   The state's actual autonomy is limited.

   (i)   The effects of international economic trends are often out of the state's control.

   (ii)   The authority of the state is often delegated to supra-national institutions such as the EU or NATO, or is constrained by treaty.

The state exercises authority and provides services in three ways:

(a)   Through direct action itself (eg defence)

(b)   Through delegation to other publicly funded bodies (such as NHS hospital trusts)

(c)   Through regulating the activities of people or organisations

The state's economic impact, such as in the determination of interest rates and tax levels, is considerable.

We now look at the size and structure of the public sector.

2.2 The growth of the public sector

Numbers employed

In the UK over five million people - over 20% of the total working population - are employed by the state sector. This is despite the recent privatisation of many of the nationalised industries.

The 1998 *Annual Abstract of Statistics* published by the UK Government reports a civil service workforce (in the ministries of central government, excluding Defence) numbering 366,000 in 1997 compared with 426,400 in 1986. Despite this reduction in numbers, it is thought likely that the growth of Executive Agencies, which are largely autonomous, will soon mean an *increase* in the number of civil servants as a result of the duplication of certain central functions. In recent years there has been a marked growth in the local government service, the National Health Service and other parts of the public sector. Local government now employs around two million people (including most teachers), and the Health Service employs about 1.6 million.

The privatisation of the nationalised industries has reduced the overall numbers employed by the public sector, but this number still totals over 5 million, nearly 30% of the total working population.

Public spending trends and fiscal policy

Public spending is expenditure incurred by public-sector organisations. Over the last century, public spending has risen considerably, both in absolute terms, and, more meaningfully, as a proportion of GDP. Total public spending was around 10% of GDP in the late 19th century, and is now around 40% of GDP. The growth has been uneven, with particularly sharp increases in times of war. The composition of public expenditure has also altered markedly over the period, with big increases in public spending on social services, and economic and environmental services.

It should be noted that this general increase has been given effect in recent years by very specific targeting of increases and by attempting to impose strict controls in all other areas, imposing efficiency gains across the board.

For example, Labour's 'New Deal' targets increased expenditure on initiatives designed to increase employment opportunities for the 18-25 age group. This has been funded by a 'Windfall Tax' on profits from the privatised public utilities.

Increases in National Insurance contributions from April 2003 are helping to fund increased expenditure on the health service and education.

Reasons for growth

Neither the extent nor the growth of the public sector is a purely British phenomenon. They are features of all advanced western economies. The United Kingdom spends a rather higher proportion of GDP on public expenditure than does the United States or Japan. It spends a rather lower proportion than the Benelux countries and Scandinavia. It spends about the same proportion as Germany, France and Italy.

Various reasons have been given for the growth of the public sector and public spending:

(a)   The impact of industrialisation and urbanisation, leading to pressures for increased government intervention in the economy and society

(b)   Changes in the profile of the population, particularly the substantial increase in the proportion of old people, who place major demands on social services of all kinds

(c)   Electoral and public pressures, as political parties compete for public support by promising better or increasing levels of services, such as health care or rail transport

(d)   Pressures from clients, users and associated pressure groups (eg Shelter, Child Poverty Action Group, Help the Aged) to improve services

(e)   The fact that the *welfare state*, with guaranteed benefits, was designed for a society in which most people had *paid* employment, not one in which there are high levels of unemployment, as is now common

FOR DISCUSSION

The creation of autonomous executive agencies, internal markets and compulsory competitive tendering has led to improved efficiency and a more 'business-like' approach by public sector organisations.

Discuss whether this is in fact true and whether the efficiency gains have led to improved services for the public.

Political debate

The size of the public sector has become the subject of considerable political controversy.

From the Second World War until the 1970s there was a broad political consensus over the welfare state and the mixed economy. There was then little fundamental disagreement over the extent of the public sector and the kind of services that the state should provide. The 1980s opened up differences in policies between those who supported increased state provision across a whole range of services, and those who advocated a drastic reduction in collective provision and the size of the public sector.

The debate today is not only about how public services should be delivered, but also about whether they should be supplied by the state at all. This fundamental question has affected virtually all public-sector organisations to some degree and has provoked considerable internal self-examination as well as external criticism.

Currently, a new consensus might see the state's role as an enabler rather than as a direct provider of services. This could lead to further reduction in provision of welfare, housing and education. A debate of particular interest to the current Government is related to the issue of state pensions and whether these should be provided by private insurance held by individuals.

> **Activity 1** [10 minutes]
>
> (a)   Which publicly provided services have you used?
>
> (b)   What benefits do you think you have gained from using them?
>
> (c)   What do you expect to have gained in 40 years time?
>
> (d)   How might this change if the services are privatised
>
> (e)   Find two examples of privatised services. Have they improved under private management?

We now explain the economic reasons for the state to engage in public-sector activity.

2.3   The role of the public sector

The economic rationale for the public sector as a whole has two main elements: a requirement for *equity* and the existence of *market failure*.

Equity

An equitable distribution of resources is one which people think is 'fair'. However definitions of equity vary. Here are two contrasting interpretations.

(a)   *Full equality* in either income distribution or access to services (eg so that exactly the same standard of health care is available to all).

(b)   *Minimum standards* so that everybody can enjoy a minimum amount of consumption of a particular good (eg food, clothing, housing), in other words a safety net.

Full equality requires greater state intervention than does the setting of minimum standards. We look further at the role of the state in the next chapter.

Market failure

Markets are supposed to allocate resources efficiently, so that the output of a good or service can be matched with the demand for it. Thus society's resources are allocated efficiently. In practice, things do not always work this way, and the state interferes to correct market failure. Various factors can lead to market failure.

(a)   *Imperfect competition* can lead to monopoly. The state can regulate the monopoly or produce the goods or services itself.

(b)   *Externalities* (eg social costs) arise as producer and consumer decisions only include private costs. For example, people who drive cars to work only pay for petrol and insurance. They do not pay compensation to those inconvenienced by the noise or traffic exhaust. State intervention to deal with these can include regulation and taxes (eg a 'pollution tax'). See recent developments as regards toll roads, park and ride schemes and restricted access to city centres.

(c)   *Public goods* (eg street lighting) are available to all, and consumption does not depend on paying a price. In a market system, individuals could get away with paying nothing.

(d)   *Imperfect information*. Consumers need to know what they are buying, but often they do not have the expertise to make a decision. The state can intervene to protect consumers

FOR DISCUSSION

In the UK the state provides welfare services. Some politicians in Asia regard this as decadent, arguing that extended families should do this job.

What do you think? How do the previous government's views on 'care in the community' fit with this? Does the current government propose any changes?

We now look at how the state influences economic activity.

2.4   State influences over economic activity

The state influences economic activity in the UK in three ways:

(a)   Through its taxation and interest rate policies

(b)   Through public spending on goods and services

(c)   Through regulation

Government economic policy is conducted with at least three aims in mind:

(a)   Economic growth

(b)   Full employment (that is, the economy's resources are fully employed, and there are very few people out of work - just those between jobs, for example)

(c)   Price stability (ie no inflation)

These aims often conflict with each other, and so it can be very difficult to achieve a balance between these aims.

The state uses various policy tools to try to achieve its aims, including *fiscal policy* and *monetary policy*.

Fiscal policy, discussed below, involves:

(a)   Taxation and other sources of income

(b)   Government spending

(c)   Borrowing whenever spending exceeds income

(d)   Repaying debt when income exceeds expenditure

A feature of fiscal policy is that a government must plan what it wants to spend, and so how much it needs to raise in income or by borrowing. It needs to make a plan in order to establish how much taxation there should be, what form the taxes should take and so which sectors of the economy (firms or households, high income earners or low income earners etc) the money should come from. This formal planning of fiscal policy is usually done once a year. The taxation aspects are set out in the Budget.

This annual review of taxation means that a government's review of its fiscal policy can normally only be done once a year. In between Budgets, a government must resort to other non-fiscal policy instruments to control the economy, such as influencing interest rate levels.

Fiscal policy, then, covers a government's income and expenditure. In the UK, the policies adopted are intended to promote high and stable levels of growth and employment.

In the *2002 Spending Review,* the Chancellor of the Exchequer announced an increase in the annual education budget of an average 6 per cent per year, to £57.8 billion by 2006. Transport spending is set to increase by 12 per cent per annum in real terms between 2002 and 2006. Defence spending is also set to increase, by 1.2 per cent, in response to the worsening international situation.

In the *2002 Budget,* the Chancellor had announced significant increases in spending on health, financed in part by increases in national insurance contributions.

Government expenditure is set to be increased by about £93 billion between 2002 and 2006, to £511 billion. these plans showed that increases in public spending, with education and health at the centre, would be a central issue in the next General Election.

Monetary policy

Monetary policy involves attempts to influence economic activity through:

- (a) Interest rates
- (b) Exchange rates
- (c) Control of the money supply
- (d) Controls over bank lending and credit

Monetary policy can be made to act as a subsidiary support to fiscal policy and demand management. Since budgets are usually once-a-year events, a government must use non-fiscal measures in between budgets to make adjustments to its control of the economy.

- (a) A policy of low interest rates or the absence of any form of credit control might stimulate bank lending, which in turn would increase expenditure (demand) in the economy.
- (b) High interest rates might act as a deterrent to borrowing and so reduce spending in the economy.
- (c) Strict credit controls (for example restrictions on bank lending) might be introduced to reduce lending and so reduce demand in the economy.

Alternatively, monetary policy might be given prominence over fiscal policy as the most effective approach by a government to achieving its main economic policy objectives. This might not however be possible: from 1990 to 1992, for example, monetary policy in the UK was heavily constrained by the need to set interest rates at levels which maintained sterling's position in the European exchange rate mechanism (ERM). From 1997, the Government has given the Bank of England the role of setting interest rates, although it is still the government which sets an inflation target. If the UK joined a single European currency, interest rates would largely be determined at the European level.

Demand management

Economic growth is measured by increases in any of the following:

- (a) Total expenditure in the economy - ie 'aggregate demand'
- (b) Total income for individuals and companies in the economy
- (c) Total output in the economy

Definitions

There are various measures available:

1   GDP (gross domestic product) is the result of all economic activity in the economy (even though UK citizens or organisations may receive income from assets abroad, or make payments to foreign individuals or organisations).

2   GNP (gross national product) is GDP inclusive of amounts earned by the UK from overseas assets, but exclusive of amounts paid to overseas holders of UK assets.

3   A formula for measuring total national expenditure is:

$$E = C + I + G + (X - M)$$

where:
- E   is the total national expenditure
- C   is the total domestic consumption
- I   is the total industrial investment
- G   is the total government spending
- M   is total imports

The government sometimes likes to limit the amount of money that people spend, to ensure economic growth without doing too much too quickly. This is known as *demand management*. In the formula above, this involves the manipulation of E (ie achieving economic growth) by influencing C, I, G or net imports/exports. People's consumption can be limited by taking more in taxation.

Fiscal policy

Businesses are affected by a government's *fiscal* or *tax policy*. The levels of taxation and the methods through which they are collected - on individual earnings, on savings, through VAT, on business profits or upon inheritance of wealth - illustrate the power of the state to determine the operating environment and thus the strategy of firms at any given time.

Fiscal policy and macroeconomic objectives

Fiscal policy is concerned with government spending (an *injection* into the circular flow of income) and taxation (a *withdrawal*).

(a)   If government spending is increased, there will be an increase in the amount of injections, expenditure in the economy will rise and so national income will rise (either in real terms, or in terms of price levels only; ie the increase in national income might be real or inflationary).

(b)   If government taxation is increased, there will be an increase in withdrawals from the economy, and expenditure and national income will fall. A government might deliberately raise taxation to take inflationary pressures out of the economy.

Achieving growth in national income without inflation has been a problem bedevilling governments for many years. Certainly, government spending and government taxation policies can affect economic growth (ie the national income level in real terms) but it can also stimulate further inflation.

Fiscal policy can be used to reduce unemployment and provide jobs.

(a)   More government spending on capital projects would create jobs in the construction industries.

(b)   Government-funded training schemes are a means of spending by government to improve training, so as to make people more qualified for jobs in private industry.

(c)   A government might tax companies on the basis of the numbers and pay levels of people they employ (as with employers' national insurance contributions). Lower 'employment taxes' would possibly make employers more willing to take on extra numbers of employees.

Government spending, however, might create inflationary pressures, and inflation tends to create more unemployment. Fiscal policy must therefore be used with care, even to create new jobs.

Since government spending or tax reductions might be inflationary, and higher domestic prices make imports relatively cheaper and exports less competitive in foreign markets, fiscal policy has possible implications for the balance of payments.

If macroeconomic objectives are economic growth, full employment, low or no inflation and equilibrium in the balance of payments, fiscal policy can certainly influence those objectives, and governments use fiscal policy to do so (as well as to help achieve other non-economic objectives). However, the impact of changes in fiscal policy is not always certain, and fiscal policy to pursue one aim (eg lower inflation) might for a while create barriers to the pursuit of other aims (eg employment).

Taxes on business

Taxation is effectively a cost. It is resources generated by the business and then appropriated by the state.

Many countries offer low taxation in certain regions as an incentive for businesses to locate their activities there.

Taxes on people (eg income tax)

A high proportion of tax reduces the amount people have to spend on certain kinds of goods rather than others. In other words, low tax might mean more spent on consumer goods and less, say, on education provided by the state.

Certain types of tax, such as Employers' National Insurance Contributions, make it more expensive for employers to hire workers.

Activity 2   **(10 minutes)**

(a)   Mrs A earns £30,000 per annum and Mr. B earns £10,000 per annum.
        Calculate the amount of tax each would pay if:

        (i)   A flat rate of 20% applied

        (ii)   There were a tax allowance of £5,000 with the remaining
                 earnings taxed at 25%

(b)   If the government wanted to increase the spending on luxury goods,
        which method of taxation ((i) or (ii)) would be most likely to achieve
        this?

(c)   If the government wanted to safeguard the net income of people on
        low earnings, which method ((i) or (ii)) would be most likely to achieve
        this?

Public spending

The economist John Maynard Keynes claimed that if the economy is operating at less than full employment there is scope for increasing national income, preferably through new investment. If the private sector will not invest enough, the government can. According to this view, government policies for boosting G (extra government spending, financed by borrowing) need not cause off-setting reductions in C, I or (X – M) and so national income will grow.

What form does government spending take?

Governments, like other organisations, spend money on the following:

(a)   Payments of wages and salaries to employees, and pensions to old age pensioners

(b)   Payments for materials, supplies and services

(c)   Purchases of capital equipment

(d)   Payments of interest on borrowings and repayments of capital

Expenditure has to be allocated between departments and functions - eg health, social services, education, transport, defence, grants to industry, and so on. Expenditure decisions by government are of great significance to companies that are major suppliers to the government - eg producers of defence equipment, medicines and medical equipment, and school text books.

More indirectly, government spending decisions affect companies and other organisations. Government spending has a 'knock-on' effect throughout the economy - companies supply companies which in turn supply the government. A lot of government work is subcontracted to private sector firms. For example, recently the British arms industries have been heavily affected by government cut-backs in arms expenditure and contracts.

Private sector and public sector investment

Extra investment means an increase in total expenditure in the economy, which in turn means an increase in national income. There are certain differences between public sector and private sector investment however.

(a)   Investment by the public sector will tend to be directed towards industries in which the public sector is involved, and towards industries supplying public sector industries (eg new roads) or on fulfilling social needs.

(b)   Public sector investments might have a longer time scale (eg health) or have fewer quantifiable economic benefits (eg education, basic research) than the private sector is willing or able to accept.

(c)   Public sector investment is financed differently from private-sector investment. In the public sector, investment could be financed even if the government did not have sufficient income from taxation. To pay for a budget deficit, the government can borrow large amounts of money.

(d)   Increasingly, the UK government is involving the private sector in the funding of public sector projects. This is called the Private Finance Initiative. An example of this is the railway link to the Channel Tunnel and the building of the Millenium Dome.

FOR DISCUSSION

Do you consider that increases in profitability and efficiency resulting from changing ownership from the public to the private sector are worth the loss of accountability to Parliament? How do you think these issues can be reconciled?

Various areas of the public sector (eg water, gas, electricity and telecommunications) have now been delivered to the private sector in a process of privatisation.

2.5   Public ownership and privatisation

Nationalisation

After World War II, the state, or state bodies, became responsible for:

(a)   Utilities (such as telecommunications, water, gas)

(b)   Extractive industries (coal and oil, to a certain degree)

(c)   Transportation (British Rail, National Bus, British Airways)

(d)   Various 'high-tech' industries (such as Cable and Wireless, Amersham International)

(e)   Other commercial operations felt to be of major economic importance, such as British Aerospace, British Steel, British Shipbuilders

The motives for state control were mixed.

(a)   Some industries had always had heavy government involvement. For example, gas and electricity were once run by local councils. The government felt that running them on a nation-wide basis would be more efficient.

(b)   Some industries offered important social benefits but could not survive as private companies (for example, the railways).

(c)   Some industries, such as coal, were nationalised because the government felt it had a responsibility to the workforce in terms of working conditions and job security.

(d) Some industries were nationalised to prevent them becoming bankrupt, which would have caused major political problems for the government of the day. British Leyland, the predecessor to Rover Cars, was nationalised for this reason.

(e) Some failing industries were nationalised in order to be 'turned round' and made profitable again.

(f) State control of an industry enabled the government to control the pay of a large proportion of the workforce, and hence the overall level of demand and even the rate of inflation.

Privatisation

Privatisation: the transfer of enterprises owned by the state into private hands.

Definition

Since 1979 the government has set about a process of reversal of nationalisation.

The process of privatisation has a number of, sometimes conflicting, objectives.

(a) Short-term *reductions in public sector borrowing and expenditure* to finance tax cuts.

(b) *Greater investment*. One reason for privatising the water industry was that the government at the time was unwilling to finance, from general taxation, the investment necessary to maintain and improve the system and bring it into line with EU requirements.

(c) Removing industries from the *control of civil servants*. Privatised utilities are free to borrow (they were previously restricted by Treasury controls) and spend as they wish. Unpopular commercial decisions or operating practices can no longer be blamed on the government.

(d) *Efficient management*. Some people believe that the private sector is necessarily more efficient than the public sector. Although there is some evidence that some privatised industries have become more efficient, many efficiency savings were made *before* privatisation to make them attractive to private investors; it may therefore have been the *threat* of privatisation that achieved the improvements in efficiency.

(e) *Competition*. Privatisation was held to encourage competition, but some public utilities were sold off as private monopolies and this has generated criticism.

The telephone industry is a good example where increased competition has led to price cuts and improved services.

(f) *Reducing costs by contracting out*. Where work was previously done by government employees (eg refuse collection, hospital laundry work, even prison management) contracting out this work to private firms is intended to save money.

(g) Risk capital for future investment is raised on the stock market - rather than from government.

BPP PUBLISHING

Activity 3 (10 minutes)

Think about the problems that can arise from privatising industries and services. Is the management accountable to shareholders or to customers?

How can the tension between accountability to shareholders and customers be reconciled in the supply of electricity, gas, water, telecommunications or public transport?

FOR DISCUSSION

Privatisation has had conflicting results. It has allowed the privatised utilities to expand their services into overseas markets. However, there is an argument that it is not so much privatisation as the injection of competition and private sector management techniques that have generated what performance improvement there has been. Where there is no competition, the public is represented by a regulator.

(a)   Some economic decisions have been deregulated. The UK government, for example, abolished exchange controls.

(b)   In other areas there has been an increase in regulation, supposedly in the public interest.

    (i)   Regulatory bodies oversee the activities of privatised utilities such as in telecommunications (for which the watchdog is OFTEL, which is to be merged into the new OFCOM by the end of 2003), gas supply (OFGAS), the electricity companies (OFFER) and water companies (OFWAT). The regulators can influence pricing policy, competitive strategy (eg by restricting 'unfair' competition) and, indeed, the structure of the industry.

    (ii)   The financial services industry in the City is more heavily regulated than hitherto, even though much of this regulation is carried out by the industry itself.

    (iii)   There are far tighter controls on the activities of local authorities and their financial arrangements.

(c)   Some of the UK government's regulating activities have been pooled with the European Union. Aspects of competition policy are managed by the European Union.

Activity 4 (1 hour)

Find out about the most recent activities/reports of OFWAT and OFGAS, for example by using the internet.

What issues have they scrutinised in relation to these two industries?

As well as public ownership, for a time the state became responsible for planning all economic activity.

2.6 Economic planning activities

When a government engages in economic planning, it is a director of economic activity.

Economic planning on a large scale (planning the minutiae of output, investment, fine-tuning demand to reach a growth target) is now out of favour, and has been discredited as a result of:

(a)   The failure of centrally planned command economies in Russia and Eastern Europe

(b)   Its mixed results in Western Europe

Economic planning on a lesser scale, with the government as an enabler of private sector activity and as corrector of market imperfections, still has some sort of a role, however.

Import substitution and export-led growth

Governments can raise trade barriers to imports to protect domestic industry and to ensure that domestic companies can grow. Alternatively, governments can subsidise exports, or promote them in other ways (eg by trade missions, export credit insurance and so on). The UK government's ability to do this has been somewhat curbed by membership of the European Union and the GATT agreement (General Agreement on Tariffs and Trades).

These two models, *import substitution* and *export-led growth*, have been adopted with varying degrees of success by various developing countries.

Inward investment

Governments can also encourage inward investment by foreign countries. This has been UK government policy since the early 1980s. It has had considerable success in attracting investment by, for example, US motor and banking, and Japanese electronics, and companies in various parts of the UK. (See the case study in Chapter 2.)

Regional policy

Regional policy is an example of small-scale economic planning, with government as an enabler rather than a director. Regional policy can include:

(a)   Providing tax incentives for investing in certain areas

(b)   Relaxing town planning restrictions to make it easier for businesses to develop

(c)   Awarding contracts to companies in one region rather than another (eg dividing operations between shipyards in different parts of the country)

(d)   Developing new towns (eg Milton Keynes) to reduce population pressure in major conurbations. The UK government has examined the issue of whether to encourage inner city developments in order to re-generate rundown areas. They have also considered whether to develop new 'rural towns' to encourage country dwellers to stay in their local area rather than migrate to existing towns and cities.

(e)   Making infrastructural developments (eg roads, rail, airports)

Activity 5   **(1 hour)**

Investigate your own local area. What initiatives are currently in operation to encourage investment and development?

NOTES

State influences over organisations

Government economic policy affects organisations in the following ways. The variety of influences are outlined in the following diagram.

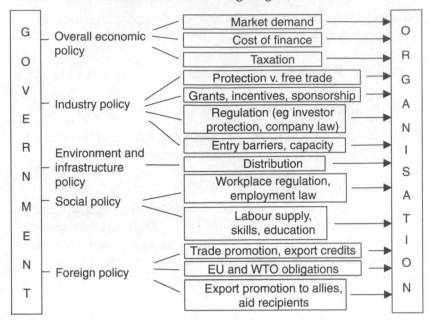

Competition policy

The government sometimes has the right to determine the structure of an industry, to ensure competition.

In Chapter 2, we discuss these issues in greater depth.

We now go on to look at private sector business in more detail.

3 PRIVATE SECTOR BUSINESSES IN THE ECONOMY

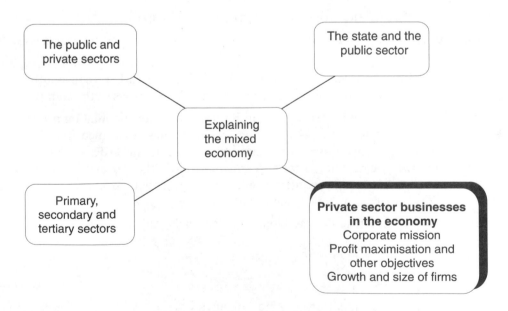

Definition

> *Firm:* a wide term for any organisation that carries on a business. In spite of their many differences, we treat firms as single, consistent decision-taking units and, for the purposes of economic analysis, we ignore any differences in decision-making procedures and economic structures between them.

We start by looking at the objectives of firms.

3.1 Corporate mission

Definition

> *Mission* 'describes the organisation's basic function in society, in terms of the products and services it produces for its clients' (Mintzberg).

The importance of mission

Although hard to quantify, the idea of a *corporate mission* is taken seriously by many firms.

(a) Values and feelings are integral elements of consumers' buying decisions, as evidenced by advertising, branding and market research. Customers not only ask 'What do you sell?' but 'What do you stand for?'

(b) A respect for quantifiable information is part of the professional culture and training of the accountant; other people have different values and priorities.

(c) Studies into organisational behaviour suggest that employees are motivated by more than money. A sense of mission and values helps to motivate employees.

(d) Many firms take mission seriously in strategic management.

Mission statements are formal statements of an organisation's mission. They might be reproduced in a number of places (eg at the front of an organisation's annual report, on publicity material, in the chairman's office, in communal work area and so on.) There is no standard format, but they should possess certain characteristics.

- Brevity – easy to understand and remember

- Flexibility – to accommodate change

- Distinctiveness – to make the firm stand out

EXAMPLE: CORPORATE MISSION STATEMENTS

The following statements were taken from annual reports of the organisations concerned.

Glaxo (now *GSK*) 'is an integrated researched-based group of companies whose corporate purpose is to create, discover, develop, manufacture and market throughout the world,

safe, effective medicines of the highest quality which will bring benefit to patients through improved longevity and quality of life, and to society through economic value'.

The British Film Institute 'is the UK national agency with responsibility for encouraging and conserving the arts of film and television. Our aim is to ensure that the many audiences in the UK are offered access to the widest possible choice of cinema and television, so that their enjoyment is enhanced through a deeper understanding of the history and potential of these vital popular art forms'.

Mission and planning

Although the mission statement might be seen a set of abstract principles, it can play an important role in the planning process.

(a) *Plans should outline the fulfilment of the organisation's mission.* To take the example of a religious organisation (the best example of a 'missionary organisation'), the mission of spreading the gospel might be embodied in plans to send individuals as missionaries to various parts of the world, plans for fund-raising activities, or even targets for the number of new converts.

(b) *Evaluation and screening.* Mission also acts as a yardstick by which plans are judged.

(i) The mission of an ethical investment trust would preclude investing in tobacco firms.

(ii) Mission helps to ensure consistency in decisions.

(c) *Implementation.* Mission also affects the implementation of a planned strategy, in the culture and business practices of the firm.

Problems with mission

(a) *Ignored in practice.* The inherent danger of mission is that it will not be implemented. *Official* goals often do not correspond with the end that seems to be pursued.

(b) *Public relations.* Sometimes, of course, mission is merely for public consumption, not for internal decision making.

(c) *Post hoc.* Missions are sometimes produced to *rationalise* the organisation's existence to particular audiences. In other words, mission does not drive the organisation, but what the organisation actually does is assumed to be mission.

(d) *Full of generalisations.* 'Best', 'quality', 'major': is just a wish list.

3.2 Profit maximisation and other objectives

Definitions

1	*Shareholder:* a person who owns a share of a company. A share entitles the owner to a share in the company's profits. The management of a company are appointed, indirectly, by shareholders and run the company on the shareholders' behalf.
2	*Stakeholders:* the many different groups and individuals whose interests are affected by the activities of a firm.

Most economists assume that the aim of any business is to make as much profit as possible over the long term. (Profit is the excess of revenue over costs.) In firms where the entrepreneur or owner is in full managerial control, as in the case of a small owner-managed company or partnership, this assumption seems very reasonable. Even in companies owned by shareholders but run by non-share-holding managers, if the manager is serving the shareholders' interests, we might expect that the profit maximisation assumption should be close to the truth. However, firms might pursue objectives other than profit maximisation.

Many managers acknowledge that the interests of some *stakeholder groups* - for example the managers themselves and the employees - should be recognised and provided for, even if this means that the interests of shareholders might be adversely affected. Not all stakeholder group interests can be given specific attention in the decisions of management. A list of stakeholders is given below.

Stakeholder groups

Shareholders	Neighbours
Lenders (eg bank)	The immediate community
Intermediate (business) customers	The national society
Final (consumer) customers	The world society
Suppliers	Corporate management
Employees	The chief executive
Past employees	The board of directors
Retirees	Government and local government
Competitors	Special interest groups

All organisations affect and are affected by different stakeholders. Sometimes these are represented by *interest groups* (eg trade unions) and at other times their power is reflected in *commercial relationships* (eg suppliers).

The public is a 'stakeholder' to some degree and concerns might be represented by government action. There are three broad types of stakeholder in an organisation.

(a) *Internal* stakeholders (employees, management)

(b) *Connected* stakeholders (shareholders, customers, suppliers, financiers)

(c) *External* stakeholders (the community, government, pressure groups)

Activity 6 (10 minutes)

(a) Think about the different stakeholders in an organisation. List those whose interests may conflict. Try to use an organisation you know or work for.

How can such conflicts be resolved?

(b) Using the list given above, categorise the stakeholders into internal, connected or external.

Profit maximisation

If the interests of the ordinary shareholders are the only stakeholder interests that are recognised, the goal of the firm should be *profit maximisation*. There is reasonable logic to support the idea that firms must seek to maximise profits, because competition from profit-maximising firms could force non profit-maximising firms out of business.

In order to maximise profits over time, the business will have to incur costs today in order to generate returns in the future. A profit-maximising firm will seek to make investments - in physical capital (eg machines), human capital (the employees), advertising and so on - and it would be wrong to think of profit maximisation as a 'short-term' motive.

Return on capital employed

The level of profit that a business earns does not relate profitability to the amount of funds (capital) employed in making those profits. An annual profit of £1 million may sound high for a small business, but if it is the profit earned by a larger company with many assets, it may in fact represent a low rate of 'return' in capital.

The most important measure of profitability is therefore the *return on capital employed (ROCE)* - sometimes called the *return on investment (ROI)*. The ROCE is calculated as profit *divided by* long-term capital employed, expressed as a percentage.

Alternative managerial goals

In many large companies the management is divorced from the ownership. Managers and shareholders are different individuals, and managers are supposed to run the company in the interests of the shareholders.

FOR DISCUSSION

Do managers act in the interests of shareholders only? Or could they make decisions to the detriment of shareholders (ie decisions that will not result in profit maximisation) and in favour of other stakeholder groups, notably themselves?

Managers are paid to make decisions about prices and output, but it is the shareholders who expect to benefit from the profits. Managers will not necessarily make pricing decisions that will maximise profits, because:

(a)   They have no personal interests at stake in the size of profits earned, except in so far as they are accountable to shareholders for the profits they make, and

(b)   There may be a lack of competitive pressure in the market to be efficient, minimise costs and maximise profits, for example where there are few firms in the market

In theory, managers of a business are supposed to look after the shareholders' interests. But things are rarely this simple, as managers have their own interests to satisfy.

Managers' interests as stakeholders are:

(a)   Career development

(b)   Personal prestige

(c)   Financial reward

(d)   Psychological satisfaction (status, job interest)

For these needs to be satisfied, managers have an interest in the organisation's continued survival and growth. Most of the time, shareholders will benefit too, but not always: it may sometimes be better to wind a company up than to carry on business.

Of course, shareholders can dismiss directors who fail to perform, so managers have a 'stake' in keeping shareholders happy.

Some argue that there is a 'political' dimension to any business. A firm is a coalition of shareholders, managers, employees and customers, with each group having different goals. There is therefore a need for 'political' compromise in establishing the goals of the firm. Each group must settle for less than it would ideally want to have. Shareholders must settle for less than maximum profits, employees for less than maximum salaries, and so on.

Given the fact that management is separate from ownership in most larger firms, it has been suggested that price and output decisions will be taken by managers with *managerial objectives* in mind rather than the aim of profit maximisation. The obvious constraint is that managers are accountable to shareholders for their decisions. The profit level must be satisfactory and so acceptable to shareholders, and must provide enough retained profits for future investment in growth. But rather than seeking to *maximise* profits, managers may choose to achieve a satisfactory profit for a firm (this is called 'satisficing').

Baumol's sales maximisation model

One 'managerial model' of the firm assumes that the firm acts towards *sales revenue maximisation* rather than profits (again subject to the constraints mentioned above). The management of a firm might opt for sales revenue maximisation in order to maintain or increase its *market share*, to ensure survival, and to discourage competition. Managers benefit personally because of the prestige of running a large and successful company, and also because salaries and other perks are likely to be higher in bigger companies than in smaller ones.

Level of service

An organisation might also appear successful because it achieves a high *level of service* and this might be set as an objective. Good service levels will enhance *customer perceptions* of the business.

EXAMPLE: AMAZON

Amazon, the internet retailer of books, compact discs and other items, enjoys a mainly positive perception among customers for its level of service. In 2000, it made special arrangements with the Royal Mail to ensure delivery of pre-ordered and price discounted copies of the long awaited new 'Harry Potter' children's book on the date of publication to its UK customers. Such service comes at a cost, and indeed Amazon has still not become profitable. Investors' uneasiness with its continuing losses was reflected in falls in its share price during the first half of 2000.

Williamson's management discretion model

Another managerial model assumes that managers act to further their own interests and so maximise their own utility or satisfaction, subject to a minimum profit requirement. Utility may be thought of in terms of prestige, influence and other personal satisfactions.

The model states that utility, which a manager aims to maximise, is a function of the manager's own salary and also expenditure on his staff (prestige and influence depend on the numbers and pay levels of subordinate staff), the amount of perks (luxurious office, personal secretary, company car, expense account etc) and the authority to make *discretionary investments* (ie new investments other than straightforward replacement decisions). The profit aimed for will not be maximum profit, because of managers' wishes for expenditure on themselves, their staff and the perks of management.

Cyert and March's organisational coalition model

Cyert and March suggested that a firm is an organisational coalition of shareholders, managers, employees and customers, with each group having different goals, and so there is a need for 'political' compromise in establishing the goals of the firm. Each group must settle for less than it would ideally want to have. Shareholders must settle for less than maximum profits, managers for less than maximum utility, and so on.

There is undoubtedly some truth in these ideas about alternative 'managerial' objectives and it can also be noted that nationalised industries may pursue objectives other than profit maximisation. However, for our purposes here it is convenient (and broadly reasonable) to assume that firms seek to maximise profits.

Firms often have to grow to survive at all. This growth may be achieved through expanding output (ie increasing the number of goods produced or services rendered), buying other businesses, or making arrangements with them for mutual benefit.

3.3 Growth and size of firms

Definitions

1   *Economies of scale:* the reductions in the average cost of producing a commodity in the long run as the amount of output of the commodity increases. The larger a business is, the more efficiently it can produce. For example, if two competing firms decide to combine their operations, they can save money by only having one head office, rather than two; a large firm can buy its raw materials in bulk, thereby getting a cheaper price or discount.

2   *Monopoly:* a firm without major competitors in a particular line of business. Usually, a firm will be regarded as being in a monopoly position if it has at least 25% of the market share. In practical terms, the UK's water firms are monopolies; household consumers cannot switch suppliers. Monopolists can earn higher profits than non-monopolists.

3   *Oligopoly:* oligopoly may result in a market where there are just a very few large competitors. Competition may be restricted because of this, especially if this is supported by informal agreements between the competitors.

Growth

The possibility of achieving *economies of scale* through expansion should encourage firms to try to grow in size. The two broad methods of obtaining growth are as follows.

(a)   *Organic growth*. This is growth through a gradual build-up of the firm's own resources, developing new products, acquiring more plant and machinery, hiring extra labour and so on. Organic growth is often a slow but steady process.

(b)   *Growth through mergers and takeovers*. These both involve the combination of two or more firms into one.

Mergers and takeovers can be categorised further according to what firms are coming together. Are they in exactly the same line of business? Are they in very similar businesses? Are they in related businesses, but operating in different stages of the production and selling process? Are they in unrelated lines of business?

(a)   *Horizontal integration*. When two firms in the same business merge, there is horizontal integration. Horizontal integration tends to create monopolies, or at least firms with a disproportionate share of the market. If, for example, All-England Chocolate plc with a 15% share of the UK chocolate market were to merge with British Choc plc which has a 20% share of the UK market, the enlarged company might expect to hold a 35% market share. A fairly recent example was the merger between Lloyds Bank and the Cheltenham and Gloucester Building Society.

(b)   *Vertical integration*. Two firms operating at different stages in the production and selling process might merge. When they do, vertical integration occurs. For example, the stages in the production of petrol for cars are as follows.

  (i)   Oil extraction

  (ii)   Shipping (in tanker fleets, or by pipeline)

  (iii) Refining

  (iv)   Distribution (to petrol stations)

  (v)   Retail sales (at petrol stations)

  A company that operates exclusively in oil refining might take over an oil shipping company, and perhaps an oil extraction company too. This would be *backwards vertical integration*, ie back through stages in production towards the raw material growing/ extraction stage.

  The same company might take over a company with a distribution fleet of petrol tanker lorries, and perhaps a chain of petrol stations too. This would be forwards vertical integration, ie forward through stages in production and selling towards the end consumer sales stage.

(c)   *Conglomerate diversification*. A company might enter a different business altogether, perhaps through merger or takeover. A group of diversified businesses is referred to as a conglomerate organisation. Hanson and BAT are prime examples, although in the 1990s firms have increasingly sold off non-core businesses to form more 'rational' groups which focus on key strengths (sometimes called 'sticking to the knitting').

Activity 7   **(10 minutes)**

Despite the supposed advantages of large firms, many commentators see small and medium-sized firms as the engines of economic growth. Before reading the next paragraph, list six advantages of small firms.

Organisational size

Organisations grow large where economies of scale encourage the success of large firms in a market at the expense of small firms. In some markets, being large is essential. In others, small can be beautiful. Small and large organisations can coexist in a market by tackling different segments.

Advantages of a large organisation are as follows.

(a) A large-scale organisation should have access to sufficient resources to command a significant market share. This in turn will enable it to influence prices in the market so as to ensure continuing profitability.

(b) A large organisation can provide for greater division of work and specialisation. Specialisation, and the development of a wide range of products or customer services, should enable the organisation to attract continuing customer support and market shares. In contrast, a small or medium-sized business will require greater competence and versatility from its top management, because they will not have the benefits of support from functional specialists which are available to the top managers of large organisations.

(c) A large organisation with a wide variety of products or customer services should be able to offer an attractive career to prospective employees, and it is therefore likely to receive job application requests from very talented people. This in turn should enable the large organisation to recruit and develop high-quality personnel for future top management positions.

(d) Specialisation brings with it the ability to provide expert services at a relatively low cost to the customer. A large organisation is also able to make use of the advantages of efficient 'large-scale' equipment such as advanced computer systems or manufacturing equipment. For these (and other) reasons, large organisations are able to achieve *economies of scale* in the use of resources. Cheaper costs in turn mean either lower prices for customers or higher profits for the organisation.

(e) A large organisation is more likely to provide continuity of goods or services, management philosophy, customer relations and so on than a smaller organisation. A smaller organisation might be prone to sudden policy changes or changes of product when a new management team takes over.

The disadvantages of a large organisation are as follows.

(a) There is a tendency for the management hierarchy to develop too many levels. The more management levels there are, the greater the problem of communication between top and bottom, and the greater the problems of control and direction by management at the top.

(b) An organisation might become so widely diversified in the range of products or services it offers that it becomes difficult, if not impossible, for management to integrate all of the organisation under a common objective and within a single 'management philosophy' and culture.

(c) Top management might spend too much time in maintenance of the organisation (that is, with problems of administration) and lose sight of their primary tasks of setting objectives and planning for the future.

(d) There is a tendency of top management in large organisations to become 'ingrown and inbred, smug and self-satisfied'. The tendency towards 'group-think' - an acceptance by all managers of a common attitude towards problems - might introduce an unconscious resistance to necessary changes and developments.

(e)   The sheer size of an organisation may provide management with problems of co-ordination, planning policy and effective control. For example, a junior manager might find the organisation so large that he has relatively little influence. Decisions which he regards as important must be continually referred up the line to his superiors, for inter-departmental consultations. At the same time, the top management might find the organisation so large and complex, and changes in policy and procedures so difficult and time-consuming to implement, that they also feel unable to give direction to the organisation. The organisation is therefore a 'monster' which operates of its own accord, with neither senior nor junior managers able to manage it effectively.

(f)   In a large organisation, many of the tasks of junior management are routine and boring. Even middle management might be frustrated by the restrictions on their authority, the impersonal nature of their organisation, the inability to earn a just reward for their special efforts owing to the standardisation of pay and promotion procedures and the lack of information about aspects of the organisation which should influence their work.

Internal economies of scale arise from the more effective use of available resources, and from increased specialisation, when production capacity is enlarged.

(a)   *Specialisation of labour.* In a large undertaking, a highly skilled worker can be employed in a job which makes full use of his skills. In a smaller undertaking, individuals must do a variety of tasks, none of which they may do very well ('Jack-of-all-trades - master of none').

(b)   *Division of labour.* Because there is specialisation of labour there is also division of labour, ie work is divided between several specialists, each of whom contributes his share to the final product. A building will be constructed, for example, by labourers, bricklayers, plumbers, electricians, plasterers and so on. Switching between tasks wastes time, and division of labour avoids this waste.

(c)   Large undertakings can make use of *larger and more specialised machinery*. If smaller undertakings tried to use similar machinery, the costs would be excessive because the machines would become obsolete before their physical life ends (ie their economic life would be shorter than their physical life). Obsolescence is caused by falling demand for the product made on the machine, or by the development of newer and better machines.

(d)   *Dimensional economies* of scale refer to the relationship between the volume of output and the size of equipment (eg storage tanks) needed to hold or process the output. The cost of a container for 10,000 gallons of product will be much less than ten times the cost of a container for just 1,000 gallons.

(e)   *Buying economies* may be available, reducing the cost of material purchases through bulk purchase discounts.

(f)   *Indivisibility of operations.* There are operations which:

(i)   Must be carried out at the same cost, regardless of whether the business is small or large; these are fixed costs and average fixed costs always decline as production increases

(ii)   Vary a little, but not proportionately, with size (ie having 'semi-fixed' costs)

(iii)   Are not worth considering below a certain level of output (eg advertising campaigns)

(g)   *Stockholding* becomes more efficient. The most economic quantities of inventory to hold increase with the scale of operations, but at a lower proportionate rate of increase.

The advantages of small firms

If large size can give economies of scale, why do small firms continue to prosper? In some industries and professions, small firms predominate (eg building, the legal profession) and in some, small and large firms co-exist (eg newsagents). The number of small firms in the UK has grown in recent years. The reasons for the survival of the small firm may be that there are problems with large size (*diseconomies of scale*).

(a)   Small firms are more likely to operate in competitive markets, in which prices will tend to be lower and the most efficient firms will survive at the expense of the inefficient.

(b)   They are more likely to be risk takers, investing 'venture capital' in projects that might yield high rewards. Innovation and entrepreneurial activity are important ingredients for economic recovery or growth.

(c)   Management-employee relations are more likely to be co-operative, with direct personal contacts between managers at the top and all the employees.

(d)   Small firms tend to specialise, and so can contribute efficiently towards the division of labour in an economy.

(e)   The structure of a small firm may allow for greater flexibility (eg an employee or manager can switch from one task to another much more readily).

(f)   Small firms often sell to a local market; large firms need wider markets, and may incur relatively higher costs of transport.

(g)   Managerial economies can be obtained by hiring expert consultants, possibly at a cheaper cost than permanent management specialists.

(h)   Some small firms act as suppliers or sub-contractors to larger firms.

(i)   There may be insufficient market demand to justify large-scale production.

The economy operates in three distinct sectors in which public or private ownership can overlap.

4   PRIMARY, SECONDARY AND TERTIARY SECTORS

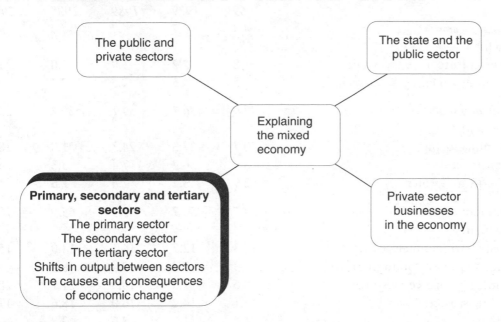

Definitions

1   *GDP:* Gross Domestic Product. A way to measure the 'size' of the economy.

2   *The primary sector:* this sector of industry consists of industries that produce raw materials, such as crops and minerals.

3   *The secondary sector:* this sector of industry consists of industries that use the raw material produced by the primary sector.

4   *The tertiary sector:* this sector of industry consists of distribution and service industries. Services include activities as diverse as banking, tourism, hairdressing, teaching, office cleaning, tax advice and the media.

Table 1.1 below illustrates the distinction between the primary, secondary and tertiary sectors of the economy and shows some trends in these sectors.

UNITED KINGDOM	% share of GDP in each sector				
	1969	1979	1989	1995	2000
Primary sector	4.3	6.7	4.4	4.4	4.1
of which:					
Agriculture, forestry, fishing	1.8	2.2	1.9	2.0	1.2
Mining, oil and gas, quarrying	2.5	4.5	2.5	2.4	2.9
Secondary sector	42.0	36.7	34.1	29.7	25.8
of which:					
Manufacturing	30.7	27.3	24.3	21.8	18.7
Construction	8.4	6.2	7.4	5.3	5.2
Energy and water	2.9	3.2	2.4	2.6	1.9
Tertiary sector	53.7	56.7	61.5	65.9	70.1
of which:					
Distribution, hotels, catering	13.3	12.7	14.1	14.0	15.7
Transport and communications	6.3	7.3	8.4	8.4	8.2
Banking, finance, business	8.6	11.0	18.5	21.1	28.2
Public services	14.1	14.2	16.9	18.6	17.4
Others	11.4	11.5	3.6	3.8	0.6
	100.0	100.0	100.0	100.0	100.0

Table 1.1 Distribution of UK national output

We will examine the primary sector first.

4.1 The primary sector

In the UK, over the long term, the trend is one of decline in this sector when measured in terms of its share of GDP. Viewed against the process of economic growth, this declining share also reflects the rising level of output of other industries that are growing faster, as well as absolute decline in output in industries such as coal.

The beginning of North Sea oil and gas production in the 1970s interrupted this trend and increased the overall importance of the primary sector within the UK economy. By 1989, however, the share of oil and gas within GDP had fallen to 56% of its 1979 share. Agriculture, forestry and fishing increased the share of GDP slightly from 1969 to 1979; the fall in share from 2.2% in 1979 to 1.2% in 2000 reflects the long-term trend of declining importance for these industries. The relatively high share of 6.7% for the primary sector as a whole in 1979 mainly reflects the advent of North Sea oil. By 1989 this had dropped to 4.4% as oil production dropped.

Next we consider the secondary sector.

4.2 The secondary sector

This sector normally grows rapidly during the early stages of economic development. The data show how the UK has reached a later stage of decline in this sector. Most of the fall in GDP share from 42.0% in 1969 to 25.8% in 2000 is attributable to a decline in *manufacturing,* (eg cars, clothes), as opposed to *construction,* (eg house or road building) and *energy* (eg electricity generation) and *water*. Manufactured goods are easy to transport and export (sell abroad). They are thus important in international trade.

The decline in the secondary sector has led to a reduction in employment in the sector bringing some severe unemployment in regions which have been heavily dependant on particular industries.

Finally, we look at the tertiary sector.

4.3 The tertiary sector

This sector is made up mainly of goods distribution and service industries. It has become the predominant provider of employment and output in the UK economy in recent decades, growing from a 53% share in 1969 to a 70.1% share in 2000. This trend is shared in other wealthy countries such as the US. Even Germany and Japan are seeing a growing service sector.

The data show that the main reason for the continuing growth during the 1980s and 1990s has been the rapid expansion in banking, finance and business activities, which expanded their GDP share from 8.6% to 28.2% between 1969 and 1995.

FOR DISCUSSION

Looking at the data set out in the UK Government publication *Economic Trends*, how might you explain the changes between the three sectors in the economy over the 31-year period?

Activity 8	(15 minutes)

Identify the key issues arising from the data on general government expenditure outlined below.

General government expenditure by function

UNITED KINGDOM	% and £ billion		
	1993	*1996*	*2000*
	%	%	%
Defence	9.4	7.8	7.3
Public order and safety	3.6	3.5	5.0
Education	4.5	5.1	11.5
Health	14.1	14.7	15.0
Social security	32.0	32.0	39.0
Housing and community amenities	2.8	2.0	1.4
Recreational and cultural affairs	0.5	0.5	1.3
Environment	3.3	2.5	1.2
General public services	3.8	3.7	5.1
Economic affairs	2.2	1.9	6.2
Other expenditure	23.8	26.3	7.0
Total expenditure (=100%) (£bn at 2000 prices)	292	326	368

NOTES

We shall now go on to explain some of the causes of the changes in the structure of the economy in recent times.

4.4 Shifts in output between sectors

Within the primary sector, the most significant factor affecting the change in GDP shares over the period from 1969 has been the discovery and exploitation of North Sea oil, and later gas. In the earlier years, as well as benefiting from the peak in absolute output from the North Sea, this sector benefited from relatively high energy prices compared with more recent years.

Definitions

> 1   *De-industrialisation:* often used to describe the long-term decline in the importance of manufacturing industry and the secondary sector in general.
>
> 2   *Trade surplus:* an excess of exports over imports.
>
> 3   *Trade deficit:* the deficit that occurs when imports are greater than exports.

Some argue that the decline of the secondary sector and the rise of the tertiary sector is an inevitable consequence of economic development. As in earlier stages of economic development, when the agricultural sector declined with the growth of the secondary sector, so the secondary sector has declined as demand has shifted, relatively, from goods to services. International comparisons offer some support for this explanation, since recent years have seen a decline in the share of employment accounted for by manufacturing in almost all advanced capitalist economies. However, the UK is unusual in that manufacturing employment reached its peak rather earlier (1955) than in many other countries, including the Federal Republic of Germany (1970), which faced major economic reconstruction following World War II. Some point out that Britain was the first country to industrialise, and during much of this century relative economic decline has been apparent in the UK, with many other industrialised countries overtaking the UK in GDP per head. One of the causes might be increased productivity: it became possible to produce more with fewer people, freeing people for employment elsewhere.

Domestic output (ie goods or services produced in the UK) supplies both domestic demand and *exports*. A relative decline in manufacturing output may result from:

(a)   People preferring goods made by overseas firms, which are imported
(b)   UK businesses' inability to make enough goods to satisfy the demand
(c)   The UK specialising in some goods and services as opposed to others

This explanation is borne out by the shift from a UK trade surplus in manufactured goods during the 1970s to significant deficits in manufactured goods during the 1980s and 1990s. This may be the result of a shift of demand away from UK manufactured goods towards foreign manufactured goods coupled with a failure of UK manufacturing industries to meet demand.

Within the tertiary sector, the rising share of banking, finance and insurance reflects a number of factors.

(a)   London has built on its reputation as one of the leading financial centres of the world, and in some areas (eg the foreign exchange markets) it is pre-eminent. The strong position of 'the City' (the London financial community) makes it a large exporter of financial services.

BPP
PUBLISHING

(b)   Increasing affluence and changing social factors (eg increasing levels of owner-occupation of housing during the 1970s and 1980s) have increased domestic demand for financial products of various kinds (eg current accounts, mortgages and insurance products).

(c)   The abolition of exchange controls (restrictions on how much money you could take out of the country) in 1979 and the deregulation of financial markets during the 1980s (for example the Stock Exchange 'Big Bang' and the Building Societies Act of 1986) encouraged greater competition between banks, building societies and insurance companies.

More recently, the trade deficits in manufactures have been offset by surpluses in oil exports, the service sector and in earnings from overseas assets. The problem then remains of how an overall balance of trade (on 'current account') is to be achieved as primary sector (oil) exports become less significant for the UK.

Activity 9   (10 minutes)

Can the tertiary (service) sector take the place of the secondary sector (manufactured goods) in ensuring a healthy balance between imports and exports?

Although the UK, with its major world financial centre in the City of London, has been very successful in international trade in financial services, the UK's share of the world market in services (or 'invisibles') still declined from 12% in 1978 to less than 9% today.

We shall now proceed to consider general problems with the changes in economic structure outlined above.

4.5   The causes and consequences of economic change

Definition

Exchange rate: the price of one currency in terms of another. If £1 can buy you $1.50 in US dollars, then the pound-dollar exchange rate is 1.50.

The economic structure of an economy may make it hard for the economy to adapt to future economic changes. For example:

(a)   The discovery of North Sea Oil and gas led to increased employment in these industries.

(b)   Furthermore, it meant a rising exchange rate. This made UK manufactured exports too expensive for overseas customers to buy, whereas manufactured imports became much cheaper.

(c)   Many firms failed and went out of business.

(d)   With the oil and gas resources running down, the diminished manufacturing industry is poorly placed to take advantage of the new situation; it is unable to make up for the lost oil and gas output rapidly enough. Domestic manufactured goods have been replaced by imports, so the UK has to export something else or rebuild its factories.

35

Activity 10 (10 minutes)

Describe what will happen when the oil supplies in the North Sea run out.

World market conditions may adversely affect an economy in which economic activity has become concentrated in particular sectors. Some poorer countries depend on exports from their primary sectors. Sri Lanka and Kenya, for example, export tea. If the price at which tea is traded on world markets begins to fall, the wealth of those economies will also fall. Issues of ethical trading practices have also been an issue for such countries. An economy may gain in the long run from having a widely based economic structure rather than one that is heavily reliant on particular sectors. You might note that both Sri Lanka and Kenya have attempted to diversify into tourism, a tertiary sector industry.

Technological progress brings about changes in economic structure, sometimes quite dynamically. Competition from overseas producers is also important. We discuss technology later.

Definitions

1   *Sunrise industries:* rising new industries, such as information technology and genetics. Their importance is increasing worldwide.

2   *Sunset industries:* gradually dying industries. In the western economies they include heavy industries such as steel and shipbuilding, whose prices have been undercut for many years by more efficient producers in Korea and other countries in the Pacific.

The decline of industries can have the following consequences.

(a)   Unemployment can be severe in the regions affected, particularly where there is heavy geographical concentration (as was the case with shipbuilding and coal mining) and if the industries on which a region is economically reliant are closed down rapidly.

(b)   There may be knock-on effects for the rest of the region's businesses, as consumers' spending power is reduced and people begin to leave the area.

Activity 11 (10 minutes)

Suggest some ways in which the government might be able to intervene in order to alleviate the effects of a decline in a particular industry.

Just as the run down of certain industries brings problems for the regions in which those industries are concentrated, so too the rapid expansion of certain sectors may present problems. In Britain during the 1980s, the rapid expansion of the banking, finance and insurance industries put strains on the economic infrastructure and brought high house price inflation in the South East region, where these industries are concentrated.

Chapter roundup

- In a mixed economy, total economic activity is managed both by private and public sectors. In theory, the public sector gets involved in areas where there is market failure.

- Economic activity can be analysed into primary, secondary and tertiary sectors. To simplify, the primary sector deals with raw materials, the secondary sector with making goods and the tertiary sector with services. The tertiary sector is likely to be the main engine of growth in the future.

- The firms in an economy pursue a number of goals. They are supposed to try to maximise profits over the long run, but there may be other objectives imposed by stakeholders other than shareholders. These might be represented by pressure groups. Most businesses like to grow.

- The state has grown a lot in recent times, particularly in its role as provider of health services and as operator of the social security system.

Quick quiz

1   List three different types of economy.

2   Give two examples of private-sector organisations.

3   Give two examples of public-sector organisations.

4   What does the term privatisation mean?

5   List three ways in which the state exercises authority.

6   Name the three sectors of industry.

7   What are the two main elements of the role of the public sector?

8   What are the policy tools used by the state to regulate the economy?

9   Which sectors of the economy can you identify?

10   What are stakeholders?

11   List some of the objectives of a private-sector business.

Answers to quick quiz

1   Free enterprise economy, command economy, mixed economy.

2   Sole trader (greengrocer), public limited company (Marks and Spencer plc).

3   Civil Service agencies, the armed forces.

4   The process of turning public-sector organisations into private-sector ones.

5   Direct action, delegation, regulation.

6   Primary, secondary, tertiary.

7   The principle of equity, the correction of market failure.

8   Fiscal policy, monetary policy.

9   Public and private sectors.

10   Stakeholder - a person whose interests are affected by the activities of a firm.

11   Profit maximisation, protection of the interests of stakeholders, provision of services.

Answers to activities

1   (a)   You may have used a number of public services. The most likely ones are the National Health Service and education.

        (b)   You may have gained the following benefits: from the Health Service - better health care, less serious illness and preventative care. From education - improved literacy and numeracy, greater knowledge and the skills and confidence to engage in lifelong learning.

        (c)   You may have said that in 40 years time you expect these services to have enabled you to have a better and longer life.

        (d)   If health services were privatised, only wealthy people might then be able to afford certain kinds of medical treatment. If education were privatised, schools might not be available for all.

        (e)   Transport - some transport has been privatised. There has been criticism of the fact that some less profitable routes have been axed. There have also been concerns expressed over issues of safety on the rail network and general standards of service on particular lines.

                 Education - some schools have 'opted out' and are now more selective about who they admit, resulting in restricted choice for some pupils.

2   (a)   **Mrs A - £30,000**

                 Method (i)   £30,000 – 20% = £24,000 net

                 Method (ii)   £30,000 – £5,000 allowance = £25,000 taxable.

                                 £25,00 – 25% = £18,750

                                 £18,750 + £5,000 = £23,750 net

                 Mr B - £10,000

                 Method (i)   £10,000 – 20% = £8,000 net

                 Method (ii)   £10,000 – £5,000 allowance = £5,000 taxable.

                                 £5,000 – 25% = £3,750

                                 £3,750 + £5,000 = £8,750 net

        (b)   Method (i) would be best for ensuring maximum expenditure on luxury items.

        (c)   Method (ii) would be best for safeguarding the net income of people on low earnings.

3   Management is accountable to shareholders but must keep in mind the quality of service and value for money offered to customers. This remains a highly political issue. For example, if the water industry is 'private' why do government ministers get involved in customer complaints about such matters as the use of garden hoses during

summer droughts? One problem is that customers have until recently had little real choice in supplier. Furthermore, the utilities used to be owned by the public, whereas they are now accountable to shareholders. The tension can be managed by increased competition - customers will go to where they get the best service, regulatory bodies such as OFWAT, OFTEL, Government intervention - eg taxation on profits.

4   OFGAS is the regulatory body for Gas Suppliers. It has investigated pricing issues, anti-competitive practices and has commented on the pay awards given to top executives of British Gas.

OFWAT is the regulatory body for the Water Authorities. It has investigated pricing, water metering, problems with cutting off customers' water supplies and problems with supply – for example, Yorkshire Water's problems of drought in the summer of 1995 and 1996.

5   You might find initiatives such as urban regeneration schemes, 'areas of extreme rural deprivation' that receive European Social Fund monies, Enterprise Zones, local initiatives to encourage inward investment, or bids to host major events, e.g. Millennium bids.

6   (a)   Shareholders may want as much profit as possible distributed as dividends. The government might want to see investment in industry instead, or higher tax revenues. Management and employees will probably want higher wages.

For private sector businesses, this conflict is usually resolved in the shareholders' interest. For other concerns, however, the matter is not as simple, especially for businesses with a public service element. Some decisions are subject to public enquiries (eg building new roads) and consultation. In other cases, conflicts of interest are managed by regulation.

(b)   (i)   Internal stakeholders - employees, past employees, retirees, corporate management, the chief executive, the board of directors.

(ii)   Connected stakeholders - shareholders, lenders, customers, suppliers, competitors.

(iii)   External stakeholders - neighbours, the immediate community, national and world society, central and local government, special interest groups.

7   Small firms are usually competitive, encourage entrepreneurial behaviour, provide personal contact with customers, provide specialist services available that larger firms may not cater for, may be local, can offer flexibility.

8   The table gives some indication of the activity of government as a whole. Key issues of comparison include the following.

(a)   Public expenditure has increased in cash terms - but of course you will have to take inflation into account.

(b)   The significant increases have been in health, and especially social security (eg benefits for the unemployed).

(c)   Relative falls include defence, housing and industrial activities, and 'other expenditure'.

9   To a certain extent, the tertiary sector can take the place of the secondary sector in ensuring a healthy balance between imports and exports. However a major problem is that many services cannot, by their

very nature, be traded internationally. This problem accounts for the international market for manufactured goods being larger than the international market for services. The exception to this would be financial services which have done very well in the international market.

10   When North Sea Oil runs out, other forms of economic activity will make up the difference. Energy will be obtained from other sources.

11   The government could:

- Initiate training programmes in new skills

- Offer support for new employment opportunities in the affected areas

- Encourage geographical and occupational mobility of labour, making it easier for people to change where they live or the jobs they do

- Subsidise loss-making industries (this is not done for either shipbuilding or mining in the UK)

Assignment 1   **(2 hour)**

Scenario

Dolminia is a small country located on the Adriatic Coast. It has a population of about 12m. At the end of the Second World War the country was part of the Soviet Bloc and until twelve months ago had a communist government in spite of changes elsewhere in Europe. The economy of Dolminia was and is centrally planned, and economic control for all but a very few small agricultural units is owned and directed by the state. Last year, after nearly fifty years of communist rule, elections were held and a Christian Democratic government was elected with a policy of introducing free enterprise into the economy.

Dolminia has few natural resources apart from some undeveloped oil reserves under the southern continental shelf and long stretches of beautiful beaches to the north. Gold mines, once an important source of revenue, are now all but depleted given the current level of extractive technology in Dolminia. The north of the country is reckoned to be amongst the most attractive in this part of the Adriatic, and there are several state-owned 'Dacha' or country houses used in the past by party officials from Dolminia and other eastern bloc countries. There is little industrialisation, with most of the population working in the primary sector. In particular the central areas contain underdeveloped agriculture, with fruit and vine predominating. Dolminia had, until the ending of the Warsaw Pact, been described as the 'fruit box of the East'. There has been some interest from French and Australian wine makers for developing a Dolminian wine industry. The only major industry in Dolminia is based in the capital of the country - Dolman - and is the state-owned moped manufacturer Hosper, which is troubled by low investment and industrial unrest. The European Union, through its support for the newly democratised nations of eastern Europe, has made some funding and support available to develop the economy of Dolminia.

Tasks

(a)   Identify three areas of the economy that Dolminia should choose to 'privatise'. Justify your choice.

(b)   Identify those areas of the economy that should remain under state control for the foreseeable future, given the need of the government to accelerate the development of the economy in a fairly short time scale.

(c)   What type of incentives might be appropriate in Dolminia given the government's intention to reward free enterprise and initiative in economic affairs and develop a modern economy?

Chapter 2:
THE ROLE OF THE STATE

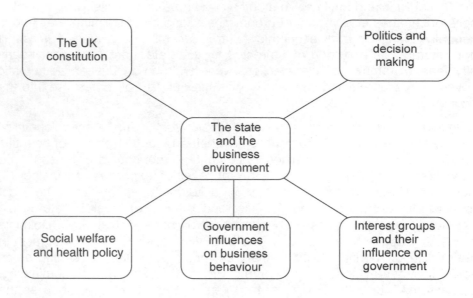

Introduction

In Chapter 1 we discussed certain general features of government policy. This chapter narrows the focus onto politics and the legislative process. We discuss the constitution of the UK and how government policies are made and implemented.

Government policy is subject to many influences, including interest and pressure groups who seek to ensure that key decisions are taken to their advantage. Such pressure groups maintain a constant dialogue with Ministers, MPs and other opinion formers, such as the media, to reach the wider public.

Government activities can influence an industry in many ways. There are some specific examples of legislation at the end of this chapter and some of these are explored in more detail in later chapters.

Effective management of organisations requires a general understanding of the processes of government, even though each area of legislation may require more specialised study.

Your objectives

In this chapter you will learn about:

(a)   Some of the basic principles of the constitution of the UK

(b)   How political decisions are taken

(c)   How interest and pressure groups can affect the decision-making process

(d)   How the state can affect the activities of individual firms

(e)   The extent of legislation

1 THE UK CONSTITUTION

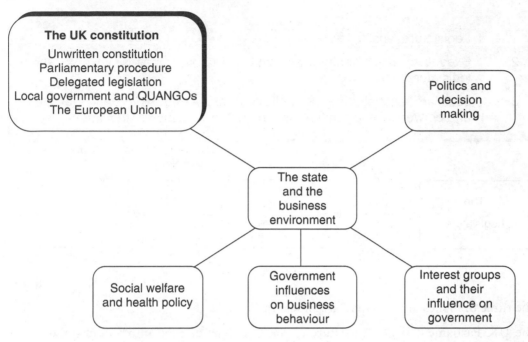

The UK constitution

Unwritten constitution
Parliamentary procedure
Delegated legislation
Local government and QUANGOs
The European Union

Politics and decision making

The state and the business environment

Social welfare and health policy

Government influences on business behaviour

Interest groups and their influence on government

1.1 Unwritten constitution

Definition

Constitution: the fundamental principles by which a state is governed. This includes the organisation and structure of government.

A number of countries have a written constitution, in which the rights of the citizens and the powers and the structure of state institutions are outlined. The constitution has a special status. It is a higher type of law than other legislation. The US Constitution is a good example: the US Supreme Court can rule other legislation 'unconstitutional'. It is harder to amend the constitution than it is to amend normal laws.

The UK is rare amongst democracies in that it has no written constitution. There is no document in which the rights of the citizen are outlined, nor can any law be ruled unconstitutional. However, the Human Rights Act 1998 effectively incorporates the European Convention of Human Rights into British law. Judges must interpret legislation in the light of this Convention. The Convention was established by the Council of Europe, which is quite separate from the EU. If a court finds that UK legislation does not fit with Convention rights, Parliament must decide what to do. It is unlawful for a public authority to breach the Convention rights unless an Act of Parliament says it could not have acted differently.

The foundation of the UK constitution is parliamentary sovereignty (more precisely, the supremacy of the Crown-in-Parliament). Parliament can do what it likes, and pass or repeal any law it chooses (limited only by physical possibility - it cannot repeal the law of gravity for example!). The only real restriction is that no Parliament can bind a future one - for example, it could not pass a law that included a statement to the effect of 'this law can never be repealed'.

Local government in the UK only exists insofar as powers are delegated to it by Parliament.

Definitions

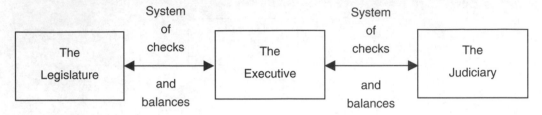

1   Legislature: enacts laws.

2   Executive: implements laws, and perhaps proposes laws to the legislature.

3   Judiciary: arbitrates between citizens, between the state and citizens, and between the legislature and executive branches of the state.

| The Legislature | System of checks and balances | The Executive | System of checks and balances | The Judiciary |

Figure 2.1 The UK constitution

The three branches of the system are shown in Figure 2.1.

The UK Parliament is the legislature of the UK. It is divided into two chambers, the House of Lords and the House of Commons.

At 2 July 2002 the *House of Lords* contained:

- 90 hereditary members

- 26 bishop

- Law Lords

- 546 members appointed for life

Before the 1999 reforms made by the Labour Government, there were many more hereditary peers – those who had the right to sit and vote by virtue of inheritance.

The House of Lords Act 1999 removed the right of most hereditary peers to sit and vote in the House. An amendment to the House of Lords Bill enabled 92 hereditary peers to remain until the House was fully reformed.

A Royal Commission, chaired by Lord Wakeham, was set up to consider the role, functions and composition of the second chamber. The Royal Commission report was published in January 2000 and put forward, amongst its recommendations, three options for composition involving varying numbers of appointed and elected members.

The Government published a White Paper in November 2001 entitled 'Completing he reform', and is planning to introduce the following changes in legislation.

(a)   The privileges of hereditary peers will be removed.

(b)   The eventual size of the House of Lords will be 600, with approximately 750 members in the interim.

(c)   An Independent Appointments Commission will decide how many seats each major political party is entitled to nominate, in proportions intended to reflect shares of the national vote in the General Election.

(d)   There will be approximately 120 appointed members without political affiliation, 120 directly elected members to represent the nations and regions, and a continuing role for Law Lords and Bishops of the Church of England.

The *House of Commons* is directly elected. The House of Lords can only *delay* legislation by the House of Commons.

Parliament includes the Monarch, who is part of the legislative process. The monarch has extensive powers in theory, but in practice these can only be exercised on the advice of his or her ministers, who normally sit in the House of Commons.

The UK's parliamentary system means that the centre of the *executive* branch (the Prime Minister and Cabinet) has effective control over the legislature. They decide the legislative programme for Parliament. The majority party in the legislature controls executive power. (In the USA, the opposite often holds: for example, President Clinton from the Democratic Party faced a legislature in which the Republican Party is the majority. However, party discipline is far less strict in the USA than the UK.) The centre of power is the Cabinet, whose members are members of the legislature.

When it comes to the *judiciary*, there is greater independence. The Lord Chancellor sits in the Cabinet, and the UK's final 'court of appeal' comprises certain members of the House of Lords and part of the legislature. Judicial independence is strictly enforced (a judge cannot be sacked because the government disagrees with his or her ruling). Judges can also be 'creative' in their interpretation of statute law. Remember though that Parliament can always change any law it dislikes. In the case of *Burmah Oil Company v Lord Advocate 1965*, a court decision was effectively rendered invalid by an Act of Parliament that was passed to override it retrospectively (the War Damage Act 1965).

The UK constitution operates what is called a system of 'checks and balances' to ensure that no branch of government can abuse its power. Each branch is supposed to be independent of the others so that abuses of power can be identified and dealt with. This is based on the doctrine of the 'separation of powers'. However, in reality certain members of government, for example the Lord Chancellor, are members of all three branches or have influence over them. Therefore, the branches are not strictly separate.

Devolution

Significant events since Labour took power have been the referenda on devolution. The 'yes' votes in both of these meant that both Scotland and Wales have directly elected assemblies. These are the National Assembly for Wales and the Scottish Parliament, which has legislative powers. An elected mayor for Greater London was supported in a public referendum in 1998, and Ken Livingstone was elected to the job in 2000.

We will now briefly discuss the process by which laws are made.

1.2 Parliamentary procedure

A proposal for legislation is originally aired in public in a government Green Paper. After comments are received a White Paper is produced, which sets out the intended aim of the legislation. It is then put forward in draft form as a Bill, and may be introduced into either the House of Commons or the House of Lords. When the Bill has passed through one House it must then go through the same stages in the other House.

In each House the successive stages of dealing with the Bill are as follows.

(a) *First reading*. Publication and introduction into the agenda; no debate.

(b) *Second reading*. Debate on the general merits of the Bill; no amendments at this stage.

(c) *Committee stage*. The Bill is examined section by section and amended if necessary by a Standing Committee of about 20 members, representing the main parties and including at least some members who specialise in the relevant subject. Sometimes it is a larger committee - on rare occasions it could be a committee of the whole house.

(d) *Report stage*. The Bill as amended in committee is reported to the full House for approval. If the government has undertaken in committee to reconsider various points it often puts forward its final amendments at this stage.

(e) *Third reading*. This is the final approval stage at which only verbal amendments may be made.

These stages are shown in Figure 2.2.

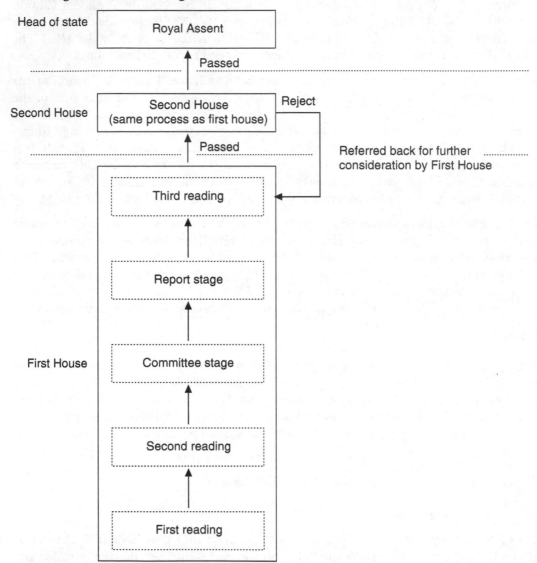

Figure 2.2 Stages of a Bill in Parliament

When it has passed through both Houses, the Bill is submitted for the Royal Assent, which in practice is given on the Queen's behalf by a committee of the Lord Chancellor and two other peers. It then becomes an Act of Parliament (or statute) but it does not (unless the Act itself so provides) come into operation until a commencement date is notified by statutory instrument.

BPP
PUBLISHING

> **Activity 1** **(1 hour)**
>
> Find out the difference between a government sponsored bill and a private member's bill. Give some examples of private members' bills that have been successful.

Acts of Parliament do not go into every detail and often give powers to ministers to clarify their meaning and application.

1.3 Delegated legislation

To save time in Parliament, it is usual to set out the main principles in the body of the Act as numbered sections and to relegate the details to schedules (at the end of the Act) that need not be debated, though they are visible and take effect as part of the Act. Even with this device there is a great deal that cannot conveniently be included in the Act. To provide for these and other matters a modern Act usually contains a section by which power is given to a minister, or public body such as a local authority, to make subordinate or *delegated legislation* for specified purposes only.

Local government has some authority but this is granted by Parliament.

1.4 Local government and QUANGOs

In the UK, the roles of *local government* have been curtailed, as have their powers to raise taxation. In some cases, over 75% of the revenue from a local authority will be provided by central government. There have been considerable upheavals in local authority structure in the past decade.

> **Activity 2** **(10 minutes)**
>
> Why is it necessary to delegate legislative power to local government? What is the advantage of this? Why is local government necessary?

Local authorities are responsible for the provision of state education, refuse collection, libraries, some roads, town planning and some social services.

Central government has taken to itself many of the functions of local government. Local government used to levy rates on business, but this is determined centrally. Some schools can opt out of local authority control, and be funded by central government. Central government can assess desirable levels of spending. The introduction of the National Curriculum has reduced the freedom schools had to choose the way and mix of teaching.

As well as local authorities there exist QUANGOs (an unofficial term referring to Quasi-Autonomous Non-Governmental Organisations). There has been a recent explosive growth in QUANGOs. They are normally funded by central government and are responsible for particular areas of policy. They are free to run their own affairs up to a point. Under the 1979-97 Conservative administrations, QUANGOs proliferated offering increased opportunities for political patronage, and critics argued, a decline in democratic accountability. Examples include the Welsh Development Agency, many NHS Hospital Trusts, and English Heritage.

NOTES

Activity 3   **(10 minutes)**

What is the advantage to the state of setting up QUANGOs to look at particular areas of policy? What are the disadvantages of this type of body?

The European Union has an increasing effect on UK laws. It is mentioned here, but gets a more detailed treatment in Chapter 3.

1.5 The European Union

The UK has certain obligations arising out of its membership of the European Union (formerly the European Community) as laid down by the treaties of Rome and Maastricht. European law is now as important as our own domestic law. We are obliged to obey European law in the same way as we have to comply with UK law.

It is important to understand the basis of the UK's membership of the European Union (EU) because EU legislation is of great importance to all business decisions and operations. This is because the EU is essentially economic in nature. The objective of a single European Market will require harmonisation of laws relating to business and trade.

There has been a steady increase in the importance of European Union Directives, which are incorporated into British law, arising from the UK's membership of the EU. This process has continued as a consequence of the decision to implement the Single European Market at the end of 1992. The fifteen member states of the EU (total population 370 million) now form one economic region in which goods, services, people and capital may move freely. The necessary legislation was introduced as a result of the passing of the Single European Act in 1986.

Activity 4   **(30 minutes)**

Find out the differences between a regulation, a directive and a decision in European Law.

Examples of aspects of legal harmonisation relevant to business.

- Company law
- Consumer rights
- Data protection
- Employment law

We now look at how policy and decisions are made.

2   POLITICS AND DECISION MAKING

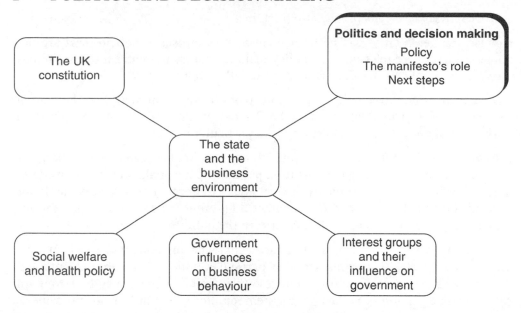

2.1   Policy

Definition

Policy: a way of expressing the broad purposes of government activity in a particular field, with some desired outcome in mind. The word 'policy' is used in a variety of ways.

(a)   A policy may be a *specific* proposal (eg to raise revenue by indirect as opposed to direct taxation).

(b)   A policy may *establish procedures* to achieve specific objectives such as parental choice in education (eg enabling schools to opt out of local authority control).

(c)   A policy can also be a vague direction for change with no *specific* outcome intended.

In the UK, political parties direct government policy and state activity.

Policies often end up as compromises between different interest groups. Political decision making on a national scale cannot really be compared to the decision making framework in a business. This is because governments have to take into account the interests of all citizens.

Public sector policies, therefore, always have some element of overt political choice attached to them. Responsibility for the actions taken by the public sector ultimately rests at the highest political level (ie the Cabinet and its committees). Ministerial decisions are made within an agreed policy framework. At this level the Treasury is also involved to assess the financial implications of policy.

The government can solicit advice from a number of sources, or in turn it may be lobbied.

(a)   The Civil Service exists to advise the government.

(b)   Academics and 'think tanks', for example, may be asked for their views.

(c)   Royal Commissions may be set up.

    (d)   *Special interest groups* may also pitch in.

Few policies are 'new'. They may be built upon an existing set of policies that are not working or are no longer relevant. The policy-making process is a pattern of continuous readjustment. Few policies run their course to the full without change.

Policy *formulation* is not always the responsibility of one single ministry. (In launching major initiatives the Prime Minister may be flanked by ministers who are associated with the bundle of policies aimed at dealing with particular problems.)

Policy *implementation* is not always the responsibility of a single organisation either. For example, the release of long-term patients from psychiatric hospitals into the community means the co-ordination of a number of policy areas (the organisations responsible for health, social welfare, housing and employment). The funding for these organisations may not be properly related to or co-ordinated with the policy objectives.

With the intermingling of policies, and of the agents who implement them, it may be difficult to identify clearly the impact of a particular policy or its implementation. Policies that have elements of political and resource choice in them may be strong on rhetoric but weak on funding, as the power system for allocating funds is not the same as that for getting the issues onto the political agenda. The Treasury wishes to control public spending in the interests of managing the economy, whereas other departments of state can think of good reasons for spending more money. For example the Chancellor of the Exchequer may wish to implement tax cuts in the next budget in order to enhance the government's image before the next election. However, the Treasury will want to know how the shortfall in 'income' can be made up.

Activity 5   (15 minutes)

If your student union wanted to propose a policy on smoking on college premises, which interest groups would it need to consult?

The election manifesto and the voting process are the links between the parties and the policies underlying them.

Political parties

The apparatus of government is headed by ministers who, unlike the civil servants advising them, are elected, and whose jobs as ministers can be terminated every so often by the electorate. Ministers direct the apparatus of government.

Definition

Party: 'a body of men and women united for promoting, by their joint endeavours, the national interest according to principles upon which they are all agreed'. (Adapted from Edmund Burke)

In the UK a political party is an organisation whose members share:

    (a)   Values or interests

    (b)   Views as to how society should be run

(c)   A desire to work together to ensure that they achieve control over policy making and the apparatus of government

In the UK, political parties compete for representation in Parliament and local government.

(a)   They are normally organised at constituency level - in order to promote their candidate for that particular seat.

(b)   However, all parties have a central organisation (eg Conservative Central Office).

A political party:

(a)   Aims to take over the whole of government, and be in charge of a variety of public policy areas from crime prevention to arts sponsorship

(b)   Draws its members from any section of society

The national parties in Britain are governed on different bases.

(a)   The *Labour Party* is composed of local parties, which send delegates to the party conference. The party conference also contains representatives from trade unions. Conference elects a *National Executive Committee*, responsible for most policy making. The leader is elected by MPs, party members and trade unionists.

(b)   The *Conservative Party* is in theory a federation of local associations which select candidates, normally from a short list, for the parliamentary seat. The Conservative MPs elect the leader, who appoints a chairman. This party's constitution is at the time of writing undergoing a fundamental review.

(c)   The *Liberal Democratic Party* has no trade union connection. Its formal constitution requires the leader be elected by a national conference. The Liberal Democrats maintain separate organisations for England, Scotland and Wales. They form a federal party.

The system of electing a leader is perceived as fair but can nonetheless have damaging consequences.

Following Labour's success in the 1997 elections, the Conservative Party witnessed a major battle between senior members who all wanted to succeed John Major as party leader. Although William Hague emerged as the ultimate victor, the whole internal election process revealed deep divisions within the Conservative Party, and reinforced a negative public image of a party preoccupied with internal squabbling.

2.2   The manifesto's role

The manifesto

In the UK, the existence of a proposal in the winning party's election manifesto is a powerful spur for implementing that proposal. A manifesto contains the promises a party makes to the voters in order to get elected. However, an election manifesto cannot cover every aspect of government activity in the right detail.

(a)   Policy objectives might be diffuse, unclear, unspecific or internally inconsistent.

(b)   The implementation process may well involve another tier of political decision makers (eg local government, appointed boards who have their own set of priorities). It is the field officers, street level bureaucrats or teachers who have to put the policy into practice. A simple example is the sale of council houses, implemented far more swiftly by some local authorities than others. Recently, the government has had some difficulty in implementing its 'nursery voucher' scheme as local authorities are reluctant to join in the pilot scheme.

The organisation implementing the policies has to make decisions about priorities from among several objectives, which may all be equally desirable but which cannot be achieved due to limited resources.

Activity 6 (30 minutes)

Your college has had its annual budget cut by central government. It has been approached by three different bodies who would like the college to run some new courses. These courses are as follows.

- A local group representing Asian women from your local community. They feel that there is a need for a course in English for women whose first language is Punjabi and who are finding it difficult to cope in the community or gain employment. They would not be in a position to pay for the course.

- A local business who wants some tailor-made in-company courses in communication skills for its staff. They are willing to pay a premium price for these courses.

- A professional body that would like to run its accountancy course in your area. They feel that there is a demand and are willing to make your college an accredited centre for this. Students would pay normal part-time rates.

The college represents itself as one that is responsive to the needs of the community and business. However, owing to the cutbacks you cannot afford to do everything that is proposed to you. How do you decide which of these proposals to implement? You would like to please everyone if you can.

To make administration more efficient, the government set up Executive Agencies through the 'Next Steps' process, which separates policy from administration.

2.3 Executive Agencies

The government has taken the steps of divorcing the making of policy from implementation or operational matters. Ministers decide the broad thrust of what is to be done, and administration is left to managers in *Executive Agencies*. The idea was to make government more efficient by introducing new management techniques. The problems of this approach, whereby policy is separated from day-to-day management, are shown by the recent controversy following the dismissal of the head of the Crown Prosecution Service.

A number of groups can influence government policy. We shall go on now to look at these.

3 INTEREST GROUPS AND THEIR INFLUENCE ON GOVERNMENT

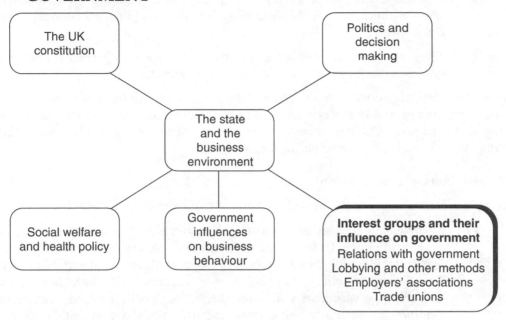

```
                                              ┌──────────────┐
                                              │  Politics and │
                                              │   decision    │
                                              │    making     │
                                              └──────────────┘
┌──────────────┐
│   The UK     │
│ constitution │
└──────────────┘
                        ┌──────────────┐
                        │  The state   │
                        │   and the    │
                        │  business    │
                        │ environment  │
                        └──────────────┘
┌──────────────┐   ┌──────────────┐   ┌──────────────────────────┐
│Social welfare│   │  Government  │   │ Interest groups and their│
│and health    │   │  influences  │   │ influence on government  │
│policy        │   │  on business │   │ Relations with government│
└──────────────┘   │  behaviour   │   │ Lobbying and other methods│
                   └──────────────┘   │  Employers' associations │
                                      │      Trade unions        │
                                      └──────────────────────────┘
```

Definitions

> 1   *Pressure group:* a collection of people promoting some particular course or objective. Examples are Greenpeace and Friends of the Earth.
>
> 2   *Interest group:* a group that represents the wider interests of a particular group of people, such as a Trade Union.
>
> Some groups may be both pressure groups and interest groups, and the terms are often used interchangeably.

Interest groups and pressure groups have an interest in matters of public policy but do not aspire to control the machinery of government.

Many pressure/interest groups seek to influence business indirectly by influencing government - but not all their groups' concerns are relevant to business.

Pressure groups in Britain

Significance of pressure groups. Pressure groups, according to an Economist survey (13 August 1994), 'are one of the growth industries of late-20th century Britain. The Royal Society of the Protection of Birds (RSPB), for instance, has more members than the Labour, Conservative and Liberal Democrat parties combined'. In the past 30 years, hundreds of pressure groups representing interests from pedestrians to civil liberties have emerged to compete for the attention of the public, civil servants and politicians.

Causes of pressure groups

(a) Disillusionment with government policy, and 'many conscience-driven activists found they could wield more influence by joining a pressure group than a party'.

(b) They 'offer citizens a direct and immediate voice in a permanent political process in ways that a vote every five years cannot'.

The effectiveness of pressure groups varies. Few succeed overnight. The most effective are run by a core of highly professional activists. However, too many groups, according to the Economist survey, seek merely to get the attention of the media rather than relying on the more sophisticated political strategy.

3.1 Relations with government

A group can have one of two sorts of relationship with government, as follows.

(a) *Insider groups* are regularly consulted by government as a matter of routine in areas of policy. In fact, some insider groups expect to be consulted. Note that insider groups do not necessarily support the government of the day. The British Medical Association, for example, although not always supporting government policy on the NHS, is still regularly consulted. *Charities* are currently being consulted over the Government's review of taxation of charities. A draft document is planned by Autumn 1998 and, again, interest groups will be invited to respond to the draft.

(b) *Outsider groups* do not have an 'inside track' to government. Many unions which used to have an inside track were marginalised and became outsider groups during the long rule of the Conservatives. Some of the activities of outsider groups are:

  (i) To promote interest in their cause outside government (eg in the media) so that the issue is raised in the public arena

  (ii) To gain credibility in the eyes of the public and recognition of their importance by the government, so that their pronouncements are taken seriously

The role of interest and pressure groups is controversial. Some argue that the existence of interest and pressure groups means that power is diffused widely, and that they are an informal check on the ever-increasing power of the state. They also help to protect minorities.

However, some interest groups representing business may be more influential than others and this can be anti-democratic. For example, some supporters of rail transport believe that 'the road lobby' has undue influence on UK transport policy.

In the US it is sometimes alleged that lobbying by the National Rifle Association against firearm restrictions has impeded gun control legislation which might have helped to reduce the US's high murder rate.

The power of vested interests can often prevent radical policy reviews that might adversely affect them. That said, there are many cases when powerful interest groups are overridden.

(a) The brewing industry in the UK was radically reshaped by a government review, in order to introduce competition.

(b) Government policy on broadcasting is another example. The auctioning of franchises to run UK television stations was opposed by many in the industry.

(c) Sunday trading legislation was passed only after a long battle between supporters and opponents of Sunday opening for most retailers.

The main associations reflecting economic interests are as follows.

(a) *Businesses:* Confederation of British Industry (CBI), Institute of Directors (IOD). There are also smaller more specific trade associations in particular industries, which group together to promote common interests (eg newspapers to oppose VAT on the press). There are many other organisations such as chambers of commerce and specialised areas such as the food and drink industry, chemicals, motor manufacturing and engineering.

EXAMPLE: CBI

An example of an interest group representing business is the Confederation of British Industry (CBI).

Objectives

To support and represent industrial and commercial organisations in the private sector.

Activities and concerns

- Government relations

    - Draft legislation

    - Economic policy

    - Training and education

- Commercial opportunities

    - Exports

    - Inward investment

    - Regional development

- Inter-organisational relations

    - Professions

    - Trade unions

    - Local governments

- Public relations

    - Research

    - Publications

    - Media appearances

(b) Professional associations are groups of people who do the same job or the same skill, for example:

(i) Accountants (with several professional bodies)

(ii) Doctors (British Medical Association)

Professional associations are generally involved in setting standards of skill and enforcing adherence to good practice (eg through disciplinary schemes).

(c)   *Trade unions* are similar to professional associations, in that they represent people who work. Their function is to negotiate terms and conditions of employment for their members. They are described in more detail later.

(d)   *Consumers' associations* represent people as consumers, campaigning on issues such as product pricing, safety and quality. Consumers' associations have campaigned for labelling on food, for example.

Activity 7 (30 minutes)

Under the procedures of the European Union, interest groups such as the CBI and the Trade Unions are recognised as 'social partners' in the process of creating economic policy and legislation. Does this idea accord with UK practice? Identify UK practices to support or contradict the assumption that social partnership has an economic function.

In the near past, it was relatively easy to identify the relationship between political parties and groups in society.

The Labour Party used to represent the organised working class, and the Conservatives represented business. In practice, this simple division did break down as, for example, there were many Conservative trade unionists and socialism had a lot of middle class support. These days, as witnessed in the 1997 General Election, party support is more volatile.

The source of funding of political parties is not exactly a known quantity. This issue has received media attention over the last year, provoking calls for stricter rules to govern the acceptability of certain sources of funding. For example, Tony Blair was strongly criticised for accepting a significant political donation on behalf of the Labour Party from Bernie Ecclestone, the insinuation being that it influenced his decision on exempting the motor racing industry from a ban on tobacco advertising. The result was that the donation was handed back.

(a)   Labour has traditionally enjoyed the financial support of the Trade Unions. However, the power of Trade Unions over decision-making has been reduced and the Labour Party has been trying to increase income from other sources (eg reversing the decline in membership). The Labour Party publishes comprehensive accounts.

(b)   The Conservative Party's financial affairs are more complex. Each constituency party is autonomous financially. The party as a whole also receives income from business sources. However, the Conservative Party does not yet publish comprehensive accounts as a whole, which critics within the party would like it to do.

We now discuss how interest/pressure groups can influence the government.

3.2 Lobbying and other methods

Definition

> *Lobbying*: a method used to influence political decision making. It involves maintaining regular contact with ministers or members of parliament, to put forward a case.

The UK government has itself issued details on how to influence government bodies - in this case the EU processes of the European Commission, but it applies at national level too.

It is much better to influence the *drafting process* of new regulations than to try and get them changed once they have been implemented.

Step 1 Get in early. Make your views known at the drafting stage. Work with officials rather than ministers.

Step 2 Work with others. 'A spread of opinion carries more weight than a lone voice.' UK businesses should thus work with European trade associations.

Step 3 Think 'politically'. A firm's lobbying will be more effective if it can be demonstrated that the issue is relevant to government or EU policy (eg single market program).

Step 4 Be prepared. Monitor what is going on, and the issues that are being dealt with by the Commission and government.

Step 5 Think long-term. A long-term presence (eg in Brussels) can be of immense benefit, given that the lobbying process can be a long standing one.

Interest groups can use a number of techniques when dealing with their own national government.

(a) They can employ lobbyists to put their case to individual ministers or civil servants.

(b) Businesses can give MPs non-executive directorships, in the hope that the MP will take an interest in all legislation that affects them. This is now subject to Parliamentary rules. However, it should be noted that a business is just as entitled to approach its constituency MP as any other constituent is.

(c) They can sit on consultative committees.

(d) They can donate money to (or withdraw funds from) the political party they support. Companies spending such funds must report the amounts involved. Rules on donations are now stricter than ever to prevent allegations of bribery.

(e) Some businesses have considerable influence/contact with government as they are involved in contracts directly with them, eg the defence industry.

The Department of Trade and Industry also recommends that having a long-tcrm presence in Brussels to influence the European Commission can be of immense benefit, given that the lobbying process can be a long standing one. Moreover, a business might be in a position to initiate the legislative process if it has unique information about a particular trading issue.

However, all businesses should be very careful when taking part in such activities - there are now strict boundaries imposed as a result of the various 'sleaze' allegations concerning MPs and others who were felt to be too highly influenced.

Some interest groups can act as both insiders and outsiders. When not walking up and down the corridors of power, members of an interest group can do the following to influence government policy.

(a) They can try to influence public opinion and the legislative agenda by advertising. The RSPCA advertised (unsuccessfully) for a dog registration scheme in the UK. This was more than just an appeal for donations. The advertising was specifically designed to change government policy.

(b) Few organisations can afford expensive press advertising. However, there are other ways of getting publicity.

    (i) Demonstrations get media publicity, and are a means by which sufficiently committed people can demonstrate support. Involvement by celebrities can also add to media interest.

    (ii) Petitions are a way of dramatising a problem.

    (iii) Direct action, as practised by Greenpeace against whalers, puts certain issues on the agenda.

    (iv) Effective public relations are important. An interest group might try to convince journalists or major newspapers, or indeed television producers, that its story is newsworthy.

These methods may or may not have a direct impact. If the action is public, ministers might not wish to be seen to 'lose face' by giving in. However, they can create a climate of opinion to which politicians can later respond. The adoption of environmental issues by politicians is the result of many years of campaigning by pressure groups.

Responding to pressure groups

For businesses, pressure groups are a fact of life. Some activists become shareholders to raise matters of concern at embarrassing moments (at board meetings).

For many firms, this is a tricky problem, so here are some examples.

Possible approach	Comment
Sue for libel	McDonald's suffered greatly from bad publicity, suing two penniless activists. Their allegations received far more publicity thanks to the 'McLibel' trial yet McDonald's management felt they had to protect their brand.
Public relations management	Greenpeace's PR over the disposal of Brent Spar in the North Sea was far more effective than Shell's - even though the ecological case for disposal was, according to many scientists, better than breaking up the rig on shore.
Consultation	Shell has agreed to consult activists on human rights and ecological issues.
Endorsement	A firm can ask for the endorsement of a pressure group on specific products.

Possible approach	Comment
Respond to their concerns	Firms may implement what the pressure groups demand in the hope that the problem would go away. Barclays 'disinvested' in (apartheid) South Africa after years of adverse publicity. Activists attempted to discourage students from opening new bank accounts.

Activity 8   **(45 minutes)**

Find a recent press article that concerns pressure-group activity designed to make either the government or a business organisation change its policy. Précis the article, listing the main points made by the pressure group.

We now discuss interest groups directly related to the business and the workplace.

3.3 Employers' associations

Definition

> *Employers' association*: an interest group that is 'an organisation of employers that seeks to assist, influence or control the industrial relations decisions of member firms and/or engage in trade activities on behalf of members'.

Employers' associations have a role similar to that of trade unions, insofar as they protect and promote the interests of their members; however, their membership and aims are very different. They represent the employers (the 'management side' of the industry), they promote the interests of the industry as a whole and they protect their businesses in relation to the workforce.

Eligibility for membership depends on:

(a)   Participating in the relevant industry

(b)   Acceptance of the policy of the association

(c)   The member having a 'reputable business'

Discipline over members is exercised by the threats of: exclusion from membership, loss of the member's share of the association's strike fund, and denial of other services.

Sometimes labour and trade matters are managed by two different associations.

(a)   On labour matters, associations are organised by industry. These issues fall into two categories:

        (i)   Collective bargaining, in which employers in an industry meet employees' representatives to hammer out pay, productivity and conditions agreements

        (ii)   Assistance to individual firms on management/labour issues

(b)   Their trade related activities include:

        (i)   Representing employers' interests to government and the European Commission

(ii)   Collating and publishing information and statistics

    (iii)   Providing joint training arrangements

    (iv)   Engaging in joint research and development activities

    (v)   Drawing up codes of conduct (eg to avoid regulation being imposed by the state)

As well as associations for particular industries there are wider bodies, such as the Confederation of British Industry, which exist to promote the aims of industry as a whole to government.

Trade unions represent the other side of industry, although they have diminished in importance in recent years.

3.4   Trade unions

Definition

> *Trade unions*: organised associations of working people in a trade, occupation or industry (or several trades or industries) formed for protection and promotion of their common interests, mainly the regulation and negotiation of pay and conditions.

There are four main types of trade union.

    (a)   *Craft or occupational unions.* Mainly catering for skilled workers, such as printers, engineers, building trade craftsmen, for example the Amalgamated Union of Engineering and Electronic Workers.

    (b)   *General workers' unions.* Mainly semi-skilled and unskilled workers across the full range of industry, for example the Transport and General Workers Union, which has about one million members.

    (c)   *Industrial unions.* Covering many of the workers of all grades and occupations within a single industry, for example the Rail and Maritime Transport and the National Union of Mineworkers.

    (d)   *White collar unions.* A growing sector of trade unionism covering technical, professional, supervisory and managerial staffs. Since 1945 white collar unions have been the main growth area in trade union membership. Trade union membership as a whole has been in severe decline since 1979.

We have seen how various groups can influence government policy. Now we look at how government can influence business behaviour.

4 GOVERNMENT INFLUENCES ON BUSINESS BEHAVIOUR

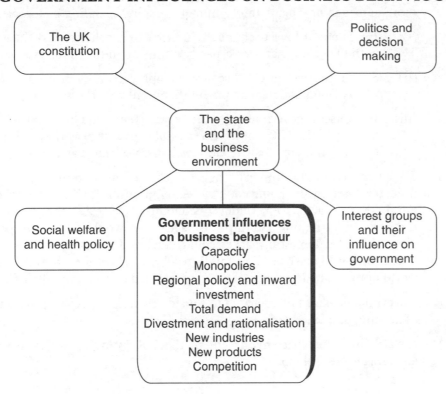

Government policy affects firms:

(a) By influencing consumer demand

(b) By increasing or decreasing the cost of funds (interest rates)

(c) By increasing/decreasing the amount of money taken from the business as taxation

(d) By regulating what, and how much, the business makes, and how it goes about it

We are concerned here with item (d) in the list above.

4.1 Capacity

Definition

> *Capacity:* the maximum amount of goods a firm can make. A bakery whose ovens are big enough to bake 3,000 loaves a day would have a daily output capacity of 3,000 loaves. A firm (or industry) with overcapacity is able to produce more than it actually needs to satisfy customers. A firm that is operating at less than full capacity is producing less than it can. If there is undercapacity in a firm or industry then the firm or industry is unable to produce enough to meet the demand.

Government policy can encourage firms to increase the amount of goods they are able to produce (ie by increasing their output capacity).

(a) The government might offer cash grants or tax incentives to firms to invest more money in new plant and equipment ('capital spending'). However:

    (i) Firms might invest too much, in order to get the grant or incentives, with the result that over-capacity builds up in the industry

    (ii) Such incentives might discourage employment, by making it cheaper to buy labour-saving equipment than to hire workers

    (iii) If overseas governments offer investment support, foreign firms trading in the UK will have a possible advantage as they will be able to access this source, whereas locally based firms may not

(b) To avoid paying for imports, government might want to build up an industry based in the home country (eg by granting it all the government's purchase contracts). To achieve economies of scale, the home-based industry might require an output capacity that would force it to produce more than the domestic market could take, and to try to sell the excess output on world markets. This might result in a short-term over-capacity in world output. The less efficient or protected firms will eventually fail.

(c) Governments might be prepared to subsidise excess capacity in the interests of keeping people in work.

(d) Inward investment (ie investment in the UK by overseas firms) may be encouraged (see below).

One aspect of business that governments may seek to control is the existence of monopolies.

4.2 Monopolies

There are several different ways in which a government can attempt to control monopolies. (See Chapter 1 for definitions of monopoly and oligopoly.)

(a) It can stop them from developing, or it can break them up (eg 'trust-busting' in the USA).

(b) It can take them over. Nationalised industries were often government-run monopolies, and central and/or local government also have virtual monopolies in the supply of other services, such as health, the police, education and social services. Government-run monopolies are potentially advantageous because:

    (i) They need not have a profit-maximising objective so that the government can decide whether or not to supply a good or service to a household on grounds other than cost or profit

    (ii) The government can regulate the quality of the good or service provided more easily than if the industry were operated by private firms

    (iii) Key industries can be protected (for example health, education)

(c) It can allow monopolies or oligopolies to operate, but can regulate them (as in the water and electricity supply industries).

(d) It can forbid mergers. If a single firm controls a big enough share of the market, it can begin to behave as a monopolist even though its market share is below 100%. An example was the government's actions to prevent Bass and Carlsberg-Tetley from merging.

(e)   It can outlaw other anti-competitive practices. (For example, several firms could behave as monopolists if they agree not to compete, or if they co-operate to divide the market between them.)

Or it may set up regulatory bodies are 'consumer watchdogs' to protect consumers' interests where conditions of natural monopoly apply, as in the recently privatised utility industries of the UK. The pricing of products in such industries may be controlled: in the UK, many of the large utilities have been required to limit price increases to a specified percentage below the Retail Prices Index over a number of years.

Mechanisms need to be set up to ensure that these areas are controlled. In the UK this is done by the Competition Commission (formerly called the Monopolies and Mergers Commission) and the Office of Fair Trading.

In the UK, the Monopolies and Restrictive Practices Act 1948 provided that any firm controlling more than one third of the market for its goods should be investigated as a potential monopoly which was against the public interest. Under the Fair Trading Act 1973, the Director General of Fair Trading is allowed to refer cases to the Competition Commission if any firm controls one quarter of the market, or if any proposed takeover or merger would create a firm that controlled more than one quarter of the market. The Commission will then investigate the proposed merger or takeover and recommend whether or not it should be allowed to proceed.

Another aspect of the work of the Competition Commission is to investigate cases where a monopoly is suspected of operating against the public interest and to recommend to the government the steps that should be taken to make the monopoly alter its practices.

Public policy in favour of monopolies and mergers

One aspect of the UK government's policy has mainly been one of trying to control the development of monopolies that are 'against the public interest'. But opinions differ about what monopolies would be good for the country and which ones would be harmful. Another aspect in recent years has been the establishment of 'watchdog' bodies such as OFTEL (for telecommunications) and OFWAT (for water supply), as already mentioned, to regulate the recently privatised utility industries where there are usually conditions of natural monopoly.

In the modern world of multinational companies, companies need to be big to survive and prosper. Arguably, the UK's industrial strength has declined over the years because the country has failed to nurture enough multinational companies (strengthened by virtual monopolies in their own country) to compete successfully in world markets. Compare Rover cars, as just one example, a very small car manufacturer in world terms, with Fiat, a big multinational with a virtual monopoly in the Italian car market.

There have been signs in recent years that the UK government has wanted to encourage the growth of companies in the UK, and many of the proposed 'mega-mergers' between large companies have not been referred to the MMC/Competition Commission. Government anti-monopoly policy in the UK has accordingly been relatively mild in recent years.

EXAMPLE: BUSINESS BANKING

In March 2002, the Competition Commission reported under the Fair Trading Act on the supply of banking services to small and medium-sized enterprises (SMEs).

The Commission judged that many of the banks' practices made up a complex monopoly situation which restricted price competition. The banks distinguished between personal and business accounts and generally paid no interest on the latter. The structure of charges was found not to reflect the structure of costs.

The Commission recommended that the main banks should give undertakings to complete a substantial proportion of account transfers within five to ten working days, and to pay compensation if these timescales were not met. It was also proposed that the banks should compile information to enable customers easily to make price comparisons.

European Union regulations on mergers

The European Commission has the power to intervene and to either block or to authorise mergers above a certain threshold size within the European Union (EU). If the Commission finds that the merger raises serious doubts as to its compatibility with the European common market, it will initiate proceedings to block the merger.

EXAMPLE: COCA-COLA/CARLSBERG

As it had done on previous occasions, in 1997 the European Commission forced US drinks giant Coca-Cola to change its plans for new bottling operations in Europe.

In May 1997, regulators started a four-month investigation into the creation of a joint bottling venture and transfers of asset between the Coca-Cola Company and Denmark's Carlsberg. The venture combines the companies' soft drinks activities in Sweden, Denmark and the Baltics with licence agreements and a distribution joint venture with the Swedish brewer Falcon, a company owned jointly by Carlsberg and the Finnish brewing company Sinebrychoff.

The Commission defined the relevant product market as that for cola-flavoured carbonated soft drinks rather than that for soft drinks in general. Once this controversial approach was adopted, investigators found that the market shares of the firms were more than 60% in the Danish cola market, more than 50% in an overall Danish carbonated soft drink market, more than 40% in non-cola soft drinks in Denmark, and above 70% in the Swedish cola market.

Government may also seek to influence business within particular disadvantaged regions.

4.3 Regional policy and inward investment

> **Activity 9** (10 minutes)
>
> Some regions of England claim they need special economic aid. How can government set about evaluating relative needs, and how can resources be redistributed from wealthy to less wealthy regions?

Government can promote particular regions to foreign investors, as the two examples below demonstrate. INWARD is a regional agency promotion for the North West of England.

EXAMPLE 1: INWARD INVESTMENT BRIEF

During 1993-94, INWARD and its partners assisted 36 companies to invest in 19 different locations across North West England, coming from 10 different countries of origin: USA, Japan, Taiwan, Germany, France, Spain, Switzerland, Eire, and Bermuda, as well as the UK.

This clearly underlines both how attractive the entire region is to potential international inward investors, and that one of its strengths is the variety of business locations that can meet the needs of international companies in a broad range of manufacturing and service sectors.

Of the 36 investment decisions, 25 of them resulted from enquiries directly generated by INWARD's efforts, and 10 of the total were expansions by companies already based in the region. Having long-established links with the region's international business community, INWARD has a pivotal role in ensuring that overseas companies continue to invest in North West England, rather than any other European region.

A third of the inward investment successes were from North America, and these included some of the year's largest projects. 1993-94 saw a regional team led by INWARD attract MBNA American Bank to Chester. This was one of the largest North American inward investments to the UK in recent years.

Chief Executive of MBNA International Bank Ltd, Thomas P McGinley, commented, 'MBNA selected Chester for the right people and education infrastructure, high quality business environment, and first class transport and communication links.'

INWARD was delighted to have provided assistance, particularly in the project's early stages, to attracting US-owned manufacturer of environmental control equipment, Omega Engineering, which decided to locate at Northbank Industrial Estate, Irlam, after lengthy negotiations with Trafford Park Development Corporation.

500 jobs will be created over the next decade, and £11 million is being invested in the first two stages of this investment project. Mr Ralph Michel, Omega's Vice-President, said: 'The high calibre of workers in the Manchester area was very influential in the company's choice for its headquarters. We have chosen Northbank because of its excellent location close to the motorway network and Manchester Airport.'

Taken with the siting of the new Euroterminal at Trafford Park, this area is truly a 'Gateway to Europe', which is particularly important for companies such as ours whose customers are based in the UK and Europe.'

Among the other 10 US-owned companies which were attracted to North West England in 1993-94, 30 jobs were safeguarded in Preston by manufacture of printed bar code labels, Zebra Technologies. Car seat manufacturer, Johnson Controls, brought 145 direct jobs to Speke with its £5.8 million investment in Merseyside. Commented Plant Manager, Steve Spratt, 'The local knowledge that our INWARD assigned project manager had would have been difficult, if not impossible, to create ourselves. It also meant that we had no need to tie up full time resources in the early stages of the project.'

NOTES

EXAMPLE 2: MERSEYSIDE

There can be no greater expression of confidence in Merseyside than the surge of inward investment. Merseyside comprises the City of Liverpool and the four Metropolitan Boroughs of St. Helens, Sefton, Knowsley and Wirral.

With more than 75% of Merseyside's workforce employed in service industries, Liverpool itself is a thriving services sector and manufacturing city. Its position today as one of the busiest ports in the UK, with the country's most successfully freeport, as well as the motorway infrastructure on its doorstep, is proving an attractive combination for investors and corporates.

At Hamilton Oil's shore supply depot in Bootle Docks, £75 million has already been invested with an anticipated further £40 million a year on goods and services. The enormous potential of the Irish Sea oil industry is opening up, with Sefton MBC spearheading the initiative.

In 1994, Sony Electronics announced that it will be basing its European software development and support centre at Wavertree Technology Park. This £35 million investment, bringing with it 250 jobs, illustrates the success of the Park which is let to companies such as Barclaycard, Rank Xerox, GEC Marconi and Siemens. The latest announced arrival is National Westminster Bank, underpinning Merseyside's claim as an ideal location.

One of the biggest developments Merseyside will see is the multi-million pound transformation of the Twelve Quays site in Birkenhead on the Wirral. This prestige development on the 60 acre site includes a roll-on roll-off ferry terminal servicing Belfast and Dublin, a maritime village and a four-star hotel. Liverpool John Moores University and a joint venture London development company are looking to create a science park in a venture funded by a combination of European Objective One money, the Merseyside Development Corporation and the private sector.

But it's not only large corporates and multi-nationals that are investing in Merseyside. It has a growing number of small companies and considerable incentives available to them. A good example is Allanprint, which is one of the UK's largest web offset presses, brought about with assistance from English Partnerships and St Helens Council.

Investment in innovative management and supportive training packages is also giving a number of Merseyside companies a competitive edge under difficult market conditions. Stoves, for example, manufacturing cookers in Knowsley, is seeing a 40% growth in a shrinking market sector, having created 200 extra jobs during the last recession.

The automotive sector continues to provide an important source of investment for Merseyside, supplying the likes of Ford at Halewood and Vauxhall in Ellesmere Port, as assemblers implement their sequencing strategies. Most recently, Raybestos US, automotive components manufacturer of clutch plates, has announced an investment of £32 million in a new factory in the Speke Hall Industrial Estate in Liverpool.

Merseyside's economy is growing and will be boosted further by the arrival of Objective One status. This brings special grants from the European Union and the UK government worth up to £1.26bn over five years. In part this will fund an image campaign aimed at encouraging the upward trend in investment and relocation. The campaign will be run by the Mersey Partnership whose specific remit is to boost the image of Merseyside and achieve inward investment by working closely with private-sector businesses, government authorities and development agencies such as INWARD.

To quote the then Environment Secretary, John Gummer, commenting on a re-investment project, 'This is another vote of confidence in Merseyside and the people of

Merseyside. They have created a remarkable new image for the area as a place to come and invest.'

Activity 10   **(30 minutes)**

Your home area wishes to create a campaign to encourage inward investment from overseas companies. List the positive factors in your area that could encourage a company to re-locate there.

Government may also have an influence on the total demand for particular products or services.

4.4   Total demand

Government policy and laws can have a direct influence on the total volume of market demand and hence the total demand for the products of individual firms and industries. For example, the tax differentials on lead-free petrol have increased demand for lead-free petrol as a whole and reduced demand for leaded petrol.

Government may seek to influence business policies that may lead to job losses.

4.5   Divestment and rationalisation

Definitions

---

1   *Divestment*: a firm gets rid of one of its businesses by closing it down or by selling it to another company. This is often the opposite process to diversification

2   *Rationalisation*: the reorganisation of a business's operations, often to cut costs and improve efficiency, or to reduce the number of businesses in which the firm operates.

Divestment and rationalisation decisions by a firm can mean putting people out of work. 'Rationalisation' of a business inevitably means closures and redundancies. A government might bring pressure to bear on a firm to dissuade it from making the divestment or rationalisation decisions that would be in the firm's best strategic interests.

(a)   Laws on redundancy payments might raise the costs to a firm of making employees redundant, and so create 'exit barriers' that dissuade a firm from divesting.

(b)   Government ownership of nationalised industries and government-run industries (eg health) means that a government can make decisions for or against divestment and rationalisation.

Government may seek to encourage or discourage the development of new industries.

BPP
PUBLISHING

4.6 New industries

Government *industrial policy* might either hamper or promote the growth of new industries.

    (a)   Restraining growth: 'green belt' policies prevent the location of industry in certain areas.

    (b)   Encouraging an emerging industry: for example the decision by the UK government some years ago to adopt the BBC microcomputer in state schools.

Government policy might make it difficult for new firms to gain entry into an industry or market. Examples of how this could be done are as follows.

    (a)   By placing restrictions on foreign firms that wish to set up business in the country, or by putting import tariffs on the goods of overseas suppliers

    (b)   By subsidising, directly or indirectly, domestic firms that are already in the industry

    (c)   By imposing product standards requiring a particular level of safety. One of the aims of EU harmonisation is the elimination of national differences, and hence the creation of economies of scale. However, this will also mean that products previously banned as not meeting UK safety requirements will be brought up to the correct standard and so can enter the UK market.

Government may also seek to encourage or discourage new products.

4.7 New products

In some industries, governments regulate the adoption of new products.

    (a)   In the pharmaceuticals industry new drugs or medicines must undergo stringent testing and obtain government approval before they can be marketed. (The stringency of controls varies from country to country, and so drugs companies may sell a product in one country that has been banned in others.)

    (b)   The food industry is subjected to strict controls on products and also manufacturing processes. Consequently, companies in the food industry have less freedom to move to any new technology, or to change material mixes, than firms that are in other industries. A current issue in this area is the recent debates about the safety of genetically-modified food products.

Government can influence the degree and nature of competition within an industry.

4.8 Competition

As a buyer, controller and supplier in a mixed economy, the government can bring considerable pressure to bear on competition within an industry. Moreover, changes in policy can result in a change in the industry and competition. As an example, the government in the UK decides what television and radio companies are permitted to broadcast; changes in policy - eg to permit more local commercial radio stations or to take away the franchises of existing ITV companies - have brought about significant changes in the industry.

Governments might impose policies that keep an industry fragmented and prevent the concentration of too much market share in the hands of one or two producers. In the UK, the Monopolies and Mergers Act is intended to regulate the growth of monopolies in an industry.

FOR DISCUSSION

Should the government interfere in the marketplace if a monopoly becomes obvious? Why should the strongest companies not be able to reap the benefit of eliminating the competition?

Definition

> *Substitute product* (or service): a product or service that can stand in for another product or service in satisfying a customer need. For example, should you wish to travel from London to Paris you can go by boat, plane or train (via the Channel Tunnel). These are substitutes.

Government policy can affect the position of products in one industry with respect to the position of substitute products. More stringent safety regulations on one type of product might weaken its competitive position against substitute products. For example, strict controls over products that use asbestos would weaken the position of asbestos producers against producers of substitute materials. On the other hand, subsidies for one industry would put that industry at an advantage against other industries producing substitute products.

Definition

> *Global industry* and *global competition* imply an industry in which producers in different countries compete with each other, with the emergence of multinational or international companies. A government can put restrictions on global competition by favouring its domestic industries.

Just as a government can put restrictions on global competition, it can encourage it too, by removing the restrictions and regulations. For example, it has been the removal of exchange controls by various countries such as the UK that has permitted the international money markets and capital markets to develop rapidly in the 1980s.

> **Activity 11** **(20 minutes)**
>
> For some years the Daily Planet has been increasing its circulation, now standing at 4 million daily. The publishers, My Words International, want to bid to take over their principal rival Newsday, which has sales of 3.5 million. Both companies have interests in commercial TV and radio and My Words is also in book publishing. If My Words' bid were acceptable to shareholders the company would be the biggest media organisation in the UK. What considerations should the Department of Trade and Industry have in mind before making a decision as to whether to allow the bid to go through?

There are a number of areas where politics and business interact. These relate to legislation governing business activities that may require new business practices and that may affect costs. The examples given are typical of the issues with which employers' associations, Trade Unions and political parties are constantly involved. They are brief outlines and many of the issues raised are covered in more detail in later chapters.

5   SOCIAL WELFARE AND HEALTH POLICY

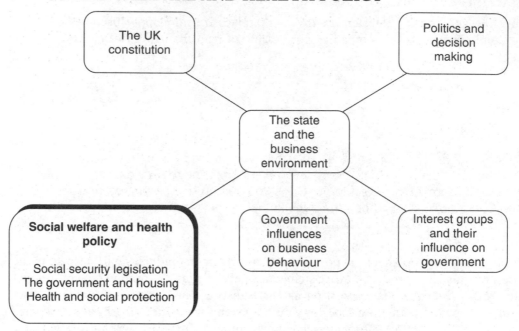

5.1   Social security legislation

Much social security legislation, including the law on statutory sick pay and statutory maternity pay, was consolidated into the Social Security Contributions and Benefits Act 1992.

This area is constantly changing and is often subject to controversy. For example the recent government decision to cut single parent allowances led to much protest.

Trends to watch are:

(a)   Greater equality between the sexes

(b)   Cuts in the levels of spending

(c)   On current policies, a replacement of public entitlements by private insurance schemes

(d)   Means testing (people's financial circumstances are assessed before they are offered any help)

Social security

Contributory benefits are benefits that an individual has paid for, rather like an insurance policy. Payment is made by national insurance contributions (NICs), which are compulsory deductions.

(a)   *Retirement pension* is a taxable benefit. Broadly, the level of pension depends on the number of years for which NICs have been paid (the individual's *contributions record*).

(b)   *Incapacity benefit* is paid when an individual cannot work because of incapacity (eg illness, disability etc).

(c)   *Maternity allowance* is a tax-free benefit paid to mothers for 18 weeks. It can start between 6 and 11 weeks before the expected date of the birth.

(d)   *Jobseekers' allowance* is for those who are looking for work.

In addition, there are several *non-contributory benefits*, available regardless of whether or not the claimant has made contributions. These include the following.

(a)   The *working families tax credit* is for working people on low income who have children.

(b)   *Housing benefit* is a tax-free contribution to rent paid by local authorities to people on low incomes.

(c)   *Council tax benefit* is a tax-free contribution to the council tax liabilities of people on low incomes.

(d)   The *Social Fund* is a source of tax-free payments for specific needs, such as things for a new baby. Loans may also be made from the fund.

(e)   *Child benefit* is a tax-free weekly payment to people bringing up children. *Guardian's allowance* may be added to child benefit.

(f)   *Attendance allowance* is a tax-free benefit for people disabled after age 65 who need a lot of help. *Disability living allowance* is a tax-free benefit for people disabled while under 65 who need a lot of help.

(g)   *Invalid care allowance* is a taxable benefit for people aged between 16 and 65 who spend at least 35 hours a week caring for a sick or disabled person, subject to an income test.

(h)   *Industrial injuries disablement benefit* is a tax-free benefit paid to people disabled by accidents at work or by industrial diseases.

The social security system provides a safety net for those on low incomes. It has the effect of redressing some of the inequalities in society as a whole.

5.2   The government and housing

In the past, governments and local authorities were suppliers of housing. During the 1950s both the Labour and Conservative governments realised a need for a mix of housing tenures. The Conservatives, between 1952 and 1959, ensured that 61% of construction was in local authority hands and 35% in those of private builders. By 1960, 44% of homes were owner-occupied, 25% rented from the public sector and 31% were privately rented. By 1980 these figures had changed to 57%, 30% and 13%.

Government policy in the 1980s and 1990s has been to reverse this trend radically. Council houses have been sold and, whilst council houses are still being built, there are far fewer of them.

Home ownership

The previous government offered tax relief and other inducements to encourage owner occupation. However, the cost of this relief has been so severe that it has been curtailed over time, so that tax relief is only granted at basic rate on interest on the first £15,000 of a loan (significantly less than the cost of a house).

The Conservative governments in the 1980s decided radically to extend owner occupation by offering council tenants the right to buy their own property. The Housing Act 1980 introduced significant direct subsidies to those buying council houses, with discounts of up to 50%. Such discounts were subsequently increased to 60%. The availability of such dwellings to prospective purchasers was later restricted by 'pre-emption' clauses, preventing further sales for fixed periods and giving local authorities 'first refusal'.

Private rentals

The government has also intervened to control the private rented sector. Although private renting was already in decline, rent controls and 'secured tenancies' (which made eviction difficult) discouraged landlords. Recent government policy has been to revive the private rented sector by making it easier for landlords to control tenancies. There are also tax reliefs available to people who let out a room in their house.

Activity 12 (30 minutes)

The students union has asked you to produce a report detailing common problems encountered by students with regard to private rented accommodation. The union intends to use your report as the basis for a code of conduct for landlords. List the main points of concern that you would include in such a report.

Other controls

Other regulations include:

(a) Planning permission, which controls the use of land

(b) Standards and regulations for new housing

(c) Safety standards

(d) Environmental health officers

Housing benefit is provided as part of the social security system. This enables people to pay their rent if they are on low incomes.

Housing has a wide significance for the UK economy and for business.

5.3 Health and social protection

The *welfare state* seeks to provide citizens with benefits they would find it hard to purchase as individuals. The National Health Service was set up to provide health care free at the point of delivery, funded by taxation. People are free to purchase private medical insurance if they so wish.

Life expectancy has increased steadily since 1901, when it was 45.5 years for males and 49 years for females; it now it stands at around 75 year for males and 80 for females. This is likely to add significantly to the cost of the welfare state. This is why the government is seeking to encourage people to make their own pension arrangements rather than relying on the state. The 'ageing' of the population, discussed earlier, will put significant pressure on the existing health system and other social benefits.

In 1995-96, just over 9.6 million people were in receipt of a retirement pension, an overall increase of 9% since 1981-2. The UK is not especially generous by the standards of other countries in the EU. Details of benefits were given in an earlier section of this chapter.

Furthermore, demands on the health service have increased. Expenditure on the NHS, after adjusting for inflation, has increased from around £28 billion in 1981 to £43 billion in 1996.

The National Health Service has now been re-organised. At one time, it was managed centrally. Hospitals and doctors did what they were told to do by regional health authorities. Now, many hospitals are managed independently, as NHS Hospital trusts. Area health authorities and some 'fund holding' general practitioners (GPs) now purchase services from hospitals. The aim is to ensure that 'market' mechanisms ensure an efficient allocation of resources.

A problem is that hospitals are more 'glamorous' than preventative medicine, which might improve people's health more effectively in the long term.

The number of elderly residents of both local authority and private sector homes has increased from under 200,000 in 1980 to over 272,000 in 1996. This trend is almost certain to continue.

Chapter roundup

- The state has grown in size and function in this century. The state contains a variety of institutions serving a number of purposes. The relationships between the state and other areas of the public sector are characterised by varying degrees of regulation and control.

- The UK is unusual in that it has no written constitution, and does not practice effectively the 'separation of powers'. Central government has since 1979 undermined other sources of political authority, such as local government, leading to an increase in the power of the state.

- The state is accountable, through the political process, to the electorate. Political parties have goals that may or may not be relevant to business decisions. Such commitments are outlined in each party's manifesto.

- Politics influences decision-making processes in the public sector.

- Government influences business indirectly through its general conduct of economic policy affecting investment and demand, and directly through company law, corporation tax, VAT and other regulations. The government can also be a major buyer from, or supplier to, particular industries. Regional policy towards industry is an example of government influence. Interest and pressure groups use direct and indirect means.

- Social policy encompasses social security policy, housing and health.

Quick quiz

1   Give an example of a country that has a written constitution.

2   List the three 'branches' of UK government.

3   Give an example of a position that is involved with all three branches.

4   What is meant by 'parliamentary sovereignty'?

5   What is the difference between a 'green paper' and a 'white paper'?

6   List some bodies with power to make delegated legislation.

7   What is a QUANGO?

8   What is meant by 'policy'?

9   Who directs government policy in the UK?

10   List some sources of advice for government.

11   What do interest groups do to influence legislation?

12   How can the state influence monopolies?

13   List some ways in which government could promote or hamper the growth of new industries.

14   How can the government influence competition in the economy?

15   List the two types of relationship a pressure group can have with government.

16   How can business influence government?

17   Give some examples of bodies that represent employers.

18   Give some examples of bodies that represent employees.

19   List some examples of legislation protecting the rights of citizens.

20   List examples of legislation affecting business practices.

21   What are the main aspects behind the re-organisation of the National Health Service over recent years?

Answers to quick quiz

1   USA.

2   The legislature, the executive, the judiciary.

3   The Lord Chancellor is a member of all three 'branches'.

4   Parliament cannot be overruled by any other body.

5   A green paper is merely a discussion document. A white paper is a draft bill.

6   Secretary of State, County Councils, District Councils.

7   Quasi-autonomous non-governmental organisation.

8   Policy is a way of expressing the broad purposes of government activity.

9   Political parties.

10   The Civil Service, 'Think Tanks', academics, Royal Commissions etc.

11   They can lobby, sit on committees, donate money, influence public opinion, take direct action.

12   Prevent them from developing, impose strict controls, take them over, outlaw anti-competitive practices.

13   Restrain growth, place restrictions on import tariffs, subsidise domestic firms, impose standards.

14   Prevention of monopolies, provide substitute products, insist on stringent safety regulations, provide subsidies.

15   They can be 'insiders' or 'outsiders'.

16   Lobbying, representing members of employers' associations, joining committees, non-executive directorships.

17   CBI, Institute of Personnel Development, industry-wide associations.

18   Trade Unions, Staff Associations, TUC, Professional Bodies.

19   Consumer Credit Act 1974, Sex Discrimination Act 1975, Race Relations Act 1976, Employment Rights Act 1996.

20   Employment Rights Act 1996, the Companies Act 1985, Working Time Directive.

21   Decentralisation and 'market mechanisms' through NHS trusts and fundholding GPs.

Answers to quick quiz

Answers to activities

1   A government sponsored bill is one that is being put forward by the government of the day and forms part of its general legislative programme. It has the backing of the government and will be allocated parliamentary time for discussion and debate. A private member's bill is one that is put forward by an individual MP. There are limited opportunities for doing this and such bills do not always have government backing. However, despite their lack of time allocation some important laws have been made or amended following private member's bills; for example divorce reform and laws relating to abortion.

2   It is necessary to delegate legislative powers for a number of reasons. Some of these include the fact that Parliament hasn't enough time to achieve all it wants to during the normal session. Some of the work has to be done outside. Also, local authorities are more aware of the particular needs and problems of their areas. The councillors elected to local authorities are local people and are thus in touch with local issues. Local government is essential to ensure that suitable local services are provided. It is also part of the philosophy of government 'for the people by the people' - local government may be seen as more representative of the ordinary person in the street.

3   The main advantage of QUANGOs is that they can allow experts in a particular field to contribute to the policy making process. They can also allow people with particularly relevant skills to contribute to community organisations. The main disadvantage is that they can sometimes be seen as little more than a system of rewarding friends of the government and a means of ensuring that the political views of the current government are able to dominate decision making at all levels.

4   All of these are types of European Union legislation. A regulation is directly applicable in all member states - ie they have to obey it once it is passed. There is no need for it to be ratified by member states' governments. A directive is basically an instruction to member states to revise their law to enable harmonisation across Europe to occur. Everyone is told that they have to achieve a particular task within a specified time limit. The new law is enacted via the domestic legal system of each state. A decision is a decision of the court of justice. This could be addressed to a particular state, a company or an individual.

BPP PUBLISHING

NOTES

5   The union would need to consult a number of different groups; for example the student body as a whole, the management of the college, the staff of the college, possibly the governors, smokers and non-smokers. They may also wish to take advice from outsiders such as the community health council.

6   Your college needs to make a policy decision on which type of course it wishes to support. Some are obviously more lucrative than others, but there is a need to fulfil the needs of the community as well. The college has its image to protect as well as its financial needs. It may be appropriate to reach some sort of compromise. For example, could the income from the business courses be used to subsidise the community programme? Could the college charge more to those who can afford it in order to help those who cannot? By looking for a compromise the college may be able to please more people than initially seems possible.

7   Many multinational companies have complied with the EU's Works Council Directive to provide for consultation with employees - but the argument and debate continues as to whether there are 'social partners' in the economy. Read the business press to follow the debate between the British government, industrial organisations such as the CBI, TUC etc and the European Commission's proposal for social and employment legislation about minimum standards and consultative processes in the work place.

8   You might have found an article on any of the following (or on another issue): animal rights protesters trying to halt the transportation of veal calves - they were trying to lobby government to ban the process and also to make businesses realise that this was not an attractive business proposition; Greenpeace mounting a very successful campaign against Shell regarding its disposal of the Brent Spar platform - the government intervened in the dispute and eventually Shell decided to abandon their previous plans.

9   One approach is self-help and private/public partnership. See the Inward Investment Brief and the Merseyside example that follow this activity.

10   Your answers will depend on your home area. You might want to stress things such as the skills available in your area, the natural environment, the facilities available in terms of industrial premises or new building, transport networks, social facilities for staff etc.

11   The DTI should bear in mind the extent of media oligopoly in ownership. They should also take into account political considerations and competition law.

12   Students would probably comment on the lack of decent affordable accommodation. Common problems with student accommodation include the following, all of which would need to be covered by any code of practice:

(a)   Affordable housing is in short supply in most popular university towns and cities.

(b)   Cheap accommodation tends to be of poor quality (in 'rough' areas, or poorly furnished and maintained).

(c)   Many student houses suffer from poor heating and damp – for example, there have been problems with gas heaters, with deaths caused by carbon monoxide fumes emitted from poorly maintained fires.

(d)   Landlords are often reluctant to carry out repairs when asked.

(e)   Many landlords do not issue proper tenancy agreements.

Assignment 2   **(1 hour)**

(a) *Scenario*

As a group of students you have decided to protest over the proposal put forward by the Government that all students be charged a £2,000 tuition fee in order to be able to attend university.

You do not feel that the charge is fair and fear it may prevent students without the money from attending university.

Task

Working in small groups, prepare a plan of action to enable you to put forward the students' point of view. Your aim is to achieve as much publicity as possible and to put our views across to the most influential people involved in the issue.

(b) *Scenario*

The management of your company have recently issued a memorandum stating that compulsory drug-testing will become part of the company's Health and Safety Policy. Staff are to be selected at random and will be asked to provide blood or urine samples for testing. Failure to comply will result in instant dismissal. A positive test will also result in dismissal.

A number of staff in your office feel very unhappy about this - they feel it is an invasion of privacy which goes beyond reasonable employment practice.

Task

Working in small groups, prepare a plan of action to enable you to put forward the employee's point of view to management. Identify the key personnel to 'target' with your campaign and produce a plan of action to apply pressure on management to reverse the decision.

(You may wish to use your own workplace as a basis for your plans.)

Chapter 3:

THE EUROPEAN UNION AND THE BUSINESS ENVIRONMENT

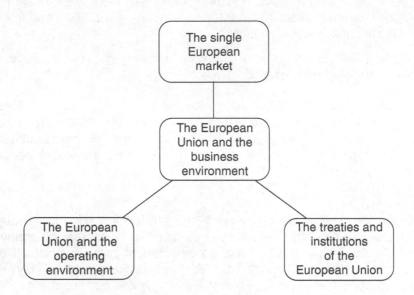

Introduction

This chapter explains how the Single European Market relates to business activities. If you follow the news, it can sometimes seem that the UK's relationship with its European partners is controversial for all the political parties. However, a lot has been achieved over the years in which we have been members of the EU.

The wars of 1914-18 and 1939-45 devastated Europe, and one of the reasons for setting up the precursor to the European Union was to build links that were so tight that yet another war would be unthinkable. Since 1945, *Western* Europe, certainly, has seen one of the longest periods of continuous peace in its history. (The example of the former Yugoslavia indicates the dangers of nationalistic rivalries getting out of hand.) The Western European economies are becoming interlinked: French companies supply water to British consumers; German companies such as Siemens are investing in the UK; most of the UK's trade is with the EU. The UK's traditional partners, such as the US and Commonwealth countries, see trading opportunities elsewhere (eg in the Asia-Pacific region). For global investors the UK provides a useful entry point to the wider European market. Given the centrality of European issues in the economic and political life of the country, we devote a whole chapter to the subject.

Your objectives

In this chapter you will learn about:

(a)   The basic structure of the European Union

(b)   The importance of the EU in world trade

(c)   How the single market works for business

1 THE SINGLE EUROPEAN MARKET

We start with some basic information about the EU.

1.1 Basic facts

Land area

(a) The European Union (EU) member states cover 3,235,000 square kilometres.

(b) The USA is around three times larger than the EU. Japan is 11.7% the size of the EU.

(c) Within the EU, Sweden (450,000 square kilometres) is the third largest country after France (544,000) and Spain (505,000).

Population

The total EU population is approximately 370,000,000. This is over 40% more than the USA and three times as much as Japan. Germany has the most people (around 80 million).

At the time of writing, the member states are: Austria, Belgium, Denmark, Finland, France, Germany, Greece, Ireland, Italy, Luxembourg, the Netherlands, Portugal, Spain, Sweden and the UK. Other states hope to join include Hungary, Poland and the Czech Republic.

History

The idea of creating a single 'common market' goes back to the time when the European Economic Community (EEC) was set up in 1957. This is now referred to as the European Union. Before the EEC was set up, co-operation had commenced with the European Coal and Steel Community in 1955.

The following key dates concern developments that are explained later in this chapter:

THE UK AND THE EUROPEAN COMMUNITY - Key dates

1957	Treaty of Rome established - the UK did not join.
1961	UK instrumental in creating EFTA, a rival to EEC.
1963	UK applied to join EEC. President De Gaulle of France feared US links and vetoed UK entry.
1966	The UK applied again. De Gaulle opposed.
1973	The UK was finally accepted into membership.
1975	The UK membership was ratified by referendum.
Mid 1970s to mid 1980s	European Community issues had a low profile.
1986	The Single European Act was passed to open the Single European Market.
1989	The Social Chapter was accepted by 11 members but the UK opted out.
1991	Maastricht Treaty. Became European Union.
1992	Single European market
1997	Treaty of Amsterdam. Amends the Treaty on European Union and the three Community Treaties.
1998	Establishment of European Central Bank running a single monetary policy
1999	Launch of single European currency (the 'euro')
2002	Launch of 'euro' notes and coins

Activity 1 (10 minutes)

Could there be a time when the EU becomes too big? If so, what might its priorities be for considering new applications for membership?

The aim of the Single Market is to create an area in which goods, capital, people and services can circulate freely without the restrictions imposed by frontiers, subject to certain essential safeguards.

1.2 The single European market

The EU consists of:

    (a)   The European Economic Community or EEC (the 'common' market or customs union)

    (b)   The European Coal and Steel Community (to control iron, steel and coal resources)

    (c)   The Atomic Energy Community or Euratom (to control the peaceful use of atomic energy)

In addition, there are two more recent areas of intergovernmental cooperation in the fields of Common Foreign and Security Policy (CFSP) and Justice and Home Affairs (JHA).

The European Union has a common market, including a free trade area and a customs union.

(a) A *free trade* area exists when there is no restriction on the movement of goods and services between countries. Such freedom exists on trade within the EU, but there are restrictions on trade between the EU countries and other countries.

(b) The customs union of the EU:

(i) Establishes a free trade area between member states

(ii) Erects common external tariffs to charge on imports from non-member countries.

The EU thus promotes free trade among member states while acting as a protectionist bloc against the rest of the world.

FOR DISCUSSION

What does the internal market mean for the EU citizen? Prioritise the following according to your own values:

- Better value for money

- Greater choice of goods and services

- Improved job opportunities

- Trouble-free travel within the EU

- Unlimited cross-border shopping

- Right to work and live in another EU country

Import duties and levies in the EU

No customs duties are levied within the Union. All states levy VAT. All EU countries charge the same duty (which is a tax people have to pay to bring their goods into your country) on imports from elsewhere in the world. This has been very important in opening up national markets to firms in other EU countries. Governments in the past often protected their own industries by charging high duties, which had the effect of making, say, a foreign car too expensive to buy. Such protection led to customers paying higher prices than they needed to. Free competition is basic to good quality, wide variety of choice and value for money. When they face competition, firms have to make sure that they are efficient and are producing what customers want at a price they are prepared to pay.

This has been an issue for the car industry because differential pricing in member states has led to customers buying where it is cheapest and driving the car to their home state in order to save money.

FOR DISCUSSION

The single European market only benefits firms from the member states of the EU. Do you agree?

How the single market works for business

A *common market* encompasses the idea of a customs union but has a number of additional features. In addition to free trade among member countries there is also complete mobility of funds and labour (ie the factors of production - see Chapter 6). A British citizen has the freedom to work in any other country of the European Union, for example. A common market will also aim to achieve stronger links between member countries, for example by harmonising government economic policies and by establishing a closer political confederation.

The reduction of *frontier controls* on goods and people will affect businesses in a number of ways.

On goods:

 (a) An end to customs documentation

 (b) No need for traders to submit tax declarations

For people:

 (a) Few limits on the amount of purchases that people can carry across borders, for private consumption.

 (b) The Schengen agreement abolishes border controls between eight member states, although France is delaying implementation,

 (c) No passport checks on EU citizens travelling between member states,

 (d) Co-operation between police and immigration authorities.

The internal market might have the following general effects.

 (a) Firms learn to compete more effectively, and can benefit from economies of scale.

 (b) Open trade policy makes EU firms match the world best.

 (c) Stable exchange rates cement the internal market.

 (d) Supporters hold that the Social Chapter, which enshrines basic workplace rights, will bring economic prosperity accompanied by better living and working conditions. Others consider it bad for business.

 (e) Internal market rules embody a high level of environmental protection.

Elimination of trade restrictions covers the following areas.

 (a) European regulations and standards mean that products approved in any one EU country can be freely marketed throughout the Union.

 (b) There is a progressive opening up of government and other public body contracts to all EU contractors on an equal basis.

 (c) There is more competition and efficiency in Europe-wide services in telecommunications and information technology by developing common standards for equipment.

(d) The road haulage market is being liberalised by eliminating bureaucratic 'red tape'. Shipping services between member countries are to be provided on equal terms. Competition on air routes should increase, resulting in lower fares.

(e) Banks and securities houses authorised in their home country should be free to provide banking and investment services anywhere in the EU. Insurers will have greater freedom to cover risks in other member countries. All restrictions on the movement of capital are being removed.

(f) Protection of ideas will become easier through harmonisation of national laws on patents, trade marks and copyright.

(g) Professional qualifications obtained in one country are generally acceptable in all other countries.

Activity 2   **(15 minutes)**

Citizens of the European Union are entitled to work in any of the EU countries. In the past, individual countries made rules about residence or qualifications which, in effect, prevented people from other countries getting jobs. What opportunities exist for UK residents to find jobs in other EU countries? List some of the difficulties involved in going to work and live in another country.

Nearly 300 new laws had to pass through Parliament to complete the single European market. These cover standards for goods (for example food additives and hygiene) and measures to enable EU citizens to carry out their trade or profession anywhere in the EU by ensuring that their qualifications are recognised.

1.3 The single European market in action

Elimination of trade restrictions covers the following areas.

(a) Physical barriers (eg customs inspection) on good and services have been removed for most products. Companies have had to adjust to a new VAT regime as a consequence.

(b) Technical standards (eg for quality and safety) should be harmonised.

(c) Governments should not discriminate between EU companies in awarding public works contracts.

(d) Telecommunications should be subject to greater competition.

(e) It should be possible to provide financial services in any country.

(f) There should be free movement of capital within the community

(g) Professional qualifications awarded in one member state should be recognised in the others.

(h) The EU is taking a co-ordinated stand on matters related to consumer protection.

At the same time, you should not assume that there will be a completely 'level playing field'. There are many areas where harmonisation is a long way from being achieved. Here are some examples.

(a)   *Company taxation.* Tax rates, which can affect the viability of investment plans, vary from country to country within the EU. A number of directives on *tax harmonisation* had to be dropped because it was not possible to reach agreement between all member states.

(b)   *Indirect taxation (eg VAT).* While there have been moves to harmonisation, there are still differences between rates imposed by member states.

(c)   *Differences in prosperity.* There are considerable differences in prosperity between the wealthiest EU economy (Germany), and the poorest (eg Greece). The UK comes somewhere in the middle.

   (i)   Grants are sometimes available to depressed regions, which might affect investment decisions.

   (ii)   Different marketing strategies are appropriate for different markets.

(d)   *Differences in workforce skills.* Again, this can have a significant effect on investment decisions. The workforce in Germany is perhaps the most highly trained, but also the most highly paid, and so might be suitable for products of a high added value.

(e)   *Infrastructure.* Some countries are better provided with road and rail than others. Where accessibility to a market is an important issue, infrastructure can mean significant variations in distribution costs.

Below are some examples of issues that affect our everyday lives.

Trading standards

Toys within the EU should nowadays have the letter CE (which stands for 'Communauté Européenne') on them to show that they meet the safety standards recognised by the EU.

The Food Law programme

The composition of certain food products, such as fruit juice, jam and coffee, has to be shown clearly on the packaging. All ingredients should be listed. Weights and measures are now harmonised across Europe. Goods have to be labelled and sold packaged in metric measures.

Transport

Laws have been introduced to make aviation, shipping and road transport more competitive. This should lead, among other things, to cheaper air fares.

However, the single market is not just about 'harmonisation' or making everything the same. Above all, it is about maximum choice, achieved by the greatest possible acceptance of each others' products and standards.

Agriculture

The *Common Agricultural Policy* (CAP) was designed to ensure a stable supply of food at reasonable prices while, at the same time, providing farmers with an adequate income. This was a major priority for the Community in the early post-war years when food shortages were a recent memory. However, the high price paid for food products under the CAP encouraged farmers to expand their production. By the 1970s this had led to large food surpluses - the 'wine lakes' and 'butter mountains'. The high prices paid to farmers for food have placed a considerable burden on the community budget which also has to subsidise sales of surplus food to countries outside the European Union. This has led to complaints from other agricultural trading nations such as Australia and New Zealand, which do not subsidise their agriculture and are suffering as a result.

To tackle this range of problems, the EU has begun to reform the CAP. The prices paid to farmers are being cut, for example by nearly 30% for wheat. This should bring food prices within the EU closer to the levels in the rest of the world, reduce costs to the EU budget and reduce prices in the shops. At the same time, farmers are being compensated for the loss of income (but this is less expensive in the long run than subsidising excess food production).

Further reforms are required, but an important step in the right direction has now been made. This is especially important as cutting agricultural subsidies is a key ingredient of the GATT agreement.

European Monetary System

The European Monetary System (EMS) was set up in 1979. Its purpose is to establish greater monetary stability in the European Union. The exchange rates between currencies can fluctuate considerably. For instance, the number of pounds needed to buy a hundred Deutschmarks has changed a lot in the past. This resulted in extra costs for businesses which sold goods or services in more than one country. Exchange rate changes could turn a profit into a loss, or vice versa. Businesses either had to accept this risk or take special measures to reduce it.

At the heart of the EMS was the Exchange Rate Mechanism (ERM). Members of the ERM have agreed to make sure that the value of their currencies do not change much in relation to each other. Within the system, a form of money called the European Currency Unit (ECU) was used as a measure of value and a means of making loans between member states. But the ERM did not work for the UK, which withdrew from it in 1992. The UK had pegged its exchange rate too high and the UK entered at the wrong time (just after German re-unification).

Consequences of membership of an exchange rate system

Exchange rate stability within an exchange rate regime may help dampen inflation by preventing a government from allowing the currency to drift downwards in value to compensate for price inflation. At the same time, it means that interest rate policy must be consistent with keeping the currency stable. If interest rates are too high, foreign investors will buy sterling, leading to capital inflows, much of which may be of short-term 'hot money', and there will be upward pressure on the currency. If interest rates are too low, there will conversely be downward pressure on the currency.

Other possible consequences of stabilisation within an exchange rate system are that there may be effects on people's expectations and on the perceived risk of exchange rate movements between member currencies. As well as allowing firms to plan and forecast with greater certainty, exchange rate stability ought to make a currency less risky to hold.

An important development is the Single European currency. This has been a controversial issue. We discuss this in more detail later.

The environment

Pollution respects no frontier, as Chernobyl, acid rain and damage to the ozone layer have all shown. It is crucial that international agreements are reached and acted on.

There is a long way to go on the whole question of protection of our natural environment and the Union has decided to establish the European Environment Agency to help it to develop policies in this area.

Activity 3	(30 minutes)

Find out what objectives were laid down for environment protection within Europe by the Maastricht Summit.

There are other international trade groups for comparison with the EU. One, EFTA, has become part of the EU. Others are developing for other parts of the world.

1.4   European Free Trade Area (EFTA) and the European Economic Area (EEA)

The *European Free Trade Area (EFTA)* was established in 1959, originally with seven member countries, including the UK. The UK, Denmark, Portugal, Austria, Finland and Sweden have since transferred to the EU. Iceland, Norway and Switzerland now constitute EFTA.

EFTA countries account for less than 6% of world export trade. There is free trade between EFTA member countries but there is no harmonisation of tariffs with non-EFTA countries.

Definition

European Economic Area (EEA): In 1993, EFTA forged a link with the EU to create a European Economic Area (EEA) with a population of 380 million, so extending the benefits of the EU single market to the EFTA member countries (excluding Switzerland, which stayed out of the EEA).

The EEA has 10.4 million non-EEA citizens, but nearly 96% of all people in EEA live 'at home'.

Latest estimates by EUROSTAT* (the EU statistical office in Luxembourg) indicate that 2.8% (nearly 10.4 million people) of the total population (370 million) of the EEA are non-EEA citizens. They also show that most EEA citizens prefer 'home'. 95.7% of the EEA population are people living in their own country. The remainder - 1.5% or just over 5.6 million people - are EEA citizens residing in another EEA country.

The percentages are similar within the EU. Non-nationals form over 4% of total population of the European Union.

Turks form by far the largest group of non-EU nationals in the EEA: 2.5 million, 70% living in Germany. Also there are 1.14 million citizens of the former Yugoslavia. 68% are in Germany and 17% in Austria. 1.09 million Moroccans live in the EEA, mostly in France (53%), the Netherlands (15%) and Belgium (13%).

Of EU nationals living away from home, Italians form the largest group, of which 45% live in Germany and 20% each in France and Belgium (1.2 million).

The second largest group from the EU living in another EEA country are the Portuguese (0.86 million). Most (75%) live in France. Next come the Irish (0.54 million), most (94%) living in the United Kingdom.

Overall, non-national citizens in the EEA are concentrated in a few countries. Germany and France host 54% of other EEA citizens; the Netherlands, Belgium and Luxembourg together account for 15%, as does the United Kingdom. Germany has 41% of all non-EEA citizens, France 22% and the United Kingdom 11%.

You can compare the EEA with the North American Free Trade Association (NAFTA) formed by Canada, the USA and Mexico in 1993. This free trade area covering a population of 360 million is similar in size to the EU. Some countries in Latin America are interested in joining.

Other trading blocs are developing in the Americas, and include Mercosur (Brazil, Argentina, Uruguay and Paraguay), the Andean Pact and Caricom.

The EU is based on two key treaties and comprises a number of institutions which were set up by Treaty.

2 THE TREATIES AND INSTITUTIONS OF THE EUROPEAN UNION

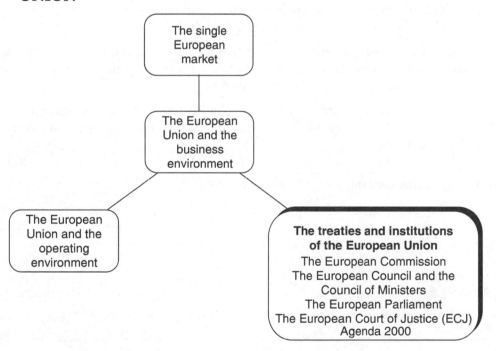

1957 - The Treaty of Rome

The Treaty of Rome setting up the European Economic Community was signed by the six founder Member States on 25 March 1957. It was then signed by new member countries, including the UK, as they joined the EC. It provides the written constitution for the Community. It established the legally binding framework for the EC and states the legal obligations and rights of Member States. The Treaty can only be changed by an Inter-Governmental Conference (IGC). Both the Single European Act Maastricht Treaty and the Amsterdam Treaty were the result of IGC negotiation.

Maastricht Treaty on European Union

The text of this Treaty was negotiated during 1991, finalised at the Maastricht European Council on 11 December 1991 and signed on 7 February 1992. It came into force in November 1993.

The Treaty is wider in scope than the Community's founding treaties or the Single European Act. The Treaty expanded existing responsibilities of the then European Community and brought in new policy areas, both within the Treaty of Rome and outside it.

The Treaty created a European Union with 3 main elements (or pillars) as follows.

1. The European Community itself - a common economic policy through the development of the European Community.

    The powers and decision-making procedures of the Community were extended and modified to allow extension of policies.

2. A common Foreign and Security Policy - Member States were publicly committed to working together.

3. A common home affairs and justice policy.

The Maastricht Treaty set out the timetable for the establishment of the European Monetary Union in 3 stages.

In addition, the Member States attempted to agree amendments to the Treaty of Rome with regard to Social Law - the 'Social Chapter'.

The UK originally negotiated to opt out of these two aspects and the 'Social Chapter' became a Protocol to the Treaty which did not bind the UK.

The election of a Labour Government in 1997 significantly altered the UK's attitude to the Social Chapter and the Government indicated its intentions to opt in to the Social Agreement at the Amsterdam Summit in June 1997.

When the Treaty of Amsterdam came into force in May 1999, the Social Agreement was incorporated into the Treaty of Rome and the UK became obliged to adopt all outstanding legislation.

The Treaty of Amsterdam

On 2 October 1997, a new Treaty was signed. This Treaty amends the Treaty on European Union. Its main purpose was to improve the efficiency, democracy and transparency of the EU and bring it up to date.

Activity 4	**(15 minutes)**

Find out the main employment rights addressed in the Amsterdam Treaty.

Definition

Subsidiarity: the principle that sets the limits of EU action. Except where the EU has exclusive jurisdiction it will act 'only if and insofar as the objectives of the proposed action cannot be sufficiently achieved by the member states and can better be achieved by the EU'. In other words decisions should be taken at the lowest possible level.

NOTES

> ### Activity 5 (5 minutes)
>
> Suggest the advantages and disadvantages of deciding issues (a) at EU level and (b) at national level.

We will now discuss the main institutions in the EU, which were set up by Treaty, beginning with the European Commission.

2.1 The European Commission

The European Commission is the executive of the EU. The main tasks of the Commission are:

(a) To ensure that Community rules and the principles of the 'common market' are observed

(b) To make policy proposals to the Council of Ministers

(c) To enforce the implementation of legislation

(d) To administer Community expenditure

The European Commission has 20 members: two each from France, Germany, Italy, Spain and the United Kingdom and one from each of the other European Union countries. The Commission's term of office is five years, like that of the European Parliament. What is more, the European Parliament is consulted before the member states appoint the President of the commission and the full Commission has to be approved by Parliament before being appointed by mutual agreement by the governments of the member states.

The Amsterdam summit addressed the issue of reviewing the future number of Commissioners but no definitive agreement was reached. A Protocol was produced which leaves the matter open for future resolution.

The general proposal is that the number of Commissioners be reduced to one per state with a weighted voting system. No decisions have been made yet but it is likely that changes will be made when the next enlargement of the Union takes place.

In carrying out their duties, members of the Commission are obliged to be completely independent of their national governments and act only in the interests of the European Union. Only the European Parliament has the right to pass a motion of censure. Each member of the Commission has special responsibility for one or more policy areas, but decisions are taken on the basis of collective responsibility.

The Commission is first and foremost the guardian of the Treaties. It is an impartial body which sees to it that the Treaties, and decisions based on them, are correctly applied. It can initiate infringement proceedings against any member state and may, if necessary, refer matters to the European Court of Justice. It can also impose fines on individuals or companies, notably when they act in breach of the Commission's competition rules.

The Commission is also the catalyst of the European Union. It has the sole right of initiative in the legislative field, and it can exert its influence at every stage of the process preceding the adoption of a new 'European law'. In the area of intergovernmental co-operation, the Commission has the same rights as the individual member states with regard to the submission of proposals.

Finally, the Commission is the executive body of the European Union. This involves issuing rules for the implementation of certain Treaty Articles and administering budget appropriations earmarked for Union operation. The bulk of these fall within one or other of the major funds: the European Regional Development Fund and the Cohesion Fund. In carrying out its executive duties, the commission is often required to seek the opinion of committees of officials from the member states.

In 1994, for example, the Commission sent 558 proposals and 272 communications, memoranda and reports to the Council. These documents are the product of intensive consultation with political, administrative, economic and social circles. The Commission has an administrative staff based mainly in Brussels (where it has its headquarters) and, to a lesser extent, Luxembourg. It comprises approximately 20,000 officials divided between some 30 *Directorates-General* and other departments. The operating expenditure of the Commission and the other institutions accounts for only 5% of the total community budget, so accusations of waste are not entirely fair.

Reform of the European Commission

The adoption of a White Paper on Reform on 1 March 2000 initiates an Action Plan on reform of Europe's public administration. The progress of implementing reforms is taking time because some changes require the European Parliament to adopt changes in the law. Some changes, particularly in the area of human resources, are being implemented during 2002.

The reform strategy centres on three main areas of change:

(a)   Balancing tasks with resources

(b)   An overhaul of management and human resources policies to make the Commission more effective as an organisation

(c)   Improving financial management, efficiency and accountability, ensuring that taxpayers have value for money.

The main source of power is still the member states (despite 'Brussels-bashing'), which participate in the Council of Ministers. However, government ministers can conveniently blame the EU when things go wrong.

2.2   The European Council and the Council of Ministers

The European Council

The Council Presidency was set up in 1986. It comprises the heads of state or government, foreign and finance ministers and two Commisioners and the President of the European Commission. It meets twice a year and its role is:

(a)   To decide on policy direction
(b)   To tackle common international problems of concern
(c)   To smooth the implementation of the single market programme

The Presidency of the Council changes every six months, as follows up to 2002.

The Council of Ministers

The *Council of Ministers* is the Union's decision-making body. It takes the final decision on most EU legislation, concludes agreements with foreign countries and, together with the Parliament, decides on the EU budget.

(a) The Council consists of one representative from each member state. Each government sends a relevant minister as its delegate, depending on the business to be dealt with. Thus foreign ministers would attend most meetings on general matters, while ministers of agriculture or finance might attend meetings on their respective areas of policy (ECOFIN is the monthly meeting of Finance Ministers).

(b) Different *voting arrangements* apply in different situations. Sometimes a unanimous vote is required; more usually a 'qualified majority' will suffice. This involves the use of a weighted voting system, based on the relative population of member states and requiring a minimum number of states to be in favour to prevent motions being carried by the larger states. In rare circumstances a simple majority suffices.

(c) Many of the Council's deliberations used to be held in secret, but this was ruled illegal when the *Guardian* newspaper took the issue to the European Court of Justice. Most of the real work is done in working groups of officials. Only unresolved issues find their way onto the agenda of ministerial meetings.

Key points - the Council as law maker

(a) The most powerful institution of the EU
(b) Community's legislative body - adopts EU law
(c) Made up of ministers representing all member states
(d) Composition depends on subject under discussion
(e) Each State is President for 6 months
(f) Usually meets in private
(g) Speed-up legislative process
(h) 'Qualified majority voting' (see below)

Qualified majority voting: The total number of votes is 87

The qualified majority is:	65	(62 can be enough)
The simple majority is:	44	An abstention counts as a vote against.
The blocking majority is:	26	

Austria:	4	Italy:	10
Belgium:	5	Luxembourg:	2
Denmark:	3	Netherlands:	5
Finland:	3	Portugal:	5
France:	10	Spain:	8
Germany:	10	Sweden:	4
Greece:	5	United Kingdom:	10
Ireland:	3		

Table 3.1 Qualified majority voting on the Council of Ministers

The European Parliament perhaps has a less powerful role than a national Parliament has, although it has gained some new powers. Unlike the Council of Ministers, which are appointed by governments, it is directly elected by the people.

2.3 The European Parliament

The European Parliament is the voice of democracy in the EU. There have been direct elections since June 1979. 626 Members of the European Parliament (MEPs) are elected every five years. The UK has 87 MEPs. MEPs sit in political groupings, not according to nationality.

The European Parliament's activities are divided between Strasbourg (where plenary sessions are held), Brussels (where committees do their work) and the secretariat in Luxembourg.

(a) *Legislative role.* The European Parliament offers opinions about and amendments to certain proposals made by the European Commission. Legislation, drafted by the Commission, is considered and if necessary amended by the European Parliament before the Ministers can take decisions. In some policy areas the European Parliament has a power of veto. But it does not have to give a positive vote in favour of every piece of legislation for that legislation to come into force.

In legislation for the Single Market, over 50 per cent of the European Parliament's amendments were adopted and included in laws approved by Ministers.

(b) *Budgetary role.* The European Parliament adopts the Union budget, or can reject it.

With the Council, the European Parliament decides the annual budget of the EU - over £60 billion in 1994 - and has the power to reject the Council's proposals in total (but not individual items).

(c) In its *supervisory role* it confirms appointment and could dismiss members of the European Commission. The European Parliament has the right to approve each Commission and to dismiss it by a 'no confidence' vote.

(d) *Political role.* It represents the people of Europe as a whole.

There are 626 Members of the European Parliament (MEPs), with seats allocated as follows.

Austria:	21	Italy:	87
Belgium:	25	Luxembourg:	6
Denmark:	16	Netherlands:	31
Finland:	16	Portugal:	25
France:	87	Spain:	64
Germany:	99	Sweden:	22
Greece:	25	United Kingdom:	87
Ireland:	15		

Table 3.2 MEPs by nationality

(e) MEPs serve on delegations sent to countries and organisations throughout the world with which the Union is involved.

(f) Ministers from the Council and Commissioners attend the European Parliament's plenary sessions to take part in debates and answer questions from MEPs.

(g) The European Parliament can veto applications to join the Union, and trade and economic agreements with non-Union countries.

(h) The European Parliament debates, in public, major issues facing the Union. Citizens have the right to petition the European Parliament and an Ombudsman appointed by the European Parliament looks into cases of maladministration by the institutions of the EU.

Activity 6 **(5 minutes)**

Do you think the balance of power between national parliaments and the European Parliament might change over the next few years? Do you think the current UK government would oppose or agree with greater power being given to the European Parliament?

The EU has a judicial function in addition to its legislative and debating functions.

2.4 The European Court of Justice (ECJ)

The court is a court of first instance from which there is no appeal. The jurisdiction of the European Court falls under four main heads:

(a) Legal matters arising from the acts or omissions of member states, such as failure of a member state to fulfil its treaty obligations

(b) Rulings on legal issues affecting persons which arise from EU law

(c) Actions brought against EU institutions by member states, individuals or companies

(d) Disputes between the EU and its employees

The Court sits in Luxembourg and is composed of 15 judges from Member States.

The ECJ has ruled on a number of areas, including competition and employment law.

Note that the ECJ is *quite separate* from the *European Court of Human Rights (ECHR)*. The ECHR has nothing to do with the EU and was set up after the European governments signed the European Convention of Human Rights. The UK was a major contributor to the terms of the Convention, but, uniquely, these rights have not been incorporated into UK law. This is one explanation for the fact that the UK has the highest number of judgements against it in the ECHR.

A single European currency, the Social Chapter and the protection of the environment are three issues that currently influence the operating environment within the EU.

A single European currency, the Social Chapter and the protection of the environment are three issues that currently influence the operating environment within the EU.

2.5 Agenda 2000

Agenda 2000 is an action programme whose main objectives are to strengthen Community policies and to give the European Union a new financial framework for the period 2000-06 with a view to enlargement. It was launched in 1999 and relates to the following priority areas.

(a) Continuation of the agricultural reform along the lines of the changes made in 1988 and 1992, with a view to stimulating European competitiveness, taking great account of environmental considerations, ensuring fair income for farmers, simplifying legislation and decentralising the application of legislation

(b) In the area of *regional policy*, increasing the effectiveness of the Structural Funds and the Cohesion Fund by greater concentration of projects on specific objectives and geographical areas and thus improving management

(c) Strengthening the pre-accession strategy for applicant countries, to support improved transport and environmental protection infrastructures and to facilitate the adjustment of agriculture and the rural areas of the applicant countries

(d) Adopting a new financial framework for the period 2000-06 in order to enable the Union to meet the main challenges of the beginning of the 21st century, in particular *enlargement*, while ensuring budgetary discipline.

Enlargement of the EU

In March 1998 the EU formally launched the process that will make further enlargement possible. It embraces the following **thirteen applicant countries:** Bulgaria, Cyprus, the Czech Republic, Estonia, Hungary, Latvia, Lithuania, Malta, Poland, Romania, the Slovak Republic, Slovenia and Turkey.

The EU can look back on a history of successful previous enlargements:

1981   Greece

1986   Portugal and Spain

1995   Austria, Finland and Sweden

However, the enlargement facing the EU today poses a unique challenge, since it is without precedent in terms of scope and diversity: the number of candidates, the area (increase of 34%) and population (increase of 105 million), the wealth of different histories and cultures.

A single set of trade rules, a single tariff, and a single set of administrative procedures will apply not just across the existing Member States but across the Single Market of the enlarged Union. This should simplify dealing for third-country operators within Europe and improve conditions for investment and trade.

3   THE EUROPEAN UNION AND THE OPERATING ENVIRONMENT

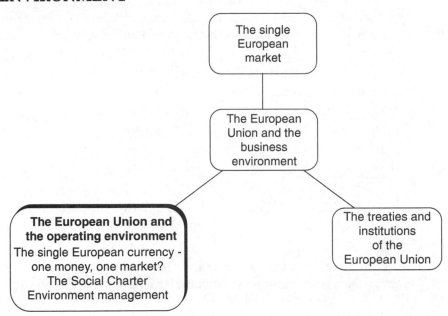

3.1   The single European currency - one money, one market?

European Economic and Monetary Union

One of the aims behind the European Monetary System has been European Economic and Monetary Union (EMU). This is a long-standing objective of the EU, reaffirmed in the Single European Act of 1985 and in the Maastricht agreement of 1991.

(a)   *Monetary union* can be defined as a single currency area, which would require a monetary policy for the area as a whole.

(b)   *Economic union* can be described as an unrestricted common market for trade, with some economic policy co-ordination between different regions in the union.

Although the whole package of measures included in European EMU is not paralleled anywhere else in the world, there have been many international monetary unions. For example, the UK and the Republic of Ireland were in currency union up to the 1970s. There are three main aspects to the European monetary union.

(a)   A *common currency*. By this, we mean that instead of using the old deutschmarks in Germany and francs in France, a common currency (the 'euro') is used for normal everyday money transactions by everyone in the monetary union.

(b)   A *European central bank*. The European central bank has the role of:

(i)   Issuing the common currency

(ii)   Conducting monetary policy on behalf of the central government authorities

(iii)   Acting as lender of last resort to all European banks

(iv)   Managing the exchange rate for the common currency

(c)   *A centralised monetary policy* applies across all the countries within the union. This involves the surrender of control over aspects of economic policy and therefore surrender of some political sovereignty by the government of each member state to the central government body of the union.

The conditions set out at Maastricht were that no EU country could participate in EMU unless the following economic 'convergence criteria' were met.

(a)   Consumer price inflation must, over the previous year, have been no more than 1.5 per cent higher than the average of the three best performing EU countries.

(b)   Long-term interest rates must, over the previous year, have averaged no more than 2 per cent more than the average of three countries with the best consumer price inflation performance.

(c)   A government's deficit should not exceed 5 per cent of GDP (gross domestic product) unless it has declined substantially or continuously or unless it is only temporarily above 3 per cent; additionally, the ratio of government debt to GDP should be no more than 60 per cent (unless it is approaching 60% at a satisfactory rate).

(d)   The currency of the country should have remained within the normal bands of the ERM for a minimum of two years, without any devaluation.

The EMU timetable

EMU is a topical issue. 1 May 1998 saw the meeting of those European Union countries wishing to join the monetary union at the outset. Italy, France, Ireland, Germany, Belgium, Luxembourg, the Netherlands, Finland, Spain, Portugal and Austria have all signed up for the first phase of EMU starting on 1 January 1999. The UK decided to opt out but retains the right to join at a later stage. The continuing timetable for EMU was as follows.

1998. Creation of a European Central Bank (ECB) running a single monetary policy. Fixing of irrevocably locked exchange rates between old currencies of participating countries.

1 January 1999. Launch of the single European currency (the 'euro') and the fixing of exchange rates between the old currencies and the euro.

2002. Introduction of 'euro' notes and coins.

The euro is thus now an established currency which has entirely replaced the old currencies of the euro zone such as French francs and German marks.

Gordon Brown, Chancellor of the Exchequer, explained in the House of Commons that in reaching the UK's decision on EMU, the Government Treasury department 'made a detailed assessment of five economic tests' believed to define whether a clear and unambiguous case could be made to support Britain joining a single currency. These are:

(a)   Whether there can be sustainable convergence between Britain and the economies of a single currency

(b)   Whether there is sufficient flexibility to cope with economic change

(c)   The effect on investment

(d)   The impact on the financial services industry

(e)   Whether it is good for employment

He concluded that applying these economic tests revealed that:

'*It is not in the interest of the UK to join in the first wave of EMU starting on 1 January 1999 and - barring some fundamental and unforeseen change in economic circumstances - making a decision to join, this parliament, is not realistic*'.

However, he went on to urge Government and business to prepare intensively during this parliament, so that Britain could be in a position to join in the next parliament, should that be desired. (Adapted from extracts of the Chancellor's speech to the House of Commons, October 27 1997, as reported in the Financial Times the next day. The Chancellor re-stated the policy in February 1999.) The Treasury is expected to complete a new assessment of the five economic tests in the near future.

The government states that, in principle, it is in favour of UK membership of EMU. In practice it takes the view that the economic conditions must be right. The determining factor stated to underpin any Government decision on membership of the single currency is the national economic interest and whether the economic case for joining is clear and unambiguous. If it is, there is no constitutional bar to joining.

For and against EMU

The arguments for and against EMU can be summarised as follows, with particular reference to the UK's position.

For	Against
Economic policy stability	*Loss of national control over economic policy*
EMU members will be required to keep to strict economic criteria.	Under EMU, monetary policy would largely be in the hands of the new European central bank.
Politicians in member countries will be less able to pursue short-term economic policies, for example just before an election, to gain political advantage.	Individual countries' fiscal policies would also need to stay in line with European policy criteria.
	The European economic policy framework would put great emphasis on price stability.
	Restrictive monetary policies could result in disproportionate unemployment and output effects.
Facilitation of trade	*The need to compensate for weaker economies*
Will eliminate risk of currency fluctuations affecting trade and investment between EMU member countries.	For the UK, the possible benefits of being economically linked to stronger European economies are reduced and possibly even outweighed by the need to compensate for weaker economies.
Will eliminate need to 'hedge' against such risks.	Stronger economies would be under pressure to 'bail out' member countries which borrow too much in order to hold the system together.
Will be savings in foreign exchange transaction costs for companies, as well as tourists.	
Will enhance ease of trade with non-EU countries.	

For	Against
Lower interest rates	*Confusion in the transition to EMU*
Will remove risk of inflation and depreciating currencies, reducing interest rates	Introduction of a new currency and coinage could cause confusion to businesses and consumers.
Will stabilise interest rates at a level closer to that of Germany, reducing interest costs for businesses and government.	Firms might use it as an opportunity to push through price rises.
Preservation of the City's position	*Lower confidence arising from loss of national pride.*
If the UK gets out of EMU, the City's position as one of the major European financial capitals will be threatened.	Sterling is a symbol of national cohesion.
In turn, the City's role as a leading global financial market would also be jeopardised	EMU puts its members on the road to a federal Europe, it is suggested, making the UK parliament into little more than a regional town hall within Europe, with no more power than local government. Such a move might dent national pride and diminish confidence.
Inward investment from the rest of the EU would also be likely to adversely affect economic	The proposal to have national variants of euro coins and notes is merely a cosmetic attempt to preserve national identities.

FOR DISCUSSION

Do you think a single currency benefits business?

What are the advantages and disadvantages for the UK, as a country, in accepting a single currency?

The extent of the EU's involvement in social issues is also a matter of dispute, as it is a source of regulation for business.

3.2 The Social Chapter

Employment practices vary substantially in EU countries.

The United Kingdom has the longest average working week in the EU by far, at 43.4 hours. It is also the only EU country in which this has increased over the past 10 years - it has in fact shortened in most of the other countries. France (39.7 hours) and Ireland (40.4 hours, now) have remained stable. Portugal is next (41.3 hours).

The EU average is 40.3 hours, 41.1 hours for men and 38.7 for women, with Belgium having the shortest working week - 38.2 hours.

In addition to the UK and Ireland, the working week exceeds 40 hours in Greece (40.5 hours). Spain (40.6 hours) and Portugal (41.3 hours). Since 1983 Denmark, Luxembourg, the Netherlands and Germany have all dropped below this threshold. Denmark and the Netherlands show the biggest reductions - 1.7 and 1.6 hours respectively. The British work longest of all by far - 45.1 hours a week. This, and other matters concerning employment, led to proposals incorporated into a Social Charter (see below). The aims of the social charter in turn provided the basis for the Social Chapter of the Maastricht Treaty. The British Labour Government has opted in to the Social Chapter which will be incorporated into the Treaty by the recently agreed Amsterdam Treaty.

Social Charter (incorporated in the Maastricht Treaty as the Social Chapter)

12 sets of principles covering the following areas.

1   The right to freedom of movement, eg recognition of qualifications.

2   Employment and remuneration, eg fair remuneration, possible minimum wage.

3   Improvement of living and working conditions.

4   Right to social protection - social security.

5   Right to freedom of association and collective bargaining.

6   Right to vocational training.

7   Right of men and women to equal treatment.

8   Right of workers to information, consultation and participation.

9   Right to health protection and safety in the workplace.

10 Protection of children and adolescents.

11 Protection of elderly - pensions.

12 Protection of disabled people.

Activity 7   **(30 minutes)**

Find out the main provisions of the Working Time Directive, which became law in October 1998.

FOR DISCUSSION

Earlier in this chapter we noted that the UK's GDP per head is lower than the European average. To what extent do you think that this calls into question the assertion that the social chapter is necessarily bad for business?

As we shall see later, ecological issues are of increasing concern for governments and business.

3.3 Environmental management

The EU has been active in raising environmental standards among its member states for many years, for example on lead in petrol and on water pollution levels. The Union wishes to encourage the manufacture of products that are less damaging to the environment.

A product may be awarded an eco-label if its manufacture does not use too much energy and raw material, or result in harmful emissions into the air, water and soil, or generate too much waste and noise. Clean, lowest-risk, sustainable technologies are to be used.

Waste is one of the main drawbacks for our environment. EU initiatives in this field are as follows.

(a) *List of hazardous waste.* The council has defined a list of different types of hazardous waste.

(b) *Waste packaging.* A new directive covers both new and used packaging. In five years the member states will have to recover between 50% and 65% of waste packaging and between 25% and 45% of it will have to be recycled, with a minimum of 15% for each type of packing material. In order to achieve this target they must set up a collection and recovery system. Each member state can manage its waste according to its own needs as long as it respects European requirements. At the end of ten years the directive will be reviewed and the targets altered.

(c) *Incineration of hazardous waste.* The EU established measurements and methods on how to avoid or reduce as much as possible the harmful effects of the burning of hazardous waste, such as the pollution of the air, the soil, the ground and surface water. Operating conditions and emission limit values were set for factories etc, as were strict conditions on waste water resulting from the purification of flue gases. For plants not specifically designed for that purpose, restrictive conditions under which the incineration of hazardous waste could take place were also set.

Activity 8 **(5 minutes)**

List three possible advantages to a firm of having an EU eco-label on its product.

Making EU industry fit for sustainable development

The Commission has decided to introduce a strategy to implement a system of monitoring and protecting the environment based on two closely related objectives.

(a) To support *sustainable development* in agriculture, energy and transport which will create jobs and improve competition in business while, at the same time, safeguard natural resources. We discuss this concept in Chapter 8.

(b) Secondly, to establish a 'satellite' national accounting framework to track the development of valuable natural resources and the corresponding environ-mental statistics as accurately as possible, since Europe-wide statistics are needed.

To achieve these objectives, the Commission intends:

(a)   To establish a joint European approach to reporting on the state of the physical environment

(b)   To create a European system of environmental pressure indices

(c)   To design a report combining economic performance with environmental degradation for each country

The aim is to come up with an idea of the cost of damage caused to the environment and the cost of the restoration work.

In order to provide accurate statistics, EUROSTAT will work with the assistance of the European Environment Agency and various other Commission services and other competent authorities. This new model will make it possible to identify the level of performance in each member state, both in economic terms and in terms of its impact on the environment. The results of this 'green' book-keeping will be available in two years and these statistics will then be used to redefine guidelines for policies such as those for transport, energy and agriculture.

Air-combating atmospheric pollution - CO2 emissions

In the context of world-wide efforts to combat climate change, the EU committed itself to stabilising CO_2 emissions by the year 2000 at 1990 levels. But the Council failed - due to the opposition of the UK - to reach agreement on a European-wide 'carbon' tax on the use of fossil fuels, such as oil or coal, as proposed by the European Commission. Nevertheless, the Commission recommends further insistence on implementing the current European and national programmes and introducing the CO_2/energy tax which it has proposed.

To overcome the political deadlock, consideration is now being given to an action by the other 14 member states. This would amount to a European Commission supervision of a CO_2 tax based on the harmonisation of excise duties in the member states.

Chapter roundup

- The European Union comprises 15 member states, with a further enlargement planned. It is a free trade area, and a customs union with a common external tariff.

- The most powerful body is the Council of Ministers representing member states. The Commission does most of the work, in drafting legislation. Parliament has the power to amend legislation and approve the budget; it is also a forum for debate.

- The single market involves a certain amount of standardisation to ensure that consumers benefit from free trade. There is free movement of goods, services, people and capital.

- There are still significant differences between the member states, in terms of GDP per head and hours worked, to mention two examples.

Quick quiz

1   Distinguish between a free trade area and a customs union.

2   List the members of the EU.

3   What are the European Monetary System and the European Monetary Institute?

4   What does the European Commission do?

5   In the European Parliament, do MEPs sit in national or political groupings?

6   List four examples of the single European market in action.

7   How do member states decide who to send to meetings of the Council of Ministers?

8   How many members sit in the European Parliament?

9   What issues have been ruled upon in the European Court of Justice?

10   List as many as you can of the 12 sets of principles laid down in the Social Charter.

Answers to quick quiz

1   Free trade area: restrictions on the movement of goods and services between countries. Customs union: establishes a free trade area between member states only.

2   Austria, Belgium, Denmark, Finland, France, Germany, Greece, Ireland, Italy, Luxembourg, Netherlands, Portugal, Spain, Sweden, United Kingdom. (15 in all).

3   See Section 3.1 for a full explanation.

4   It performs the 'executive' function of the government of the EU.

5   Political groupings.

6   Examples include: trading standards, food law, transport, agriculture.

7   They are chosen according to the matter in hand. So, for example, agriculture ministers would be sent to discuss agricultural issues.

8   626

9   Various, including competition and employment law.

10   See Section 3.2.

Answers to activities

1   Many countries in Eastern Europe, as well as Turkey and Cyprus, want to joint the EU. The main problems are budgetary. The cost of extending the Common Agricultural Policy to these areas would be prohibitive. Also, the EU is taking a stronger line over human rights and democratic issues.

2   In theory you have the right to work in any EU country, so opportunities ought to be unlimited, but each country has its own rules and procedures (eg for tax and social security). Potential difficulties include unemployment problems across Europe - there may not be a job available, language issues - UK citizens are notorious for being the worst at learning languages, and lifestyle/cultural differences.

3   The Maastricht Summit laid down the following objectives for a EU environment policy:

     (a)   To preserve, protect and improve the quality of the environment

(b)   To protect human health

    (c)   To make prudent and rational use of natural resources

4   The main areas covered in terms of employment are - opting in to the Social Chapter, promotion of employment, improved living and working conditions, dialogue between management and labour, proper social protection, equality of pay and treatment, discrimination.

5   Subsidiarity encapsulates the view that decisions should be taken at the most appropriate level. At national level, general principles can be applied in a flexible manner to deal with national differences. Decisions at EU level are needed to ensure compatibility.

6   The future powers of the European Parliament are a subject of debate, with some commentators arguing that there is a 'democratic deficit' in the way the EU is run. The UK government has opposed giving more powers to the European Parliament to rectify this deficit.

7   The main points of the Working Time Directive are - compulsory rest periods and rest days, maximum working hours per week (48), minimum periods of annual leave (4 weeks by 1999), health checks for night workers and a prohibition on overtime for especially strenuous or difficult night work.

8   Possible advantages could include enhanced reputation for environmental responsibility, ability to charge a premium (higher) price, opportunities for marketing, ability to supply goods to environmentally ethical companies.

Assignment 3   **(4 hours)**

Prepare a presentation about a local company that you feel has taken full advantage of the opportunities presented by the UK's membership of the European Union.

Your presentation should include the following points.

1   An outline of the company, its product /services and its market area

2   How it markets itself within Europe

3   Who it sees as its customers

4   Who it sees as its competitors

5   The changes the company has found necessary to make in its trading practices

Chapter 4:
MARKET STRUCTURES AND MARKET FORCES

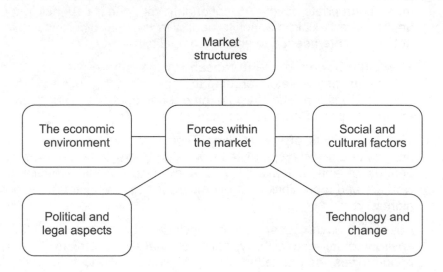

Introduction

We now look at the environment created for each buyer or seller in the market by the other people in the same market. This will focus our attention on price: how much can a company charge for its products, and how much should it charge?

Your objectives

In this chapter you will learn about:

(a) Different market structures

(b) Key factors in a company's environment

(c) The relevance of the environment

(d) Analysis of a business's environment

1 MARKET STRUCTURES

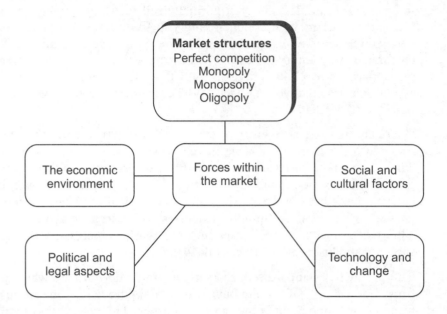

Economics is concerned with where money comes from and where it goes to: with buying and selling, with wages and profits and with wealth. Economists try to work out general laws which can be applied in a wide variety of businesses. The area of economics which is most relevant to us looks at how businesses and consumers behave in markets. The most important thing for an individual business or consumer is the number of rivals there are in the market. If you run the only supermarket in a town, you have a lot of power: people will come to you even if your prices are a bit high. If, however, another supermarket is opened next door to yours, you may have to cut your prices to keep your customers.

We will now look at the types of market which economists identify. We will start with one which has lots of businesses and lots of consumers, so that no-one has much power, and go on to consider markets with a few big players.

1.1 Perfect competition

Definition

> *Perfect competition* exists when there are so many people in the market, and other conditions are such, that no-one can influence the price, all other things being equal.

Perfect competition exists when all the following conditions are fulfilled.

(a) There are lots of buyers and lots of sellers. None of them can have any significant effect on the total quantity for sale (the *quantity supplied*) or the total amount which buyers want (the *quantity demanded*).

(b) The market price is fixed by the total quantity supplied and the total quantity demanded. If buyers want more, the price goes up. If businesses offer more for sale, the price goes down. This happens pretty well automatically. Suppose, for example, that you run a cake shop. You can only make 200 cakes a day, and you normally sell just that number at £1 each. Cakes then become more popular, and you find that 300 people come into your shop each day, each wanting a cake. You have to send the last 100 customers away empty-handed. The obvious thing to do is to increase the price, perhaps to £1.40. This will put off some of your customers (ideally 100 of them), so that you are back to 200 customers a day, but you get £280 a day instead of £200.

(c)   There are no barriers to entry or exit. This means that if someone wants to come into the market, or leave it, they can without incurring high costs. Thus the market for legal advice is not perfect, because it takes a long time to qualify as a solicitor and start offering your services to the public. Ease of entry and exit helps to keep prices under control: if the quantity demanded goes up, prices will go up and businesses will start to make good profits. This will attract new businesses into the market, increasing the quantity supplied and bringing prices back down again.

(d)   The product is standardised, so that customers do not care who they buy from. For example, if you are buying ingots of pure gold, you can buy them from anyone: one ingot is the same as another. This means that there is no point in promoting a brand: customers will only look at the price. Petrol companies have this problem - a litre of four star petrol is much the same thing, no matter who you buy it from. They therefore try to create artificial differences, using the image of the company, shops at filling stations, free gifts and so on.

(e)   There is good exchange of information: everyone knows what everyone's prices are. Real life is not like this: when you look at a bag of sugar in Sainsbury's, you cannot find out straightaway how much Tesco's would charge you for the same product.

The consequence of all the above is that there is a single market price, and there is nothing anyone can do on their own to change it. Any business charging more than the market price will lose all its customers to its rivals, and any business charging less than the market price will be swamped with customers whom it cannot satisfy.

Activity 1   **(10 minutes)**

Think about the market for new motor cars. In what respects is it like a perfect market, and in what respects is it unlike a perfect market?

It probably strikes you that the conditions required for perfect competition to exist are pretty unrealistic and in fact it would be difficult to point to a truly perfect market. In the past in the UK it has certainly been a lot easier to point to the other extreme of market structure, monopoly.

1.2   Monopoly

Definition

A *monopoly* exists when there is only one supplier of a product or service.

There are now few true monopolists. Most of those that existed were state-owned: for example, British Rail once had a monopoly on the provision of rail travel in most parts of Britain, but the Government has started to sell rail travel operations to private operators. Even where we do find monopolies, they may not be as complete as they seem - it depends on how you define the market. British Rail certainly never had a monopoly on long-distance public transport, because people could choose to use coaches or air travel instead of trains. However, some companies control large shares of their markets, and they may then be almost as powerful as genuine monopolies. The water industry is close to being a monopoly. Whilst there are many water companies, they hold a monopoly position in the area they serve. Consumers are only able to purchase from their local water provider. They cannot choose one of the other water companies no matter how better their service or cheaper their product. However, the government has recently stated that it intends to introduce competition to the water industry.

A business which has a monopoly on something which people really need could in theory charge what it liked, and still make sales, without any marketing effort. In practice, businesses cannot behave quite as badly as that. If something is really expensive, people will find substitutes. If, for example, electricity became too expensive, people would go back to gas for lighting although substitution is more difficult with water. In addition, marketing efforts are still needed to make sure that the product is what customers need, and to persuade customers to buy a bit more than they need.

Because monopolies could charge high prices, there are laws which try to control them, such as the Fair Trading Act of 1973. A company controlling 25% of the UK market is considered to be a monopoly. There is a Director of Fair Trading who can investigate unfair trade practices and monopolies and mergers which may put a company in a monopolistic position. Most service monopolies, such as water and gas, have regulators to look after the consumer's interest.

If a monopoly abuses its power and makes big profits, other businesses will want to move into the market and make big profits themselves. Thus for monopoly power to exist in the long run, the monopoly must be able to set up barriers to entry, to keep other businesses out. The most common types of barriers to entry are as follows.

(a) The business owns a key resource without a close substitute. For example, De Beers controls most of the world's supply of diamonds.

(b) There are government restrictions. For example, the Post Office has a legal monopoly on the delivery of letters for less than £1. No-one else can enter the private mail market, because few people will pay £1 for a stamp when they can buy one from the Post Office for 19p.

(c) Patents can give exclusive rights to exploit an invention for 20 years. For example, Black & Decker has enjoyed a monopoly on the WorkMate, and has been able to take legal action to stop the sale of similar, competing products. However, when the patent on the WorkMate runs out, Black & Decker will be faced with a lot of competitors producing cheap imitations.

(d) The huge amount of capital required to enter some markets can be a severe limitation. For many years the high cost of specialist cheese slicing equipment deterred competitors from entering the cheese slice market and gave Kraft a monopoly. This monopoly was lost when the cost of machinery fell dramatically.

Activity 2	**(10 minutes)**

Can you think of three ways a monopoly may abuse its power to the detriment of the customer?

Sometimes a company's monopoly power is weak, because the barriers to entry are not really effective. For example, if the monopoly is based upon product; differentiation which is primarily cosmetic, for example a brand name or fancy packaging, competitors could probably enter the market quite easily even though they could not legally copy the brand name or packaging. Only Heinz can sell baked beans under that name, but other companies can sell them under other names: if the customers do not see any significant difference between the contents of the tins, then there is no monopoly. This sort of threat may lead to the monopolist not charging too high a price, so as not to tempt competitors into the market. If a competitor does enter, a likely response is increased promotional activity. This is often in the forms of new advertising and price cuts.

1.3 Monopsony

Definition

> *Monopsony* arises when there is only one buyer for a product.

The buyer may then be able to dictate terms to suppliers. For example the manufacturers of hydraulic mining equipment at one time only had British Coal as a customer in the UK. For some manufacturers, Marks and Spencer is the sole buyer of their products. Monopsonists must remember that they need a good quality supply: if they force prices down, they may end up getting shoddy goods.

1.4 Oligopoly

Definition

> There is an *oligopoly* when there are a few large suppliers, whose business decisions affect each other.

We can distinguish oligopoly from monopoly by asking whether the businesses in the market can set their own prices (monopoly) or must take account of the prices set by other businesses (oligopoly). If an oligopolist sets a price higher than that charged by others, the company can expect to lose a lot of sales (but not necessarily all sales, unlike perfect competition).

The UK soaps and detergents market is an oligopoly, with Proctor & Gamble and Unilever dominating the market. However, this does not mean that they set out to exploit customers, nor that they could do so if they wanted to. They are both acutely conscious of the German company Henkel and have not so far set prices for their products at the level where Henkel would consider it worthwhile to compete.

Like monopolies, oligopolies can only last for a long time if they are protected by barriers to entry.

Activity 3	**(30 minutes)**

Is the United Kingdom grocery market an oligopoly? With the big three supermarket chains - Tesco, Sainsbury and Safeway - holding a combined market share of over 50%, how easy would it be for another retail grocery chain to enter the market? What specific obstacles are there?

BPP PUBLISHING

An *oligopsony* is the buyer's equivalent of an oligopoly, when there are very few customers in the market.

The context within which a business and its market operates is known as the environment. Since we have been looking at the economic explanation for market structures, we shall look first at the overall economic environment.

2   THE ECONOMIC ENVIRONMENT

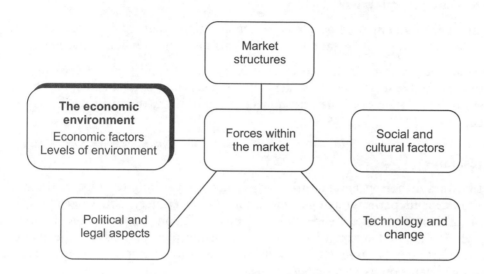

2.1   Economic factors

You will often hear reports of politicians discussing the state of the economy, and whether it is booming or in recession. We all know that this is supposed to be important, but unfortunately vague terms like 'recession' don't give us much useful information. They certainly don't give business people enough information to decide what to do. We need much more precise measures of how the economy is doing. These can then be identified as the economic factors which affect businesses and set their economic environment. For example, the rate of inflation is both a measure of how the economy is doing and an important factor for most businesses: if costs are rising, a business must either raise its own prices or save on costs in order to maintain profits. We will therefore identify a number of key measures, and look at why they are important for businesses.

The rate of economic growth

The rate of growth of the economy is the rate of increase in total economic activity. It can be measured using the gross national product, which is (roughly) the total amount of goods and services made in a year. For example, if a country has only one product, cars, and in year 1 it makes 1,000 cars and in year 2 it makes 1,200 cars, the rate of growth is 20%. The rate of growth matters to businesses because the faster the economy grows, the better off people become and the more they will buy. People can also change what they buy. For example, they might buy more cars and fewer train tickets, because they prefer private transport. This could have a knock-on effect: the demand for driving lessons might increase, and the demand for sandwiches at stalls in railway stations might fall.

The rate of inflation

This is the rate at which prices are rising. Businesses must take account of how their costs might increase, what wage rises they might have to pay and the extent to which competitors might increase their prices.

Quite apart from general inflation, the prices of certain raw materials may go up or down dramatically, having a direct effect on some businesses. For example, the price of crude oil has fluctuated sharply in the past 25 years, affecting not only the price of petrol but also the price of all goods transported by road or sea.

The level of unemployment

The number of unemployed people is particularly important for consumer markets and the retail sector. If people are out of work, they will not spend much in the shops.

Businesses may also be interested in who is unemployed, if they are looking for new workers. Some businesses need workers who already have special skills, or who can be trained quickly. If most of the unemployed are unskilled, this may make recruitment difficult.

Interest rates

Most businesses borrow money, either as overdrafts or as long-term loans. If a business wishes to expand, perhaps buying a new factory and machinery, it may need to take out a large loan. If interest rates are low, this may be easy. If, on the other hand, interest rates are high, it may be too expensive and the expansion plan may have to be abandoned. High interest rates can even drive a business to bankruptcy, if it can no longer afford the interest payments on its existing borrowings.

Taxation levels

Taxation levels and the nature of taxes can greatly affect businesses and their customers. The Conservative government of the 1980s and 1990s has reduced the rate of income tax, which increases the amount people have to spend. The same government has also cut the taxes on business profits, which gives the owners of businesses more spending money. On the other hand, it has increased VAT, which reduces the amount people can buy for their money, and has reduced personal allowances for certain people suffering income tax.

The reverse of taxes is subsidies, when the government hands out money to new businesses, businesses in poor areas and so on. Businesses who might be eligible are obviously directly affected by the level of subsidies.

The level of personal saving

If people earn money, they can either spend it or save it. If they spend it, businesses get the benefit straightaway through making sales. If they save a large part of their incomes, businesses may suffer in the short term. However, savings are ultimately invested, and make capital available for industry to expand.

The balance of payments

This is a measure of whether the country is selling more abroad than it is buying from abroad (a surplus) or the other way round (a deficit). If the UK has a surplus, this will tend to make the pound worth more, so that imports become cheaper. This will help businesses which import, for example a UK dealer in Japanese televisions. A deficit will have the reverse effect.

How other countries are doing

If a company exports to, for example, Australia, it is likely to do well if the Australian economy is doing well: Australians will have more money to spend on its output. This in turn will depend on Australian inflation, unemployment, interest rates and so on.

International barriers to trade

Some countries set up trade barriers, such as customs duties on imports, so as to make it difficult for foreigners to sell goods into the country. On the other hand, groups of countries can set up free trade areas such as the European Economic Area, and remove trade barriers within the area.

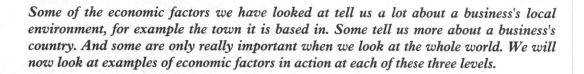

Activity 4	(15 minutes)

Think about a company which makes personal computers and give one way whereby each of the above economic factors may affect the company?

Some of the economic factors we have looked at tell us a lot about a business's local environment, for example the town it is based in. Some tell us more about a business's country. And some are only really important when we look at the whole world. We will now look at examples of economic factors in action at each of these three levels.

2.2   Levels of environment

The local economic environment

A business's local environment is most likely to have a big impact on its prospects if it is a retail business. A shop will only do well if there are customers in the town with money to spend. The most important local factor is likely to be the unemployment rate. A major industrial closure, for example of a coal mine, can destroy shops in the area. On the other hand, the opening of a new factory can bring prosperity to all businesses.

The national economic environment

The national environment affects practically all businesses. Growth, inflation, unemployment, interest rates, taxation rates and the level of personal saving are all relevant. Another factor which affects long term national economic prospects is the make-up of the population. In some countries the retired population is increasing faster than the working population, because people are living longer but having fewer children. This may mean that economic growth will slow down, because too small a proportion of the population is making things to sell.

Note that these national economic factors are things which an individual business, even a very big one, can do little or nothing about.

The world economic environment

World economic factors include the balance of payments and exchange rates, the performance of other countries' economies and international barriers to trade or free trade areas. Businesses may be affected by these things directly, if they import or export goods. They may also be affected indirectly, if they buy from an importer or sell to an exporter. For example, a printer may work only for UK publishers and may buy paper only from UK paper makers, but the paper makers will buy their raw material, wood pulp, from Sweden where the trees are grown. If the pound falls in value against the Swedish Krona, the price of wood pulp will go up in pounds and the printer will have to pay more for paper. This in turn may put up the price of books in bookshops, affecting the number of books sold and the shops' profits.

The economic state of the world as a whole is often held to be responsible for the performance of individual countries. For example, the UK's poor economic performance in the late 1980s and early 1990s was often blamed on a world recession. Such claims may be true, or they may simply reflect politicians' desire to blame anyone except themselves for poor economic performance!

FOR DISCUSSION

Do you feel that the UK economy is doing well or badly at the moment? What are the good signs and what are the bad signs? Are there any big problems looming in the years ahead?

The impact of some changes can be dramatic. Consider, for example, the UK's departure from the European Exchange Rate Mechanism (ERM) in 1992 and the subsequent fall in value of the pound against many other currencies. This provided a welcome boost to UK companies who were major exporters, because it made their goods cheaper to foreigners. On the other hand it increased the price of imported raw materials, pushing up domestic inflation.

A business buying large items of machinery from Germany, for example, may sign a contract in 2000 for goods to be delivered and paid for in 2002. If, in the meantime, the pound falls in value against the Euro, the goods will be more expensive than expected. Businesses can protect themselves against such risks, but the protection costs money.

Activity 5	**(15 minutes)**

Can you think of any other way a company may attempt to overcome the various economic problems that arise from world trade?

Social and cultural factors are the second important dimension of the external environment for a marketing business. To some extent they interact with economic factors.

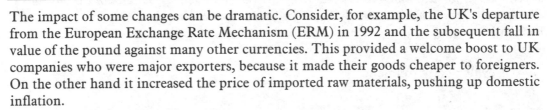

BPP
PUBLISHING

3 SOCIAL AND CULTURAL FACTORS

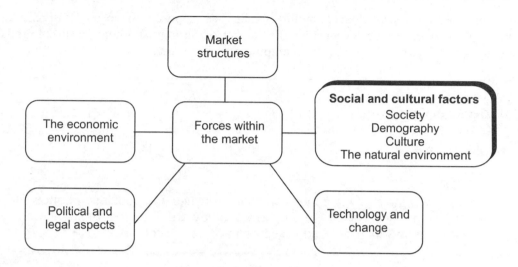

3.1 Society

People on the whole are social animals. Most of us come into contact with others fairly frequently. Society provides the framework for human behaviour and conduct. Underpinning this is a set of attitudes and beliefs. We know that if we want to be accepted by others, we should behave in certain ways. For example, when a group of friends are drinking in a bar, it is normal for them to take it in turns to buy drinks for each other. If you accept drinks from other people but never buy any in return, you will not be popular! This example of a round of drinks reflects deeper attitudes about sharing, which may go back to earliest times when people co-operated to kill and cook a mammoth, then all shared in eating it. Businesses need to take account of these attitudes. For example, bar staff need to be trained to remember an order for half a dozen different drinks.

Activity 6	**(15 minutes)**

Think of five recent advertisements which play on social attitudes.

When a business is taking account of social influences, it should consider the following aspects.

   (a)   Norms and values, such as sharing. Families influence people strongly.

   (b)   Lifestyles, for example the young, free and single lifestyle or the respectable middle-aged lifestyle. These are often influenced by the media.

   (c)   The influence of peer groups. These are groups of people of your own age, status and so on, whom you tend to mix with. There is often pressure to conform, to be like your peers in your choice of clothes, restaurants and so on.

FOR DISCUSSION

To what extent does marketing mould society, as opposed to society influencing marketing? You may wish to consider the impact of Sunday shopping, global brands such as Coca-Cola, and the targeting of computers at the young.

3.2 Demography

Definition

> *Demography* is the study of population characteristics and population trends. It is about how many people there are, how old they are, the proportions of men to women and how the population is spread across the country.

Demographic factors affect what consumers are likely to want, and the quantities they will want. For example, if the population comprises mostly young adults, demand for baby care products may be high. When planning for the future, an organisation should consider the following factors.

(a)   The rate of growth or decline of the national population.

(b)   Population changes in particular regions.

(c)   The age distribution of the population, both nationally and regionally. This will not only affect what people want. It will also affect what people can afford to buy, both individually and as a whole. If a country has a high proportion of retired people, who are not productive, the overall standard of living may be low.

(d)   Where people live (cities, small towns or the countryside), whether people live alone or in families and so on. This will affect where goods should be sold.

Activity 7 (20 minutes)

Consider the following population figures for the United Kingdom, in millions of people.

Age	1971	1981	1991	1993	2001
Under 16	14.2	12.5	11.7	12.0	12.4
16-39	17.5	19.7	20.4	20.3	19.7
40-64	16.7	15.7	16.6	16.8	18.3
65-79	6.1	6.9	6.9	6.2	6.8
80 +	1.3	1.6	2.1	2.3	2.6

What are the main trends? What are the main implications for organisations in (1) the health care sector and (2) the manufacturing sector, for example Coca Cola?

Demography has a big effect on culture, and cultures can influence demography. A mainly young society is likely to have a different culture from an elderly one, and culture influences people's decisions on whether or when to have children. The next section looks at several cultural issues.

3.3 Culture

Definition

> *Culture* is the sum total of the inherited ideas, beliefs, values and knowledge that make up the basis of social action.

A society's culture comprises three interdependent elements, as follows.

(a)   The *ideological system* represents the ideas, beliefs, values and ways of reasoning that we accept. For example, most people accept that they have some responsibility not to endanger others through carelessness, and therefore accept (at least in theory) that they should drive carefully.

(b)   The *technological system* comprises the skills, crafts and arts that allow us to make things. Thus one of the most important reasons why our culture today is very different from the culture of 500 years ago is that we have aeroplanes, computers, telephones and so on.

(c)   The *organisational system* is the system which co-ordinates people's efforts. It includes the government, companies, families and social clubs.

Activity 8   **(15 minutes)**

The role of the family and religion are two of the main indicators of what a culture is like. What do you think that the other main indicators are?

Businesses must take account of the culture of their society. It will determine what they can sell and how they should sell it. For example, an advertisement containing a shot of a semi-naked woman might be perfectly acceptable in some countries, but will be very offensive in others. Businesses must also pay attention to subcultures, the cultures of groups within a society. The culture of young students is likely to differ from that of middle aged business managers.

Attitudes to pleasure

Many people have spare money to spend as they choose, and businesses want to attract that money to themselves. There are many different ways in which they can get people to spend on things they do not really need. One approach is to appeal to self-centredness, using slogans such as 'Go on, treat yourself (to a chocolate)'. Another approach is to emphasise the benefits to others, for example by emphasising that producers of the goods in poor countries are paid a good price for their output. Which approach is best will of course depend on the product, but it will also depend on the culture. Here are some pairs of opposed attitudes to pleasure.

Other-centredness	Self-fulfilment
Postponed gratification	Immediate gratification
Hard work	The easy life

Formal relationships   Informal open relationships
Religious orientation   Secular orientation

Activity 9   (20 minutes)

Assume that you are running a bookshop. Think of one way you could deal with each of the above attitudes to attract different customers.

Changes in culture

A business must not simply find out about the state of the culture it operates in, and leave it at that. Culture can change, and businesses need to notice these changes and adapt. For example, while belief in marriage has persisted, the belief that people should marry young has not: women now have careers before they marry, and have children later than they used to.

3.4 The natural environment

The natural environment has become an important issue in the past 25 years, and pressure groups such as Greenpeace have been set up to publicise the detrimental effects that organisations of all kinds are having. Campaigning by these pressure groups has caused organisations to accept responsibility for the natural world. It is now common for big companies to take account of the environmental costs of their actions, and to publicise the steps they take to minimise the damage they do. Concern about the environment can even be turned into a positive selling point. A washing machine can be advertised as energy-saving because it automatically checks the size of the load and only heats the amount of water needed, and some airlines make the point that they use the latest quiet aircraft for the benefit of people who live near airports.

Activity 10   (15 minutes)

What are the natural environmental problems that a bus company should be concerned about? What could it do to be more environmentally responsible?

Becoming more ecologically responsible can have economic and social ramifications. Thus when Germany re-unified in 1990, the environmentally damaging use of brown lignite coal in the former East Germany was stopped. This led to increased energy prices and unemployment.

Businesses, like everyone else, have to work within the law.

4   POLITICAL AND LEGAL ASPECTS

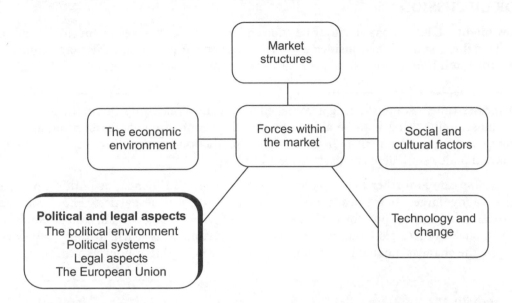

4.1   The political environment

Laws are made by Parliament for the good of society as a whole. What laws are made depends on which political party holds power. Therefore the political environment is important to businesses. However, this environment goes further than the election of governments. Although a government will come to power already committed to making certain changes, there are many other things which it might or might not do. Businesses may, either individually or though trade associations, lobby for changes they would like. In the UK, pressure groups have an important role, and businesses can hire professional lobbyists who know how to persuade politicians to do things. Even beyond legislation, businesses must also be aware of general political attitudes. For example, some governments favour free enterprise, while others prefer central control, and even nationalisation of industries. Large businesses and pressure groups may put a lot of effort into influencing such attitudes.

We will start by looking at how political systems can affect businesses. It is tempting to think that, because the UK's political system has changed only slowly over the years, with no revolutions since 1685, it can be ignored. In fact it has a big impact on business.

4.2   Political systems

The UK's political system has been remarkably stable, with no revolutionary changes for over 300 years. Over the same timespan, most European countries have experienced violent revolutions which have seriously disrupted their economies. UK businesses need not worry about revolutions. What they do need to worry about is the risk of dramatic changes in government policy, as one party replaces another in government at a general election. The UK system channels any urges for dramatic change into the voting system, which allows a change of heart by a few voters to change the whole direction of government. On a change of government, there could be major changes in the healthcare and education sectors, for example.

FOR DISCUSSION

How might a UK car manufacturer be affected by a change of government (to the left or to the right)? You might consider the effect of changed policy towards, say, company cars, road-building, green issues, personal taxation and import restrictions.

Businesses can to some extent get round the problems created by the political system. The most useful thing is to be able to predict the result of a general election, and the likely effect on government policies. Accurate prediction is very difficult, but opinion polls and policy statements by party leaders can help.

A business can go further than prediction and attempt to influence the political process itself. Many large companies contribute money to political parties. They also use political lobbyists to put forward their point of view. Some organisations, such as professional bodies, also retain Members of Parliament as Parliamentary advisors. Despite the changes mooted by the Nolan Committee, lobbying is bound to continue.

Activity 11	**(10 minutes)**

Think of one argument for allowing businesses to pay members of Parliament to act as advisors, and one argument against it.

In a mixed economy, like that of the UK, the government controls a significant part of the economy. It is the largest supplier, employer, customer and investor. A shift in political policy can change a particular market overnight. For example, the end of the Cold War has been a big problem for weapons makers.

Any business which operates abroad, or which has overseas suppliers or customers, needs to consider the political environment in the countries involved as well as in the UK. In many cases there is no special problem beyond the need to deal with different sets of rules and forms to fill in, because many countries are stable democracies. In some countries, however, one has to consider the risk of revolution, military coup or economic collapse. These can lead to assets being confiscated and debts never being paid. Even in safer environments, there can be problems. If an economy is in difficulties, perhaps suffering high unemployment, foreign businesses are often blamed. The consequence can be unexpected controls on trade. Whole industries, as well as individual businesses, can also be affected by international politics. For example, the deregulation of air travel in Europe and the USA has proceeded very slowly.

One of the main functions of the political process is lawmaking. Businesses and consumers are directly affected by the laws passed, and by the international conventions which governments agree to. We will now look at these legal aspects.

4.3   Legal aspects

Laws can affect businesses in the following different ways.

(a)   *Dealings with customers* can be affected by laws on the sale of goods and services, on advertising and trade descriptions, on product safety and on shop opening hours.

(b) *How a business treats its employees* is affected by employment legislation and trade union law, largely designed to protect employees' rights. Thus there are strict rules on the dismissal of employees and on equal opportunities.

(c) *Dealings with shareholders* are affected by the Companies Acts, which lay down how information must be given in published accounts and what dividends may be paid.

(d) The *criminal law* can affect companies. Some offences can be committed by companies as separate legal persons distinct from their directors and employees.

Some laws apply to all businesses. Others apply only to particular types of business. An example is the Financial Services and Markets Act 2000, which affects firms in the financial sector which deal with investments.

Changes in laws are often predictable. The proposals may be part of a government's declared programme or part of an opposition party's manifesto. The process of enacting laws in the UK also gives businesses time to plan for proposed changes: there is likely to be a preliminary period of consultation, followed by the Parliamentary process. This process can itself take several months.

Businesses are affected by laws made outside the UK. For example, anyone doing business in the USA must take account of US law. Even a business which has no international dealings must take account of European Union law. We will now go on to look at the effect of the European Union.

4.4 The European Union

The EU has done many things to make the sale of goods in different countries easier, and to allow the free movement of capital and labour. Here are some examples.

(a) Setting common standards on food labelling and hygiene

(b) Setting common standards for information technology

(c) Making rules to ensure that when a government needs to buy something, all EU companies have an equal chance to supply and the home country's companies are not favoured

(d) Liberalising of capital movements, so that (for example) a UK investor can freely move money to another country and invest it in a business there

(e) Removing of rules which limited access to financial services - it should soon be possible for insurance companies to sell their products anywhere in the EU

(f) Ensuring mutual recognition of professional qualifications, so that (for example) a French lawyer can practise in the UK without having to requalify as a UK solicitor or barrister

(g) Giving all EU citizens the right to work anywhere in the EU

Activity 12	(15 minutes)

A Japanese electronics company decides to set up a factory in the UK. Can you think of three political and three legal aspects that the company will need to be aware of which will impinge on the company and its products?

We discuss technology in the context of change since this is the area in which the greatest environmental developments are currently taking place.

5   TECHNOLOGY AND CHANGE

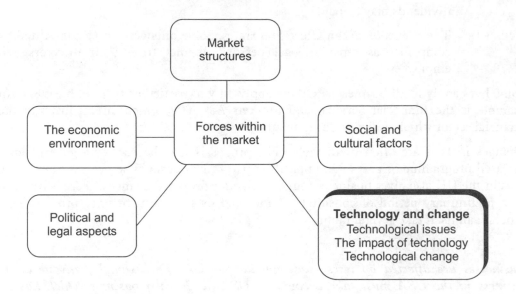

5.1   Technological issues

Definitions

> *Technology* is the knowledge which allows people to make and do things. Such knowledge often comes from scientific research and can be 'high tech', for example the use of micro chips. However, technology can also be 'low tech', for example child-proof tops on medicine bottles.

An *invention* is the product of research and development. Innovation is making commercial use of an invention, making money out of it.

Of all environmental factors, technology is the most challenging. Change is rapid, and a company which makes the right decisions early can get a big advantage over its competitors. To stay ahead, companies need effective research, planning and marketing; of new products. In some cases, if a new product is late, it may barely sell at all because better products have become available in the meantime. This has happened with personal computers: there would be little point in launching a new range of computers with 486 processors now that the more powerful Pentium processors are widely available.

The need to get the marketing right, as well as the technology and the timing, is illustrated by domestic video systems. Initially, consumers could choose between the VHS system or the Betamax system. In the end VHS won, not because it was technically better nor because it was available sooner, but because the promoters of VHS ensured that a lot of films were available on video in the VHS format. This was important to many consumers, who wanted to be able to rent films to watch at home.

FOR DISCUSSION

Digital cameras, which take still pictures but record them electronically instead of on film, are now available. Pictures taken on them can be loaded into computers and manipulated (for example, changing colours or merging two pictures). If you had to sell these cameras to consumers in high street shops, what features would it be important for them to have (for example, ability to take close-ups and panoramic views)? You can include features which may not yet be feasible, so long as they are reasonably likely to become feasible in the next ten years.

Technology can drive some companies out of business, or at least force them to change their products completely. For example, the market for mechanical typewriters is now much smaller than it was, because computers with word-processing packages are so cheap.

Activity 13	(10 minutes)

Why have electronic personal organisers (such as those made by Psion) not destroyed the market for ring-bound organisers (such as Filofaxes)?

We will now look at key areas where technology has a direct effect on our lives, both at work and in the home.

5.2 The impact of technology

Technology can affect businesses in the following ways.

(a) The *types of products* that are made have changed. In consumer markets we have seen the emergence of personal computers, compact disc players and palm held televisions. Satellite TV, received via dish or cable, is now commonplace. Industrial markets have seen the introduction of sophisticated new machines run by microchips.

(b) The *manufacture of products* has changed. Robots are now used in many factories.

(c) The *quality of products* has improved with the use of automatic testing equipment that takes away human error.

(d) The way in which goods and services are *delivered* to the customer has changed. For example, automatic teller machines are now the main route by which people get cash from their banks. Home shopping is also becoming easier and more widespread.

(e) The *availability of goods* has improved. The flow of goods can be monitored by the use of computerised point of sale equipment such as barcode readers in shops. This information can be used to re-order goods automatically when stocks are low, and also to gather marketing information. For example, a supermarket might find that chocolates tend to sell better in wet weather (perhaps because people feel that they need cheering up). The supermarket could then use the long-range weather forecast to decide on the stock levels for chocolates.

(f)   Large scale databases to monitor customer behaviour are now possible. The Barclays Bank group of companies have access to a database of over 20 million potential customers and therefore can closely monitor the individual members of its market. Direct mail can be sent to the right people, instead of to everybody.

(g)   Technology has significantly changed the way people work. Computers are used not only to create documents and to store and process data, but also to communicate using electronic mail (e-mail). Many people can now work at home, and be linked to their employers electronically. This is called telecommuting.

FOR DISCUSSION

There are now many more mobile telephones than there were five years ago, and a very high proportion are used for private, rather than business, purposes. What impact has this technology had on people's lives? How might the technology develop further?

Activity 14	**(20 minutes)**

Look at the direct mail that you or your family have received during the past few months. How do you think the senders obtained your names? How relevant are the products or services to you? Do you think that the senders have any idea of how old each of you are, of how much money you have or of your lifestyle?

We will end this chapter by looking at the broad effects of technological change on businesses.

5.3   Technological change

The effects of technological change can include the following.

(a)   *A fall in costs.* The most dramatic example is data processing costs. The cost of working out how much a customer owes, or working out an employee's pay, is now about 0.2% of what it was 40 years ago.

(b)   *Improved quality*, especially in the area of customer service. If, for example, a customer telephones with an enquiry, that customer's details can be called up on screen straightaway. The customer does not have to wait while their file is found.

(c)   *New products and services.* For example, telephone subscribers can now get itemised bills.

(d)   *Easier access to products and services*, for example using home shopping by computer.

In order to keep up with technological change, businesses must be flexible enough to change quickly. They must also plan for change and innovation. They may either invest more into research and development directly, or acquire technology by taking over other companies or arranging to share the fruits of other companies' research.

Activity 15 (20 minutes)

Think of a company which you know something about. How has it changed over the past few years in response to new technology? How might it have to change over the next few years?

Chapter roundup

- The main market structures are perfect competition, monopoly and oligopoly.

- Under perfect competition, no one buyer or seller can influence the price.

- The state of the economy is shown by a number of key indicators, including the rate of inflation and the level of unemployment.

- The economic environment can be viewed at the local, national and world levels.

- Social factors include demography, culture and the natural environment.

- The political environment is determined by the political system. This is not just the formal law-making system: it includes the ways in which politicians and public opinion can be influenced.

- The European Union has had a big impact on businesses, and will go on doing so. A lot of EU legislation is concerned with standardisation.

- Technology has led to dramatic changes in businesses. However, it is not enough to have a bright idea: it needs to be implemented in the right way, the right time and with the right marketing.

Quick quiz

1   What are the main ways of classifying factors in the environment?

2   What are the conditions for perfect competition?

3   Give five examples of economic indicators.

4   What are the main factors affecting the world economic environment?

5   What demographic factors should an organisation consider when planning for the future?

6   What are the three elements of a society's culture?

7   How can companies turn environmental concerns to their advantage?

8   How can businesses affect the political environment?

9   What are the three types of economic system which flow from different political systems?

10   In what ways can laws affect businesses?

11   Give some examples of things which the European Union has done to create a single market.

12   What is the difference between invention and innovation?

13   In what ways can technology affect businesses?

Answers to quick quiz

1   Political, economic, social and technological.

2   There are so many people in the market and conditions are such that no-one can influence the price, other things being equal.

3   Rate of growth; rate of inflation; tax levels; level of unemployment; interest rates.

4   Balance of payments; exchange rates; other countries' economies; international barriers to trade.

5   (a) The rate of growth or decline of the national population.

       (b) Population changes in particular regions.

       (c) The age distribution of the population, both nationally and regionally. This will not only affect what people want; it will also affect what people can afford to buy, both individually and as a whole. If a country has a high proportion of retired people, who are not productive, the overall standard of living may be low.

       (d) Where people live (cities, small towns or the countryside), whether people live alone or in families and so on. This will affect where goods should be sold.

6   Ideological system; technological system; organisational system.

7   Turn into positive selling point: for example, 'energy saving'.

8   Lobby political parties through trade associations or professional lobbyists.

9   Planned economy; free market economy; mixed economy.

10   Dealings with customers; treatment of employees; dealings with shareholders.

11   Easing of customs controls; common standards; recognition of professional qualifications.

12   Invention is the product of research and development; innovation is making use of an invention.

13   Types of products; manufacture of product; quality of product; delivery; availability.

Answers to activities

1   The market for new cars is like a perfect market in that there are many manufacturers, dealers and customers, and information on products and prices is widely available.

    The market is unlike a perfect market in that the product is not standardised: a Ford and a Honda are not the same. There are also significant barriers to entry: to start making cars, you must make a big investment in machinery.

2   Monopolies may keep prices high in order to make large profits, may limit the distribution system to keep sales costs low and may not update products and services as often as they if there were competitors.

3   Yes, the UK grocery market is an oligopoly. It is hard to enter the market, except perhaps by opening a local store which is open for very long hours, because the big chains charge very competitive prices. Specific obstacles to overcome include the difficulty of finding suitable sites for stores, the costs of building, stocking and training staff for new stores, and the large amounts of advertising required.

4   The rate of growth will determine the number of computers sold: if people have more money, and new businesses are being created, then sales should be good. The rate of inflation will affect costs, the price which can be charged and the profits made. The level of unemployment will affect demand: unemployed people are not likely to buy computers. Interest rates will determine the amount the company has to spend on financing its activities. If customers borrow money to buy computers, interest rates may also affect the willingness of customers to buy. The balance of payments will affect the exchange rate, and this in turn will affect the cost of imported components and revenue from export sales. International barriers to trade and the state of other countries' economies will affect export sales.

5   A company may decide to open up a factory or offices overseas. Motor manufacturers have done this very successfully in order to gain advantages of low wage rates, taxation and get round import controls.

6   Your answer will depend on what advertisements you have seen recently, but food and drink advertisements often centre on happy gatherings of families or friends. The BT advertisements also centre on family and friends as do those for package holidays.

7   In all groups except the 16-39 year olds, growth is predicted. The numbers of retired people will continue to rise with a marked growth in the 80 plus age group. The health care sector will be faced with an ageing population, but also with some growth in the child population. Child medicine and care of the elderly are likely to be the main areas for the sector to concentrate on.

8   The other main indicators of culture are language, education and material possessions.

9   A regular coffee evening with the occasional author as speaker and a club card allowing discounts would ensure that most attributes listed are met. Also ensure that there are books in stock on a wide range of subjects and an efficient ordering service for books not in stock.

10   The natural environment factors that a bus company should take account of are pollution and the consumption of a scarce resource (diesel fuel). A bus company could make sure that it uses fuel in an efficient way, could consider alternative fuels (such as natural gas), should maintain its vehicles efficiently and should ensure that its routes and timetables do not lead to undue congestion.

11   An argument for allowing MPs to be paid advisors is that they will spend time on the work, in addition to their normal duties, and that time should be paid for. An argument against allowing payment is that MPs may spend too much time working for whoever pays them the most, and may ignore their duties to their constituents.

12   Examples of legal aspects which would impinge upon the company are health and safety laws, employment law and planning regulations. Examples of political aspects are grants for companies in certain areas

of high unemployment, tax policy and relations between Japan and the UK (and EU) generally.

13   Electronic personal organisers are much more expensive than most ring-bound organisers, and some people do not like using very small keyboards.

14   Your name might have come from a list sold by another business you have had dealings with, from a membership list of an organisation you belong to or even from a telephone directory. The senders probably know something about you, if only the type of area you live in.

15   Your answer will depend on the company you have chosen. For example, a retailer might now use EFTPOS; a firm might use the internet for promotional purposes in future.

Assignment 4   **(4 hour)**

Scenario

You are employed by a company providing office services to firms in major cities in the UK. You are one of a team of people who have been given the task of investigating the potential for the company to establish a number of tele-cottages.

Your task is to investigate the tele-cottages movement and determine what would be required for such a project. In particular you should focus on the benefits for both employees and employers for involvement in tele-cottages as compared to either home working or traditional office-based work.

What factors would need to be considered for any proposed tele-cottages and how reasonable is the prospect for your company in business terms?

Task

In your group, prepare and deliver a presentation of your findings, which should also be summarised in writing for the panel.

Chapter 5:
MARKET DEMAND

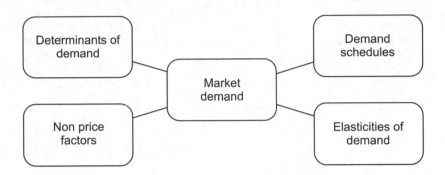

Introduction

Businesses cannot sell anything unless there is a demand for it. People must both want a product and have the money to buy it. How much people will buy depends on several things, not just the price. In this chapter we will see what affects the demand for goods and services.

Your objectives

In this chapter you will learn about:

(a)   What determines demand

(b)   Constructing a demand schedule

(c)   The concept of price elasticity of demand

(d)   Other measures of elasticity

1 DETERMINANTS OF DEMAND

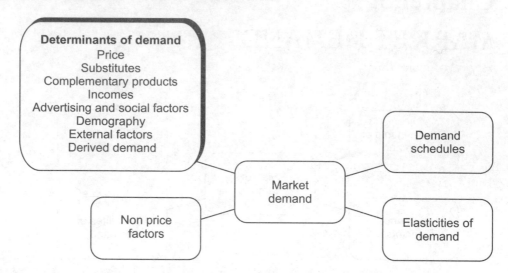

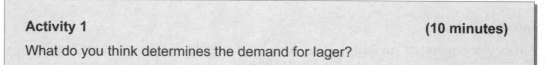

Activity 1 **(10 minutes)**

What do you think determines the demand for lager?

You should have come up with several factors. All the following are likely to be relevant.

(a) The *price of lager*. The higher the price of lager, the less will be demanded.

(b) The *price of substitutes*. The prices of other beers, spirits and soft drinks will have a bearing on the demand for lager. For example, if the price of substitutes increases while the price of lager remains the same, then people will tend to switch to lager.

(c) The *price of complementary goods*. These are goods which go with lager. Thus a rise in the price of curry should reduce the demand for lager drunk with it.

(d) The *level of incomes*. If people earn more than they used to, then they will tend to buy more of most things, including lager.

(e) *Advertising and social factors*. If lager is heavily advertised, or if it becomes a fashionable drink, demand for it will rise.

(f) *Demography*. If the population consists largely of people who are of the right age and lifestyle to go out to pubs for a drink, demand for lager is likely to be high.

(g) *External factors*. In hot weather, demand for lager is likely to increase.

The conclusions reached above are a little simplistic. We will now analyse the factors affecting demand more closely.

1.1 Price

It seems likely that as the price of something rises, the quantity demanded will fall. Eventually, it will become so expensive that no-one will buy any of it. However, it does

not follow that as the price falls, more and more will be demanded with no upper limit. There are two reasons for this.

(a) People will only want a certain amount of anything. You cannot drink an infinite amount of lager, because you will first become ill and then become unconscious.

(b) Many people assume that price indicates quality. If lager is offered at 20p a pint, people may assume that it is of poor quality, and not buy it.

1.2 Substitutes

People may change from one product to another, as the relative prices change, but they may not. Some people simply like lager, and will not change to bitter just because it becomes relatively cheap.

1.3 Complementary products

It could be suggested (rather facetiously) that if the price of curries rises, the demand for lager would fall. However, this might not happen. People might choose to eat cheaper bar snacks in pubs instead of curries, and they might then drink as much lager as before. They might even drink more, because they would be spending less on food than before.

1.4 Incomes

If someone's income rises, their spending will also rise (although perhaps not by as much as their income, because they may save some of their extra income). As a lager drinker's income rises, his or her spending on lager is likely to rise at first. However, beyond a certain point their spending on lager may actually start to fall. This is because there may be enough money to change to more expensive drinks, such as fine wines. Thus we have the paradox of demand for a product going down in spite of increased buying power.

This effect can be seen in reverse, when incomes fall and demand for cheaper products increases. People cease to be able to afford expensive products and switch to cheaper ones.

1.5 Advertising and social factors

Advertising and other sales promotional activities can greatly affect the level of demand. However, if a brewer runs a successful advertising campaign for lager, we should not automatically conclude that overall consumption of lager has risen. The campaign may simply have persuaded people to switch from other brands of lager to that brewer's brand.

Fashion can certainly affect the demand for products. It is closely linked with advertising: many advertisements deliberately suggest that in order to be fashionable, you need to buy the advertised product.

1.6 Demography

Lager is often seen as a drink for younger people. One might therefore expect that as the population ages, with fewer younger people because people were not having many babies 20 years earlier, demand for lager would fall. However, this might not happen. Current lager drinkers could continue to drink lager as they age, so that demand does not fall.

1.7 External factors

Demand for lager is likely to increase during a spell of hot weather. However, alcohol affects people more quickly when they are dehydrated, so if it is very hot demand for lager might fall.

1.8 Derived demand

Some items are not demanded for their own sake, but because of a demand for something else. For example, the demand for farming land is derived from the demand for food which will grow on the land.

Activity 2	(15 minutes)

Consider mountain bikes and suggest how demography and social factors may affect demand for them.

It is very important to be able to map out and understand how demand works, as we will later see how demand interacts with supply to determine whether price information demand is represented in demand schedules.

2 DEMAND SCHEDULES

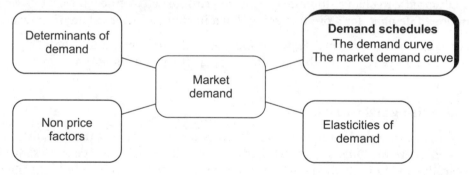

Determinants of demand

Non price factors

Market demand

Demand schedules
The demand curve
The market demand curve

Elasticities of demand

2.1 The demand curve

As we have seen, if the price of something goes up the quantity demanded is likely to go down. The relationship between the quantity demanded and the price is known as a demand schedule. It can be shown graphically as a demand 'curve'. The demand schedule for an individual is found by finding out how much of an item he or she would want to buy at various prices. Figure 5.1 is an example of a household's demand schedule for cheese and the corresponding demand curve. The curve has price on the vertical (y) axis and quantity on the horizontal (x) axis.

Price per kg £	Quantity demanded each month kg
1	9.75
2	8
3	6.25
4	4.5
5	2.75
6	1

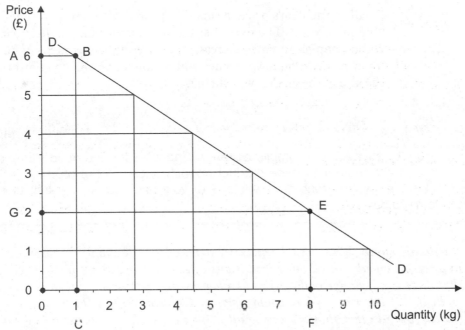

Figure 5.1 The demand curve

The extra horizontal and vertical lines are not necessary if we just want the demand curve. We have drawn them so as to see how much money in total would be spent on cheese each month at different price levels. For example, at a price of £6, demand would be 1 kg and total spending would be £6. This is represented by the area of the rectangle ABCO. Similarly, at a price of £2, demand would be 8 kg and the total spending of £16 is represented by the area of GEFO.

Activity 3   **(20 minutes)**

Choose a product that you buy frequently and estimate how much you would buy at three different price levels.

Although the demand schedule for one person or household may be interesting, a business needs to know how much will be demanded by the whole population: it needs to see the total market demand curve.

BPP
PUBLISHING

2.2 The market demand curve

The market demand curve shows the total quantities of a product that all consumers would buy together at each price level. A market demand curve is therefore the sum of all individual demand curves.

As with the individual demand curve, the market demand curve generally slopes down from left to right, reflecting the fact that at lower prices more will be sold. This is for the following reasons.

(a) For the individual consumer, a fall in the price of an item makes it cheaper compared to other goods. The individual only has a limited amount of money to spend, so expenditure will be switched to the item whose price has fallen. It is the relative price of the item that is important: a fall in the relative price of an item increases demand for it.

(b) A fall in the item's price means that people with lower incomes will also be able to afford it. The overall size of the market for the item increases. The reverse applies so far as increases in prices are concerned. As the price goes up, consumers on low incomes will no longer be able to afford the item, and the size of the market will shrink.

Activity 4 (20 minutes)

Repeat Activity 3, but compile demand schedules for five of your friends. Add up all their demands for the product at each price level to produce a demand schedule for the group as a whole. Plot your findings on a graph, to give the demand curve.

A demand curve shows how the quantity demanded will change in response to a change in price provided that all other conditions affecting demand are unchanged. This means that there is no change in the prices of other goods, or consumers' tastes and expectations, or in the distribution of household income. This condition is known as ceteris paribus (Latin for 'all other things being equal'). We now look at what can happen to demand when things other than the price of the item we are interested in change, that is when all other things are not equal.

3 NON-PRICE FACTORS

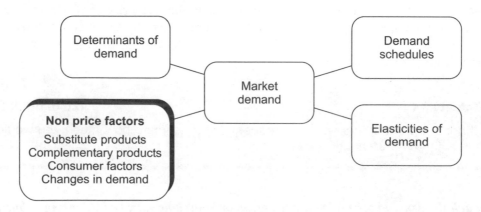

3.1 Substitute products

Most products have alternatives. These are known as substitute goods. Some are very close, for example tea and coffee, and some are not so close, such as a new car and a luxury holiday. Goods should be treated as substitutes if an increase in demand for one of them should result in a decrease in demand for the other.

Examples of substitute goods and services, to a greater or lesser extent, are:

- (a)   Rival brands of the same commodity, for example Coca-Cola and Pepsi-Cola

- (b)   Lager and bitter

- (c)   Rail travel and car travel

- (d)   Films and plays

Activity 5	(15 minutes)

For someone who commutes from a suburban home to a city centre office each day, are rail travel and car travel close substitutes? Give reasons for your view.

The next category is complementary products. When demand for a product goes up, demand for its substitutes goes down but demand for its complementary products goes up as well.

3.2 Complementary products

These are goods that tend to be bought and used together. Thus a change in demand for one item should lead to a similar change in demand for the other related product.

Examples of complements are:

- (a)   Cups and saucers

- (b)   Bread and butter

- (c)   Motor cars and replacement exhausts

In the case of cups and saucers, the maker tends to supply both goods at the same time. With the other examples the link is less close. A supplier of replacement exhausts will have to monitor the quality of the original exhausts closely so as to forecast demand for replacements.

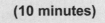

Activity 6	(10 minutes)

If the ownership of domestic deep freezers increased, would this have any effect on the demand for perishable food products?

We will now look at the effects on market demand that household income, fashion, consumer expectations and the distribution of incomes will have.

3.3 Consumer factors

Household incomes

More income will give people more to spend, and they will want to buy more goods at existing prices. However, a rise in incomes will not increase market demand for all goods

and services. The effect of a rise in income on demand for an individual product will depend on its nature.

Demand and the level of income may be related in different ways.

(a)   A rise in income may increase demand for a good. This is what we would normally expect, and goods like this are called *normal goods*. For instance, a rise in income may increase demand for moderately priced wine.

(b)   Demand may rise with income up to a certain point but then fall as income rises further. Goods whose demand eventually falls as income rises are called *inferior goods*. An example is cheap wine. The reason for falling demand is that as incomes rise, demand switches to superior products, for example better quality wines instead of cheap 'plonk'.

Fashion and consumer expectations

As already mentioned, a change in fashion will alter the demand for a product. For example, if it becomes fashionable for middle class households in the UK to drink wine with their meals, expenditure on wine will increase. There may be passing crazes, such as rollerblades or Power Rangers, and long-term trends, such as the move away from red meat for health reasons (even before the recent BSE scare).

If consumers believe that prices will rise, or that shortages will occur, they may try to stock up on the product, thereby creating excess demand in the short term which will increase prices. This can then lead to panic buying. Some years ago, a rumour was spread that the Siberian salt mines were closed. This caused panic buying of salt in the UK to the extent that most shops ran out of supplies, even though salt for the UK is supplied from enormous deposits in Cheshire and not from Siberia at all!

The distribution of incomes

Market demand for products is influenced by the way in which income is shared among households.

In a country with many rich and many poor households and few middle income ones, we might expect relatively high demand for luxury cars and yachts, and also for basic necessities such as bread and potatoes. In a country with many middle-income households, we might expect high demand for TV sets and medium-sized cars.

Activity 7   **(15 minutes)**

A food supermarket chain known for its service, up-market goods and fairly high prices is looking to build a new store in the North East. They have narrowed down their choice of area to two sites and now have to make a decision. The sites are 75 miles apart and one of their criteria is distribution of income within a five mile radius of the new store. Site A has many large, new executive housing estates within the area, but also many run down older areas with high unemployment. Site B has many well established private and council housing estates within the area. Unemployment is around average in this area.

(1)   Where do you think the supermarket chain might choose to build a new store and why?

(2)   Can you name one factor for and against each area?

Finally in this section we look at how to show the effect of changes in demand, using the demand curve.

3.4 Changes in demand

Changes in price

If the price of a good goes up or down, given no changes in the other factors that affect demand, then there will be a change in the quantity demanded, shown as a movement along the demand curve (the demand curve itself does not move).

Shifts of the demand curve

When there is a change in other factors that affect demand, the relationship between quantity demanded and price will also change, and there will be a different demand; schedule and so a different demand curve. For example, suppose that at current levels of income, the total UK demand for cheese at a price of £4 per kg is 150,000 tonnes. This will be a point on the demand curve. If incomes increase by 10%, the total demand at £4 per kg might rise to 160,000 tonnes. This will be a point on the new demand curve, which will be further to the right on a graph than the old curve.

We refer to such a change as change in demand, so as to distinguish it from a change in the quantity demanded. A change in demand involves a new demand curve. A change in quantity demanded, resulting from a price change, simply involves a movement along the old demand curve.

Figure 5.2 depicts a rise in demand at each price level, with the demand curve shifting to the right from D_0 to D_1. For example, at price P_1, demand for the good would rise from X to Y. This shift could be caused by any of the following.

(a) A rise in household income

(b) A rise in the price of substitutes

(c) A fall in the price of complements

(d) A change in tastes towards this product

(e) An expected rise in the price of the product

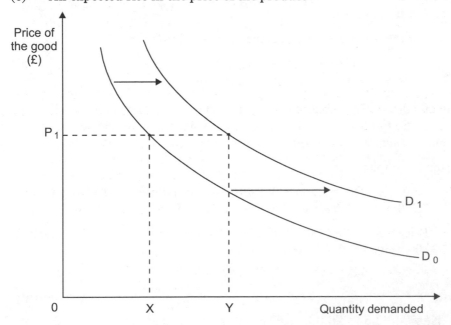

Figure 5.2 Shift of the demand curve

A fall in demand at each price level would lead to a shift of the demand curve in the opposite direction: towards the left of the graph. Such a shift could be caused by the reverse of the changes described in the previous paragraph.

Activity 8 (15 minutes)

Can you think of three reasons why it is important for a company to know how demand for their products will be affected by income changes?

We have looked at the factors affecting demand, but we have so far only discussed their effect in general terms. We will now see how to measure their effect.

4 ELASTICITIES OF DEMAND

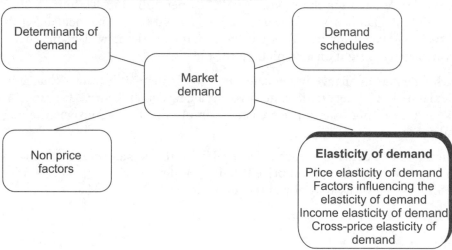

4.1 Price elasticity of demand

The price elasticity of demand measures how far the quantity demanded changes as the price changes. As explained later, the price elasticity of demand for a product is likely to be different at different prices.

The formula for the price elasticity of demand is as follows:

$$\frac{\text{Percentage change in the quantity demanded}}{\text{Percentage change in price}}$$

Because demand usually increases when the price falls and decreases when the price rises, price elasticity of demand normally has a negative value. However, it is usual to ignore the minus sign when looking at the price elasticity of demand.

Here are some examples.

    (a)   Price rises from £10 to £11, a 10% rise, and demand falls from 4,000 units to 3,200 units, a 20% fall: the elasticity is 20/10 = 2.

    (b)   Price rises from £15 to £18, a 20% rise, and demand falls from 1,000 units to 800 units, a 20% fall: the elasticity is 20/20 = 1.

Activity 9 (15 minutes)

Price rises from £5 to £6.25, a 25% rise, and demand falls from 8,000 units to 7,000 units, a 12.5% fall. What is the price elasticity of demand?

Note the following points.

(a) A product is said to have an elastic demand if the elasticity is greater than 1. A small change in price (up or down) leads to a large change in quantity demanded.

(b) If the elasticity equals 1, then a given percentage change in price leads to an equal percentage change in demand: this is called unit elasticity.

(c) A product is said to have an inelastic demand if the elasticity is less than 1. A large change in price (up or down) leads to only a small change in quantity demanded.

Why is price elasticity of demand important?

The price elasticity of demand is important when working out how much to charge for a product. If a company has a good idea of the price elasticity of demand for its products, that can help it to make sensible decisions on prices.

If demand is inelastic, then a company should seriously consider increasing the price, because it will not lose many sales: in fact, its total revenue will go up, even though it is selling less than before and therefore incurring lower costs. If you go back to the last example, where a price rise from £5 to £6.25 caused a fall in quantity from 8,000 units to 7,000 units, total revenue was 8,000 × £5 = £40,000 at a price of £5 and 7,000 × £6.25 = £43,750 at a price of £6.25.

Conversely, if demand is elastic, then a price rise may not be a good idea, because sales will fall fast and total revenue will fall. (Total costs will fall as well if less is being made, so a price rise might not be a disaster.) A price cut may be a good idea, because it will lead to a lot of extra sales, but of course costs will rise as well.

To find the elasticity of demand, a company may conduct market research to find out how much of a product people would buy at different prices.

Activity 10   **(20 minutes)**

The elasticity of demand generally changes as the price changes. Here is the demand schedule from section 2.1 with the elasticity of demand worked out for the first price. Work out the elasticity of demand for the other prices and complete the table.

Price per kg	Quantity demanded each month	Price elasticity of demand
£	kg	
1	9.75	
2	8	0.158
3	6.25	
4	4.5	
5	2.75	
6	1	

NOTES

We now need to analyse what factors are at play in determining how elastic demand for a product is.

4.2 Factors influencing the elasticity of demand

The elasticity of demand for any product depends mainly upon the availability of substitutes. If close substitutes are readily available then demand will be elastic: a small increase in price will cause many consumers to switch to the close substitutes, resulting in a fall in demand. If the price of canned spaghetti increases then people may switch to a close substitute - baked beans. If there are no close substitutes demand will be less elastic, because consumers will find it harder to switch to another product. If the price of milk goes up, people are likely to go on buying it in much the same quantities as before, because the closest substitutes (such as orange juice) are not really that similar.

	Activity 11		(10 minutes)

Do you think that demand for each of the following products is price elastic or inelastic: tick the appropriate box?

	Price elastic	Price inelastic
Petrol	☐	☐
Commuter rail tickets	☐	☐
Holidays in Spain	☐	☐
Mars bars	☐	☐

We have looked at the price elasticity of demand, making the assumption that other factors remain unchanged. We will now see how to measure the effect on demand of a change in incomes.

4.3 Income elasticity of demand

The responsiveness of demand to changes in household incomes is known as the *income elasticity of demand*. The formula for the income elasticity of demand for any one product is as follows.

$$\frac{\text{Percentage change in the amount demanded}}{\text{Percentage change in income}}$$

The income elasticity of demand may be positive, zero or negative.

(a) Demand for a good is *income elastic* if income elasticity is greater than 1 so that quantity demanded rises by a larger percentage than the rise in income. For example, if the demand for compact discs will rise by 10% if household incomes rises by 7%, we would say that the demand for compact discs is income elastic.

(b) Demand for a good is *income inelastic* if income elasticity is between 0 and 1 and the quantity demanded rises less than the proportionate increases in income. For example, if the demand for books will rise by 6% if household income rises by 10%, we would say that the demand for books is income inelastic.

(c) If the income elasticity is negative, then as people's incomes rise, they buy less of the product. This could happen if people switch to more expensive products. For example, as incomes rise people might switch from lager to wine: the income elasticity of demand for lager would then be negative.

Goods whose demand is positively income elastic or income inelastic are said to be *normal goods,* which means that demand for them will rise when household income rises. If income elasticity is negative, the commodity is said to be an inferior good since demand for it falls as income rises.

Activity 12   **(20 minutes)**

Complete the table to show the income elasticity for each product.

	Positive elasticity	*Zero elasticity*	*Negative elasticity*
White bread	☐	☐	☐
Croissants	☐	☐	☐
Salt	☐	☐	☐
Bars of chocolate	☐	☐	☐

We have seen that both prices and incomes may cause people to switch from one product to another. We will now look at the relationship between the demand for one product and the price of another.

4.4 Cross-price elasticity of demand

The way in which the price of one product affects demand for another is measured by the *cross-price elasticity of demand.* The formula is as follows.

$$\frac{\text{Percentage change in the demand for product X}}{\text{Percentage change in the price of product Y}}$$

The result may be positive, zero or negative.

(a) If it is positive, then X and Y are substitutes, like butter (X) and margarine (Y). If the price of margarine goes up, the demand for butter will rise because some people will switch from margarine to butter. A margarine maker would have to consider the sales he would lose in consequence before going ahead with a price rise.

(b) If it is zero, then the products are unrelated. For example, a change in the price of newspapers (Y) is unlikely to affect the demand for holidays (X).

(c) If it is negative, then the goods are *complements,* like tyres (X) and petrol (Y). If the price of petrol goes up, then people will drive less. This means that they will not have to replace their tyres so often, so the demand for tyres will fall.

Chapter roundup

- There are several factors that determine demand. These are price; the price of substitutes and complementary products; the level of household incomes; advertising and social factors; demography; and external factors.

- A demand schedule shows the quantity demanded of a product at each price level. The figures can be plotted on a graph, to give a demand; curve.

- The market; demand curve is found by adding up the demand curves of individual consumers.

- Shifts in the demand curve can be caused by many non-price factors.

- The responsiveness of the quantity of a product demanded to changes in its price is measured by the price elasticity of demand.

- The effect of changes in consumers' incomes on demand is measured by the income elasticity of demand.

- Demand for a product is affected by changes in the prices of related products. This is measured by the cross-price elasticity of demand.

Quick quiz

1   Why might the quantity demanded of a good fall as its price falls?

2   What are complementary products?

3   What is a demand schedule?

4   What is shown by a demand curve?

5   Which way does a demand curve normally slope? Why?

6   What does ceteris paribus mean?

7   Give some examples of substitute products.

8   How do substitute products differ from complementary products?

9   What are the social factors affecting demand?

10   How will a change in quantity demanded as a result of a price change be shown on the demand curve?

11   How will a change in demand, due to something other than a change in the price of the product concerned, be shown on the demand curve?

12   What is the formula for the price elasticity of demand?

13   Why might a company want to know the price elasticity of demand for one of its products?

14   What is the formula for the income elasticity of demand?

15   If the cross-price elasticity of demand for a product measured against another product were negative, what would that tell you about the two products?

Answers to quick quiz

1   People only want a certain amount of anything; price indicates quality.

2   Products bought and used together.

3   The relationship between quantity demanded and price.

4   The demand schedule.

5   Downwards from left to right because the lower the price, the more will be demanded.

6   All other things being equal.

7   Lager and bitter; films and plays.

8   Complementary tend to be bought and used together; substitute goods are alternatives.

9   Household incomes; fashion and consumer expectations; distribution of income.

10   Move of quantity demanded along demand curve.

11   New demand curve.

12    $$\frac{\text{Percentage change in quantity demanded}}{\text{Percentage change in price}}$$

13   To know how much to charge for a product.

14    $$\frac{\text{Percentage change in amount demanded}}{\text{Percentage change in income}}$$

15   They are unrelated.

Answers to activities

1   The answer is given in the text following the activity.

2   As the population ages it is likely that demand will fall, but as the present fashion is for health and fitness, it may be that demand will remain fairly static but with ageing customers.

3   The answer will depend on the product you have chosen and you own tastes and income.

4   Again, the answer will depend on the product and on the individuals' tastes and incomes. Did you find that everyone had a similar demand schedule? Were there any cases of demand going up as the price fell?

5   On the face of it the two products should be closely related. They both satisfy the same need, to get the commuter to and from work. There are, however, some big differences. Driving into a city and finding somewhere to park is difficult and stressful. On the other hand, trains only run at set times, which may not be convenient for the commuter. A commuter may not be able to afford the capital outlay for a car at all.

6   Domestic deep freezers and perishable food are complements, because people buy deep freezers to store perishable food. Perishable food may be supplied fresh or ready frozen. If more people have freezers, the demand for frozen produce will rise. The demand for fresh food may fall, but on the other hand it might keep up because people may buy fresh food and freeze it.

7   You may have chosen site A but B is equally possible. They may choose site B. At site B, people will have been in homes longer and may have more money to spend than those who have just taken out large

mortgages. However, Site A has high income families but high unemployment in some parts. Site B may have middle income families but no pockets of high unemployment.

8   The company may wish to make substitutes they know whether it is possible to put up prices without losing too many sales and they may decide to switch to other products.

9   12.5/25 = 0.5

10

Price per kg	Quantity demanded each month	Price elasticity of demand
£	kg	
1	9.75	0.179
2	8	0.437
3	6.25	0.84
4	4.5	1.556
5	2.75	3.182
6	1	10.5

11   The demand for petrol is likely to be inelastic within a modest range of prices: people will not cut back on their motoring significantly just because petrol goes up by 5p a litre. However, if the price were to rise a lot, people might cut back significantly, and demand would then be elastic.

The demand for commuter rail tickets is likely to be inelastic in a city with serious traffic congestion: people have to get to work, and they will pay quite a lot more to do so rather than switch to driving to work. Where car journeys take less time, there may be more substitution and demand for rail tickets will be more elastic.

The demand for holidays in Spain is likely to be elastic: many people go there simply for a beach holiday with reliable sunshine, and will happily switch to Greece or some other country if Spain becomes relatively more expensive.

The demand for Mars bars might be elastic, because there are many alternative chocolate bars which people could switch to. On the other hand, they might stick with Mars bars, because they have been made highly aware of the brand by advertising and because the cost of buying them is only a very small part of income.

12   White bread: negative, because as incomes rise people will switch to more expensive alternatives.

Croissants: positive, because people will only switch to them as incomes rise.

Salt: zero, because income levels are not likely to have much effect on consumption.

Bars of chocolate: as incomes rise, positive at first, because people feel able to indulge in chocolate more often; then negative, as people feel able to afford 'luxury' chocolates.

Boxes of Belgian chocolates: positive, because people will only switch to them as their incomes rise.

Assignment 5 (2 hour)

You have now decided on a business, considered the environment in which it will exist and your customers. Now you need to look at demand for your product or service. When you have completed this assignment you may decide to change your previous decisions.

(a)   Examine the factors that determine demand. How will your business be affected? Is there a substitute for what you are offering? Is your product/service a substitute? You will need to examine all the factors that you can.

(b)   Conduct a survey to try to assess demand at various prices and levels of income.

Present all your findings in the form of a memo to one of your partners.

Chapter 6:
MARKET SUPPLY AND PRICE

Market supply ——————————— Market price

Introduction

In the last chapter we looked in detail at demand - what the customer is willing to buy. In this chapter we will look at supply - what businesses are willing to sell. We will go on to see how supply and demand fit together to establish the market; price. We will also consider how to decide what price to charge for a product.

Your objectives

In this chapter you will learn about:

- (a) The factors that affect market supply

- (b) How to assess the impact of changes in supply

- (c) The interaction between supply and demand

- (d) Other considerations which affect pricing

1 MARKET SUPPLY

Market supply
Supply and price
The supply curve
Factors affecting supply
Responding to changes
The price elasticity of supply

Market price

1.1 Supply and price

Definition

> *Supply* is the quantity of a product that existing or would-be suppliers would want to produce at a given price. As with demand, supply is measured per time period – for example 17,000 kg of cheese a week, or 50,000 tonnes of coal a year.

As you would expect, supply depends largely on price. The higher the price that a product can be sold for, the more of it businesses will be willing to supply. The quantity of the product on offer may change because existing businesses choose to increase production as the selling price rises, or because new businesses are attracted into the market by the prospect of good profits. Conversely, if the price falls, some businesses will reduce their production and others will go out of business altogether (voluntarily or because they have gone bust).

Although a high price will attract producers, it will put consumers off. Thus a high price may result in over-supply, which means that more is being produced than consumers want. One possible result is a price war, with each producer cutting his price in the hope of attracting enough consumers. In the very short term, one producer (probably the first one to reduce the price) may benefit, but other producers will follow suit in order to win back some customers. The result is that all producers will suffer. In the long term, some producers may choose to withdraw, reducing supply and solving the problem, but before that happens some producers may run out of cash to pay their bills and be forced into liquidation. This is what happened in the package holiday business when Intasun, one of the three largest tour operators, went out of business.

Activity 1   **(20 minutes)**

The retail grocery industry suffers from some over-supply. The major supermarkets have specifically avoided using price as a weapon to beat their competitors in the fight for customers. How have they avoided this? What would happen if they decided to compete aggressively on price?

As with demand, we must distinguish between the total market supply and the individual business' supply.

    (a)   The total market supply is the total quantity that all firms in the market would want to supply at a given price.

(b) An individual business's supply is the quantity which that business would want to supply to the market at a given price.

We will sometimes find a business charging prices which are higher than those charged by other businesses in the same market, that is non-market prices. There may be many reasons why this is so. Here are two.

(a) Individual businesses may be able to use marketing, and particularly brand names, to ensure that even if they charge high prices, they can still get customers. Thus for example, Marks & Spencer can charge more than the major supermarkets for many foods, because people associate the St Michael brand with high quality.

(b) Reciprocal buying may occur, in order to maintain good business links. For example a manufacturer of computer chips may buy computers from important customers even if there are cheaper alternatives available elsewhere. Reciprocal buying may also take place between members of the same group of companies.

1.2 The supply curve

We can draw up a supply schedule and supply curve:

(a) For an individual supplier, or

(b) For all suppliers together

A supply curve is constructed in the same way as a demand curve (from a schedule of quantities supplied at different prices), but it shows the quantity suppliers are willing to produce at each price. It slopes upwards from left to right, because greater quantities will be produced at higher prices.

Suppose, for example, that the supply schedule for television sets of a given type is as follows.

Price per unit	Quantity that suppliers would supply at this price
£	Units
100	10,000
150	20,000
300	30,000
500	40,000

The relationship between output and price is shown as a supply curve in Figure 6.1.

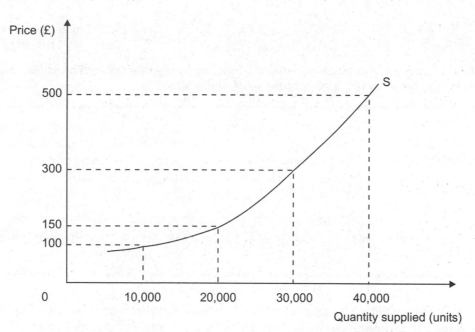

Figure 6.1 A supply curve

In the next section we look at the main factors that affect supply. Some of these are similar to those that affect demand.

1.3 Factors affecting supply

The quantity supplied of a good depends both on the market selling price and on the supplier's costs. There are five main factors as follows.

(a)   The *price* obtainable for the product.

(b)   The *prices of other products*. Increases in the prices of other products would make the supply of a product whose price does not rise less attractive: if other products become more profitable, suppliers will be tempted to switch to producing them, if they are able to. Of course, some products are produced as by-products of others, and a rise in the price of one will then increase the supply of the other. For example, if the price of beef rises, suppliers will decide it is worthwhile to supply beef and the supply of beef will rise. One effect of this will be an increase in the supply of leather.

(c)   The *costs of making the product*, including wages, raw materials and the cost of money to run the business (the interest rate). If any of these costs rise, some producers will be put off and will go out of business, reducing the total supply. They may not go out of business entirely, of course. They may simply change to products which are not so affected by the increase in production costs. Thus the jeweller, faced with a sharp rise in the cost of gold, might decide to stop making gold jewellery and switch to silver jewellery instead. See below on *productivity*, which affects cost

(d)   *Changes in technology*. Technological developments which reduce costs of production will increase the quantity of a product supplied at a given price.

(e)   *Other factors*, such as changes in the weather (very important for agriculture), natural disasters and strikes.

147

> **Activity 2** (15 minutes)
>
> Think of specific examples of products whose supply has been affected by the following: the weather, a natural disaster and a strike.

Productivity

Definition

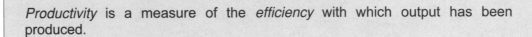

> *Productivity* is a measure of the *efficiency* with which output has been produced.

Suppose that an employee is expected to produce three units in every hour that he works. The standard rate of productivity is three units per hour, and one unit is valued at $\frac{1}{3}$ of a standard hour of output. If, during one week, the employee makes 126 units in 40 hours of work the following comments can be made.

(a) **Production** in the week is 126 units.

(b) **Productivity** is a relative measure of the hours actually taken and the hours that should have been taken to make the output.

(i)	*Either*, 126 Units should take	42 hours
	But did take	40 hours
	Productivity ratio = 42/40 × 100% =	105%
(ii)	*Or alternatively*, in 40 hours, he should make (× 3)	120 units
	But did make	126 units
	Productivity ratio = 126/120 × 100% =	105%

A *productivity ratio* greater than 100% indicates that actual efficiency is better than the expected or 'standard' level of efficiency

Management will wish to *plan* and *control* both production levels and labour productivity.

(a) Production levels can be raised as follows

- Working overtime

- Hiring extra staff

- Sub-contracting some work to an outside firm

- Managing the work force so as to achieve more output.

(b) Production levels can be reduced as follows

- Cancelling overtime

- Laying off staff

(c) Productivity, if improved, will enable a company to achieve its production targets in fewer hours of work, and therefore at a lower cost.

Labour cost control is largely concerned with *productivity*. Rising wage rates have increased automation, which in turn has improved productivity and reduced costs.

The supply curve and changing supply conditions

The supply curve shows how the quantity supplied will change in response to a change in price, provided that all other conditions affecting supply remain unchanged (the *ceteris paribus* assumption which we also made in connection with demand). If supply conditions (such as the prices of other products, costs of production or changes in technology) alter, a different supply curve must be drawn. In other words, a change in price will cause a shift along the supply curve, which we call a change in the quantity supplied. A change in supply conditions will cause a shift in the supply curve itself, which we call a change in supply. We are here making the same distinction that we made in the last chapter between a change in the quantity demanded and a change in demand.

Figure 6.2 shows a shift in the supply curve from S_0 to S_1

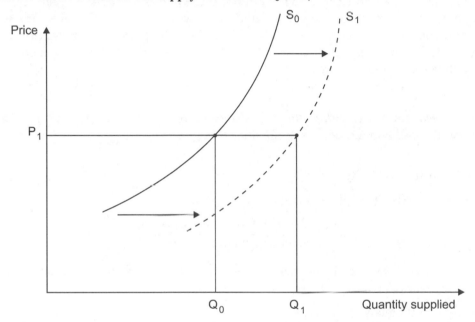

Figure 6.2 A shift in the supply curve

This diagram shows a rightward shift of the curve, representing an expansion of supply. If the market price of the product is P_1, suppliers would be willing to increase supply from Q_0 to Q_1 because of the new conditions of supply. The change in conditions might be:

(a)   A fall in costs of production

(b)   A fall in the prices of other products

(c)   Technological progress

Suppliers need to be able react to changed conditions of supply.

1.4   Responding to changes

The factors which affect supply can change very quickly. Unfortunately, suppliers may not be able to adapt to changed conditions instantly. For example, a prolonged hot sunny spell may cause a shortage of suntan lotion. The makers may be able to run their machines for longer periods, perhaps working nights and weekends, but they may already be working at full capacity. If the increase in demand were permanent, they would in due course enlarge their factories and install new machines, but that cannot be done in a few days. Even if production can be increased in the short term, it takes a little while to get the extra output to the shops.

With goods which do not deteriorate rapidly, one solution to this kind of problem is to hold substantial stocks, which can be used in weeks when demand exceeds supply and then be built up again once demand falls. Often these stocks will not be held by the manufacturers, but by wholesalers and distributors who stand between the manufacturers and the shops.

This is not a solution with products which deteriorate rapidly, such as fresh fruit, or with products which for some other reason must be sold straightaway or thrown away, such as newspapers. (How much would you pay for yesterday's newspaper?) In these cases, someone has to take the risk of either oversupplying the market, or leaving some consumers unsatisfied. With newspapers, the publisher normally takes the risk. Newsagents take more than enough copies to satisfy the customers, and then return the unsold copies to the publisher for a full refund. If the publisher refused to take this risk, newsagents would order the lowest number of newspapers they thought they would need, and some customers would not be able to buy their preferred newspapers. The result would be immediate lost sales, and possibly the loss of previously loyal customers as they changed to other newspapers.

We have seen how to calculate the responsiveness of demand to price changes using elasticity. We will now see how to do the same thing for supply.

1.5   The price elasticity of supply

The price elasticity of supply is calculated as follows:

$$\frac{\text{Percentage change in quantity supplied}}{\text{Percentage change in price}}$$

(a)   If this exceeds 1, for example when a 10% price rise leads to a 20% quantity rise (elasticity = 2), supply is *elastic*.

(b)   If it equals 1, we have unit *elasticity*.

(c)   If it is less than 1, for example when a 10% price rise leads to a 6% quantity rise (elasticity = 0.6), supply is *inelastic*.

Activity 3	**(20 minutes)**

The makers of a particular type of television set are prepared to supply 15,000 sets a year if the price per set is £200. If the price were to rise to £300, they would be prepared to supply 20,000 sets a year. What is the price elasticity of supply? (Calculate the percentages as percentages of £200 and 15,000, not £300 and 20,000.)

When we talk about the quantity supplied in the formula for elasticity, we mean the quantity which suppliers would be happy to supply at a given price. This might not be the same as the quantity they will end up supplying, because while a price rise encourages suppliers, it also puts customers off. We will now look at how supply and demand interact to set the market price and the quantity supplied and consumed.

2 THE MARKET PRICE

2.1 The equilibrium price

We have seen how, as price rises, more of a product is supplied but less is demanded. If supply exceeds demand, then suppliers will cut their prices in an attempt to win customers. This may lead to some suppliers going out of business, reducing the supply. It may also attract some new consumers, increasing demand. Conversely, if demand exceeds supply, some suppliers will raise their prices. This may put some customers off, reducing demand, and may also attract new suppliers into the market, increasing supply.

The end result of these changes will be that both price and quantity will settle down to equilibrium. The equilibrium is the point at which there are no longer any pressures to change the price or the quantity, because at the equilibrium price suppliers want to sell the same quantity as consumers want to buy.

We can find the equilibrium by showing the supply curve and the demand curve on the same graph: the equilibrium is the point where they cross (Figure 6.3).

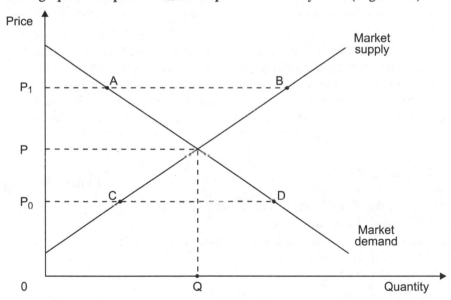

Figure 6.3 Point of equilibrium

At price P the amount that sellers are willing to supply is equal to the amount that customers are willing to buy (Q). There will be no unusual variation in stocks and, so long as nothing else changes, there will be no change in price. Customers will be willing to spend a total of £(P × Q) on buying Q units of the product. Suppliers will supply Q units and earn a revenue of £(P × Q). P is the equilibrium price.

At price P_1 sellers want to supply more than customers want to buy. The gap between supply and demand is represented by the length AB. At price P_0 customers want to buy more than sellers want to supply, and the gap between supply and demand is represented by the length CD. In either case, the market is said to be in disequilibrium. Suppliers and customers will behave as explained above, in order to get to the equilibrium price P and quantity Q.

Supply and demand can be seen working in this simple manner in commodity markets, such as the markets for gold and coffee, where prices move rapidly in response to deals done. In most markets, the mechanism may not be so obvious or efficient. For example, if car manufacturers are selling more cars than they can make, they may not increase prices straightaway because it may take them a while to realise what is happening, and because a sudden price rise may look bad. They may let waiting lists grow for a while instead.

Activity 4 (20 minutes)

Use the following supply and demand schedules to draw supply and demand curves on the same graph, and find the equilibrium price and quantity.

Unit price £	Monthly supply Units	Monthly demand Units
15	60,000	150,000
25	90,000	120,000
35	120,000	90,000
50	150,000	60,000
75	180,000	30,000

We have seen how if a market is in disequilibrium, the price will change, leading the quantity supplied and the quantity demanded to change until they are equal. Once the market is in equilibrium, we can expect it to stay there unless either the supply curve or the demand curve shifts: a change in supply or a change in demand. Either of these could happen for any of the reasons we have already covered, for example a change in consumer tastes or a change in the weather.

Activity 5 (10 minutes)

Suggest three conditions which you think determine the supply and demand curves in a retail fruit and vegetable market.

Activity 6 (15 minutes)

Customers may be prepared to wait for some products. A sports car company has chosen to supply only a fixed quantity a month which is below the current demand level. A waiting list build up and people sell their places on the list.

How do you think the price of a place on the list is determined? How do you think that the price of a place is related to the price which the company should charge to make demand equal supply? Why does the company not simply charge that price and make more money?

Prices are not always left to find their own equilibrium levels. We will now see what can happen when governments interfere.

2.2   Price regulation

A government may wish to regulate prices. This is normally done for one of two reasons.

(a)   The government may want to control inflation. It may do this by setting maximum prices for certain goods, or by ruling that prices may only rise by (for example) 4% a year.

(b)   The government may want to help suppliers. It may do this by setting minimum prices.

Maximum prices

If a *maximum price* for a product is set, but this maximum is above the market equilibrium price, there will be no immediate effect. However, people will read the maximum as a warning of future government intervention.

If the maximum price is lower than the equilibrium price, then there will be an excess of demand over supply. This is shown in Figure 6.4.

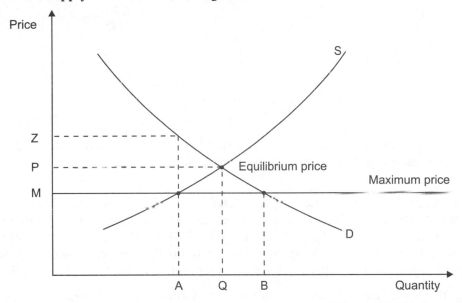

Figure 6.4 Maximum prices

The low price will attract buyers, but it will deter suppliers. The amount supplied will fall from Q, the market equilibrium quantity, to A. The quantity demanded will increase from Q to B. Demand will exceed supply by the gap AB.

The result of this gap is that some consumers will have to go without. To prevent an unfair allocation of the available supply the government might introduce rationing (so that each consumer gets something, but less than they want), or alternatively a waiting list. Unfortunately such systems rarely work perfectly. There will always be people who are willing to pay more than the maximum price, and other people (black marketeers) who will find ways to supply what they want. If only quantity A is available in the market, consumers will be prepared to pay price Z, and so black marketeers can supply at this price.

Minimum prices

Minimum prices are introduced for the benefit of suppliers. Minimum prices are the basis of the Common Agricultural Policy of the European Union: farmers are guaranteed a minimum price for their output if they cannot get a higher price on the free market. If the minimum price is set below the market price there is no effect. However if it is set higher it will result in excess supply.

The effect of a minimum price which is above the market equilibrium price is shown in Figure 6.5.

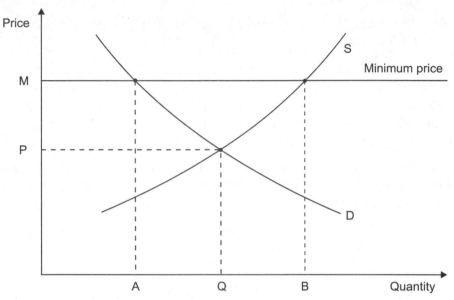

Figure 6.5 Minimum prices

The minimum price M is set above the market price P. The quantity demanded falls from Q to A but the quantity supplied increases to B. There is excess supply, represented by AB.

The excess supply caused by the Common Agricultural Policy led to the notorious beef mountains, butter mountains and wine lakes of the 1970s and 1980s. Some of these have had to be sold very cheaply to countries outside Europe. To try to prevent this oversupply, quotas have been set (limiting the amounts farmers are allowed to produce) and set-aside payments have been offered to farmers who take land out of production.

With all these problems, you may wonder why the Common Agricultural Policy exists at all. The historical reasons may be largely political, but we can say that the result has been fairly stable food prices. One of the problems which all farmers face is the danger that the weather will lead to a very good harvest, leading to excessive supply and very low prices, or a very bad harvest, leading to excessive demand and very high prices. The Common Agricultural Policy has helped to control these price fluctuations.

Activity 7   **(15 minutes)**

If there were no price regulation in agriculture, what would the implications of a very good harvest be for farmers? You should look beyond the obvious fact that prices would fall, and consider the consequences of price falls.

We have now looked at how prices are set as the result of supply, demand and government intervention. It is now time for us to focus again on marketing and look at how an individual producer should set prices.

2.3 Marketing aspects of pricing

Brand loyalty

The basic economic theory of supply and demand suggests that prices are fixed in a simple way, and that there is not much an individual supplier can do about them. If, of course, the supplier is a monopolist he has a freer hand and can set prices without fear that competitors will undercut him and take all his customers away. However, even a monopolist does not have a totally free hand because if prices are too high consumers will use their ingenuity to find acceptable substitute products or will simply do without. A supplier who wants a bit of freedom in setting his prices can do so by creating the impression that he has a unique product, so that he is a bit like a monopolist. For example, Ford do not have a monopoly on cars, but they do have a monopoly on Ford cars. If they can build up brand loyalty, so that some consumers would rather buy a Ford than any other brand of car, then they have a bit of freedom in setting their prices. In practice this is not difficult, because different makes of car are in fact different: they have different engine powers, different size boots, different safety features and so on. A Rover may be a close substitute for a Ford, but it is not an exact substitute.

Price perceptions

As well as using brand loyalty, a business needs to consider consumers' perceptions of prices. Consumers very often feel that a given product ought to cost a certain amount: they would not expect an ordinary family car to cost as little as £5,000 or as much as £20,000. They are likely to go out shopping with the intention of spending a certain amount of money and a company which does not charge a price within the expected range is unlikely to attract many customers.

Consumers also take price to be an indication of quality A very cheap product may fail to sell, not because there is really something wrong with it but because consumers assume that there must be something wrong with it.

Competitors' prices

Competitors' prices are important factors. If a business charges more than its competitors for a product which consumers see as being the same, then it cannot expect to sell much. Similarly, sales can suffer if a business puts up its prices but its competitors do not do so. Sometimes all businesses within an industry have a reason to raise prices at the same time, as when the cost of a raw material rises such as the price of oil. When this happens all the oil companies put up the price of petrol. However, no one business can rely on its competitors putting up their prices. Some will be tempted to keep their prices the same, in the hope of taking customers from those who put up their prices.

As well as considering what competitors will do before changing its own prices, a business should consider how competitors will react to its actions. In particular, a price cut which is meant to attract customers away from competitors may fail, if the competitors respond by cutting their prices: the result may be a price war, in which all the businesses involved suffer.

Maximising profit

Most businesses want to maximise their profits, or at least make reasonably large profits. The choice of prices will certainly have an effect on profits, but the effect can be hard to determine in advance. If prices are raised, revenue per unit sold will rise, but fewer units will be sold. Total revenue may rise or fall, depending on the price elasticity of demand.

Profit is revenue minus costs. If total output falls, then costs will fall, but they may not fall by much. For example, if a business needs expensive machines, the cost of those machines will stay the same even if they are not used much. The raw materials which the same company uses might be quite cheap, so that a fall in their use caused by a fall in output may make little difference to total costs. Another business with cheap machines but expensive raw materials, such as a jeweller, might find that costs change much more quickly as output changes.

The conclusion to be drawn is that before making any decisions about price changes, a business should find out what it can both about price elasticity of demand and about its own costs.

Chapter roundup

- Supply is the amount of a product that suppliers would like to produce at a given price.

- As a general rule, if the price rises, suppliers will be happy to produce more. This can be shown by a supply curve, plotting quantity supplied against price, which slopes upwards from left to right.

- Supply does not only depend on price. It is affected by the prices of other products, by the costs of production and by technology.

- The factors which affect supply can change very fast, but it can take some time for suppliers to respond.

- The responsiveness of the quantity of a product supplied to price changes is measured by the price elasticity of supply.

- The equilibrium price is determined by the interaction of demand and supply. It can be found by drawing the supply and demand curves on the same graph, and seeing where they cross.

- Price regulation can lead to excess demand or excess supply.

- When a business is working out what prices to charge, it must consider several factors, including customers' perceptions, competitors' behaviour and its own costs.

Quick quiz

1 What is a price war, and what are the likely consequences?

2 Why can some businesses get away with charging higher prices than their competitors for the same goods?

3 How can the prices of some products affect the supply of others?

4 Define reciprocal buying.

5   What is the difference between a change in the quantity supplied and a change in supply?

6   Why is holding large stocks not always a sensible response to the problem of fluctuating demand?

7   What is the formula for the price elasticity of supply?

8   Describe how price and quantity settle down to equilibrium.

9   In what types of market can supply and demand best be seen interacting to reach the equilibrium price and quantity?

10   How does a black marketeer exploit maximum prices for products?

11   What sorts of preconception held by consumers are important to producers when setting their prices?

12   If a producer doubles his output, does it follow that his costs will double? If not, why not?

Answers to quick quiz

1   Price war: each producer cuts prices in hope of attracting enough consumers when there is oversupply. Consequences: other producers follow, some withdraw from the market, some go into liquidation.

2   Brand names and reciprocal buying.

3   When some are by-products of others.

4   Buying in order to maintain good business links, or from other members of your group of companies.

5   Quantity supplied depends on suppliers' costs and selling price. Change in supply is due to other factors such as the weather.

6   Some stocks deteriorate rapidly and some go out of date.

7   $$\frac{\text{Percentage change in quanitity supplied}}{\text{Percentage change in price}}$$

8   As price rises demand falls so supply is reduced. This recurs until equilibrium is reached.

9   Commodity markets.

10   Some consumers are always prepared to pay more for goods in short supply.

11   They feel certain products ought to cost a certain amount and see price as an indication of quality.

12   No. Fixed costs remain the same.

Answers to activities

1   The major groups such as Sainsbury, Safeway and Tesco have avoided using price as a key marketing device even in the face of competitive pressures because they need high profits in order to fund their superstore programmes. Low price ranges are available, but they are not heavily promoted. Marketing strategies have been based upon quality as indicated by the range of goods and services offered to customers. If you compare the range of goods available as recently as five years ago to that available today you will see a marked change. The quality of service offered has improved to include such things as a range of different styles of shopping trolleys, more efficient checkouts, cafés and mother and baby rooms.

A price war would reduce profits. This would cause shareholders to look to invest in sectors offering a better return. They would sell their shares and the share price would fall as supply exceeded demand. A lower share price would affect the ability of companies to raise more capital to fund expansion plans. A loss of profitability could also lead to store closures, job losses and even company failures. This would lessen consumer choice.

2   The supply of coffee has been affected by frosts in Brazil. Natural disasters such as earthquakes and tornadoes affect the supply of holiday accommodation in the stricken areas. Strikes have practically closed the British Rail network.

3   The price elasticity of supply is 33%/50% = 0.67.

4   Your graph should look like this.

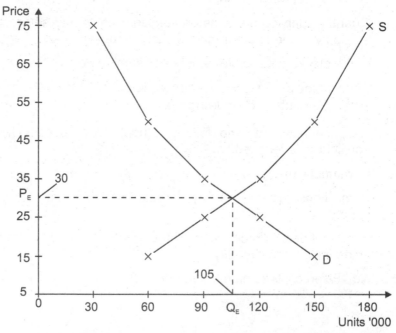

The equilibrium price, P_E is £30 and the market quantity exchanged at this price is Q_E 105,000 units.

5   A retail fruit and vegetable market will probably consist of many small traders, each with their own stall and competing directly with one another.

The conditions determining the supply curve include:

(a) Costs: the main cost to the traders will be the cost of their own wholesale supplies; although there will also be costs of renting a stall and costs of labour

(b) Availability of stalls: the prices that traders can charge will depend to some extent on the number of stalls that there are and the ease with which new traders can acquire stalls and thus enter the market

The conditions determining the demand curve include:

(a) Prices of similar goods in supermarkets

(b) Shopping habits: some people are in the habit of using markets, while others prefer supermarkets

(c) How much money shoppers have to spend

6 The price may be determined by adding a mark-up for profit on to the total costs. If the price was determined by demand it would rise until demand = supply. The company could set prices by demand and make a much higher profit which could be invested in the business. However, it may be that the company feels the cars are good value at the price they are and this is why they are so popular. By making them so desirable they are sure of sales and customers know they can obtain a good second-hand price for them. If the price were to rise, they might not appear such good value.

7 Oversupply is likely to lead to a serious fall in prices. While more may be sold at the reduced prices, it is likely that large quantities of produce will not be sold at all: the fact that food is cheap does not mean that everyone will eat much more, because each person still only has one stomach of a given size! Thus farmers' incomes may fall drastically. This may drive some farmers out of business. The result may be to reduce the supply in the following year, causing an abnormal price rise.

Assignment 6 (1¹/₂ **hour**)

Now that you have an idea of demand for your product we can turn to supply. Is what you are providing likely to be affected by the weather or other events over which you have no control? Are there barriers to entry in your market which you may be able to overcome or is it easy to enter? What would your strategy be if other suppliers entered the market and reduced prices?

Conduct an examination of all the factors covered in this chapter that may affect your business. Write up your findings in the form of briefing notes for a meeting.

Chapter 7:
COMPETING IN MARKETS

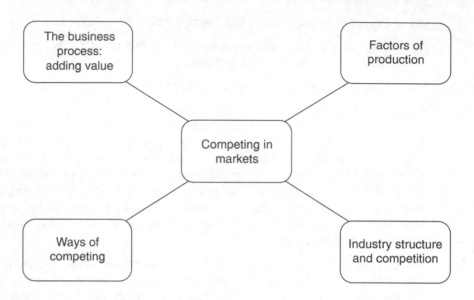

Introduction

You have already considered some of the broad economic, political, technological and social factors that businesses face. In this chapter we focus more precisely on those aspects of a business's environment that determine its success or failure - we examine competition and the approaches that firms must take in dealing with it.

We introduce 'factor markets', which economists hold are the basics of any business, from which a business gains raw materials and other inputs. (Some relevant considerations are developed further in Chapter 8, in line with current anxieties about the physical environment.) We then describe aspects of the competitive environment and the forces that make it hard or easy for businesses to compete. Next we explain some of the legislation regarding competitive behaviour. Finally we look at the 'output' end: how businesses can achieve their long-term goal of profitability by choosing their competitive strategy and 'marketing mix'.

Your objectives

In this chapter you will learn about:

    (a)   The four factors of production

    (b)   The transformation process

    (c)   The five competitive forces

    (d)   The strategies by which organisations compete

    (e)   The marketing mix

1 THE BUSINESS PROCESS: ADDING VALUE

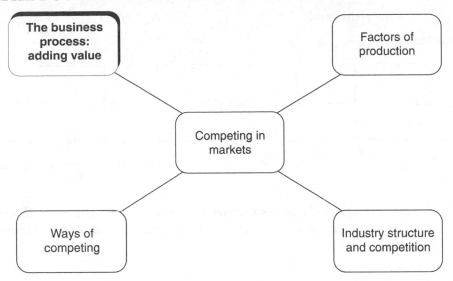

A business is a system that transforms *inputs* of various kinds into outputs that people choose to buy. This process is called *adding value*.

EXAMPLE: RESTAURANT ADDING VALUE

A restaurant buys food, cooks, and serves it. There is no reason, in theory, why its customers should not do all these things themselves. The customer, however, is prepared to *pay* for someone else to do all this. There are two points to note here.

(a)   Customers compare a firm's products and services with similar offerings by competitors.

(b)   The business creates value by either carrying out its activities more efficiently than other businesses, or by combining its activities in such a way as to provide a unique product or service.

The restaurant has a number of choices as to how to create value.

(a)   It can become more efficient, by automating the production of food, as in a fast food chain.

(b)   The chef can develop commercial relationships with growers, so he or she can obtain the best quality fresh produce.

(c)   The chef can specialise in a particular type of cuisine (eg Nepalese, Korean).

(d)   The restaurant can be sumptuously decorated for those customers who value 'atmosphere' and a sense of occasion in addition to a restaurant's purely gastronomic pleasures.

(e)   The restaurant can serve a particular type of customer (eg celebrities).

Each of these options is a way of organising the activities of buying, cooking and serving food in a way that customers will value.

The restaurant example demonstrates how a business:

(a)   Acquires inputs from its environment (eg people to work, raw materials), and

(b)   Transforms these inputs (the cooking) into

(c)   Outputs (the meal)

which customers pay for.

Figure 7.1 The business process

A business makes a profit if the prices it charges exceed the costs it incurs. However, a business cannot charge any price it likes; the price must be one that consumers are prepared to pay.

2   FACTORS OF PRODUCTION

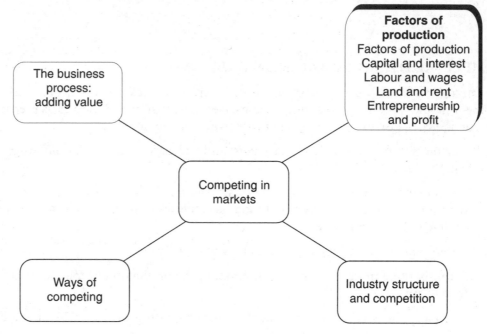

2.1   Factors of production

Firms are rewarded for the goods and services they produce by the price customers pay for them. The resources used in production, called the *factors of production*, are also rewarded, by the price that firms pay for them.

The four factors of production are defined below.

Definitions

> 1   *Land*: property (the land element only, buildings are capital) and the natural resources that grow on the land or that are extracted from it. (These include natural resources of the soil and woodlands, as well as extracted minerals such as coal.) Land is rewarded with rent.
>
> 2   *Labour*: both the mental and the physical resources of human beings. Labour is rewarded with wages (including 'salaries').
>
> 3   *Capital*: not just 'money in the bank' but also manufactured items such as plant, machinery and tools that are made and used to aid the production of other goods and services. Capital is rewarded with interest.
>
> 4   *Entrepreneurship*: the organising factor in production. An entrepreneur is someone who undertakes the task of organising the other three factors of production in a business enterprise, and who, in doing so, bears the risk of the venture. He or she creates new business ventures. The reward for the entrepreneurship is profit.

The factors of production are limited, which is why firms are driven to make the most efficient use of them. In other words, businesses have to make do with scarce resources.

FOR DISCUSSION

In what ways can technology be a factor of production?

The demand for factors of production is a *derived demand*. By this we mean that the factors of production are not demanded for their own sake; they are demanded because a firm needs them to make goods, which are then sold to consumers. The demand by firms for the factors of production is derived from the demand by consumers for goods.

Now we describe why a business might want capital and some of the conditions influencing the demand for it.

2.2   Capital and interest

Interest is the reward for capital and is determined by supply and demand.

(a)   The demand for capital comes from firms, which invest in stocks and equipment to create more output, make more sales and earn greater profits.

(b)   The supply of capital (finance to acquire stocks, equipment and so on) comes from investors.

Firms only demand capital if they can make an adequate return: the return must exceed the cost of the capital. Investors only supply capital if the interest they are paid makes it worth their while to invest.

Firms should always seek to invest in the opportunities that offer the highest returns. Once these investments have been made, the remaining opportunities will not offer such high returns. As more and more investments are made, the returns from additional capital investments gradually decline. This falling return as investment increases is called the *marginal efficiency of capital*.

Firms need to obtain money to invest. The supply of capital comes from savers. Savings lead to investment and the creation of capital, but savings are only made by 'sacrificing' some current consumption. An example of why people save is to build a pension fund.

In theory the return on capital should simply result from the supply and demand for capital. However, savers may demand a higher return (a 'price' for their savings) for investments that are more risky. Many investors will accept a lower return if that return is certain and there is no risk of loss in value of their investment.

Despite labour-saving equipment, human expertise is needed to 'run' the capital and use the machines. In service industries, such as the theatre, the human element is all important. The relative importance of capital and labour varies from firm to firm.

2.3 Labour and wages

The demand for labour is also a derived demand, as people demand the goods and services that the firm produces. All other things being equal, the more people employed, the greater the volume of goods and services that can be provided. In theory, wages are determined by the demand for and supply of labour. However, such a model does not work in practice. Wages are not always responsive to changes in supply, and people are often unwilling to adjust the price at which they offer their services.

Activity 1   **(10 minutes)**

Produce a list of factors, other than financial ones, that could make it difficult for people to change jobs.

Definitions

---

1   *Monopoly*: a single firm or organisation selling a good or service.

2   *Monopsony*: a single buyer for a good or service.

Collective bargaining is the process by which unions negotiate and reach agreements with employers. It is common for collective bargaining to involve a single monopolist seller of labour (the trade union) and one buyer or monopsonist (a single firm or an employers' federation). Annual wage claims may therefore be a trial of strength between two 'giants'.

The role of trade unions, in economic terms, has two aspects.

(a)   They erect and maintain barriers to entry into jobs in the industry, thus ensuring high earnings for the existing members.

(b)   They attempt to monopolise the supply of labour in the industry.

In some industries of some countries there is a *minimum wage agreement*, which means that all workers in the industry must earn at least the minimum amount. The purpose of a minimum wage is to ensure that low-paid workers earn at least enough in wages to have a certain standard of living.

The current UK Labour Government has introduced a statutory minimum wage which is £4.10 per hour from October 2001 and £4.20 from October 2002 for workers aged 22 or over, and £3.50 per hour for 18 – 21 year olds (£3.60 from October 2002). Casual workers, agency workers, homeworkers and those aged 16 – 17 on formal apprenticeships are excluded. Some people argue that the consequences of a minimum wage are:

(a) To raise wage levels for employed workers to above the 'equilibrium' wage rate, but

(b) To reduce the demand for labour and so cause job losses

FOR DISCUSSION

Relate the concept of labour as a factor of production to the realities of the labour market. Does supply of labour match demand for labour?

2.4 Land and rent

The price of land, which is rent, is also determined by the supply of and demand for land.

Definitions

1   *Commercial rent*: rent paid to a landlord who owns capital (for example when renting a house, a car or a television). Commercial rent is not the same as the more specific economic rent.

2   *Economic rent*: a payment made in excess of the payment needed to keep a factor of production, such as land, labour or capital, in current use.

3   *Urban sprawl*: the development of a town or city that takes over countryside and smaller communities as the town or city expands.

(a) The total amount of land available is fixed; therefore the supply of land is fixed, regardless of how much rent is paid for it.

(b) The amount of rent is determined by the price of the goods produced from the land for sale to markets.

In practice, however, the uses of land depend on social or political priorities. Planning restrictions ensure that land designated for farming cannot be used for building. The government has indicated that it plans to relax some of these restrictions to make more industry possible in rural areas. Land designated as agricultural land commands a smaller rent than land designated for housing or industrial development.

Similarly, 'green belt' land cannot be built on and is designed to prevent 'urban sprawl'. The intention is to preserve green areas around towns and cities.

> **Activity 2** (10 minutes)
>
> List the advantages and disadvantages of 'green belt' restrictions.

You have looked at the first three factors of production: land, labour and capital. Now consider the fourth: the entrepreneur who directs these factors.

2.5 Entrepreneurship and profit

The entrepreneur:

(a) Organises production and makes decisions about new business ventures

(b) Earns the reward of profit

These dual aspects of entrepreneurship are possibly most apparent in partnerships and small private limited companies, where the owners of the business (partners or shareholders) are often also the senior managers. Such managers organise production, make the decisions and earn the profits for themselves.

Unlike land, labour and capital, which are rewarded by rents, wages and interest respectively, the entrepreneur cannot be sure of gaining a reward (making a profit) because the business might make *unanticipated losses*.

FOR DISCUSSION

How do you think entrepreneurship is organised in larger businesses?

> **Activity 3** (10 minutes)
>
> What might influence a business's use of the different factors of production?

So far you have examined the individual firm in isolation, as a mechanism that converts inputs of factors of production into outputs that people will buy. No firm exists in isolation and, in practice, firms compete with other firms for resources and for customers. We will now examine how competition might be arranged in any one industry.

3 INDUSTRY STRUCTURE AND COMPETITION

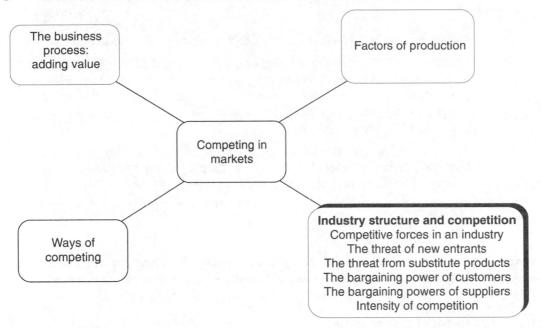

The business process: adding value

Factors of production

Competing in markets

Ways of competing

Industry structure and competition
Competitive forces in an industry
The threat of new entrants
The threat from substitute products
The bargaining power of customers
The bargaining powers of suppliers
Intensity of competition

3.1 Competitive forces in an industry

We make a distinction between two groups of factors.

(a) Environmental factors that characterise the nature of competition in one industry compared with another (eg in the chemicals industry compared with the clothing retail industry) and make one industry as a whole potentially more profitable than another (ie yielding a bigger return on investment).

(b) Factors that characterise the nature of competition within a particular industry.

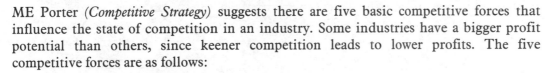

Activity 4 **(15 minutes)**

Jaspal is considering opening a new balti restaurant in Birmingham. He has seen the growth in the number of restaurants of this type over the past two years and has noticed that they all seem to be very popular. He wants to get in on the act. He realises that it is a competitive market, but is keen to join. What could influence the success of his venture?

ME Porter (*Competitive Strategy*) suggests there are five basic competitive forces that influence the state of competition in an industry. Some industries have a bigger profit potential than others, since keener competition leads to lower profits. The five competitive forces are as follows:

(a) The threat of new entrants to the industry

(b) The threat of substitute products or services

(c) The bargaining power of customers

(d) The bargaining power of suppliers

(e) The rivalry amongst current competitors in the industry

We now describe each of them in turn.

Definitions

> 1 *Capacity*: how much a firm (or industry) is capable of producing.
>
> 2 *Market share*: the sales of a good or service by one firm in the industry as a percentage of the sales of the good or service by all companies in the industry. For example, if Rover Cars had a 15% share of the European car market in 1994, this means that 15% of all cars sold in Europe in 1994 were Rovers.
>
> 3 *Economy of scale*: the more of an item you make the cheaper it becomes to produce each item. For example, if you produce enough, you might save money on raw materials by buying in bulk.

A new entrant into an industry will bring extra capacity. The new entrant will have to make an investment to break into the market, and will want to obtain a certain market share.

3.2 The threat of new entrants

The strength of the threat from new entrants is likely to vary from industry to industry, depending on two factors:

(a) The strength of the barriers to entry

(b) The likely response of existing competitors to the new entrant

Definition

> *Barriers to entry*: a term used in economics to describe the factors that make it difficult for a new entrant to gain a foothold in an industry.

Barriers to entry can be categorised as shown in Figure 7.2.

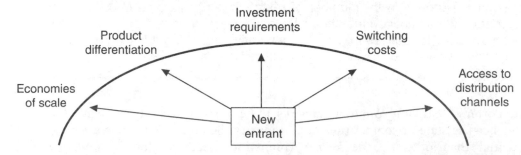

Figure 7.2 Barriers to entry

(a) *Economies of scale*. If the industry is one in which significant economies of scale can be obtained by producing more than certain volumes of output, existing firms in the industry should have a big advantage over any new entrant.

(b) *Product differentiation*. Existing firms in an industry may have built up a good image for their products through advertising, product quality etc. Customers may see no reason to change product. New entrants would have to spend heavily to overcome existing brand loyalties and to build up a brand image of their own.

(c) *Investment requirements*. The amount of capital for investment that is needed by a new entrant varies from one industry to another. When capital requirements are high, the barrier against new entrants is strong, particularly when the investment might be high-risk.

(d) *Switching costs*. A customer may have to incur costs when they switch from one supplier's products to another's. These costs are not just financial - time and inconvenience are costs in this context. The consequences of a switch might include the following.

  (i) Having to buy new ancillary equipment that is compatible with the equipment of the new supplier

  (ii) The loss of the existing supplier's after-sales service, which might include the provision of technical support

  (iii) The risk that the new supplier will be less reliable than the existing supplier.

When customers think that switching costs will be high, there is a strong barrier to entry against new competitors in the industry.

(e) *Access to distribution channels*. Distribution channels are the means by which a manufacturer's products reach the end buyer. In some industries new distribution channels are difficult to establish, and existing ones hard to gain access to. For example, food products in the UK are largely sold through supermarket chains; it can be difficult for a new producer to get supermarket organisations to agree to stock his or her product. As the supermarkets become more powerful they are placing greater demands on food producers: failure to comply can mean exclusion from the channel of distribution.

(f) *Other cost advantages of existing producers*. These include the following.

  (i) *Patent rights*. A patent is a type of intellectual property. If you invent something new you can take out a patent to prohibit other people from copying your invention without your permission. Patents expire after a certain time, but they do give an innovating firm a breathing space in which to establish their product.

  (ii) *Experience and know-how*.

  (iii) *Government subsidies*.

  (iv) *Access to sources of raw materials on favourable terms*.

Entry barriers are not permanent. Firms in an industry try to strengthen them; potential new entrants may seek to lower them (eg through the use of new technology or by bypassing them).

EXAMPLE: GILLETTE RAZORS

The Financial Times (21 March 1991) contained a report relating to the sale of disposable razors and wet shaving equipment in the UK. The Monopolies and Mergers Commission (MMC) (since re-named the Competition Commission) forced Gillette to sell its stake in its main competitor in the UK market. The Commission's report mentions a number of the issues we have discussed so far.

'There are few suppliers and a number of practical barriers to anyone wishing to achieve entry to the UK market as a manufacturer of razor blades and razors. Distribution channels do not encourage entry and strong customer loyalty makes it more difficult. There are no close substitutes for wet-shaving products...

One of the key disputed questions in the report was the height of the entry barriers.'

The report carried on to mention the different estimates of capital investment required to enter the market (which varied widely from £6m to £80m) and the numbers of blades sold to make entry worthwhile (100m-500m pa).

Competition can come not just from other firms but from other industries.

3.3 The threat from substitute products

The products or services that are produced in one industry may have substitutes that are produced by another industry.

EXAMPLE: CROSS-CHANNEL TRANSPORT

If you want to go from London to Paris there are a number of substitutes open to you:

(a)   Planes (London to Paris flight)
(b)   Trains (Channel Tunnel) from London Waterloo to Paris (Gare du Nord)
(c)   Automobiles (via car ferry or tunnel)

Customers can set the pace by refusing to pay above a certain amount.

3.4 The bargaining power of customers

The profitability of an industry also depends on the strength of the bargaining power of its customers. Are the customers in a position to drive a hard bargain? At the moment, supermarkets find it hard to increase prices as customers are unable - or unwilling - to pay more. At the same time, the supermarkets themselves are in a very powerful position with respect to their own suppliers.

The following factors can influence the relative strength and weakness of customers and sellers.

(a)   Customers are in a strong position relative to the seller when the seller makes a high proportion of their sales to that one customer.

(b)   If most of a customer's supplies come from a single industry, the customer is in a weaker bargaining position than if only a small proportion do so.

(c)   Customers who find it hard to switch products are in a weaker position.

(d)   Suppliers may try to increase their bargaining power over customers by creating a strong brand image, making customers reluctant to move.

(e)   A customer who makes low profits will be forced to insist on low prices from suppliers.

(f)   Customers may take over sources of supply if suppliers charge too much.

(g)   The skills of the customers' purchasing staff, or the price-awareness of consumers, can be a strength.

(h)   When product quality is important to the customer the customer is less likely to be worried about price.

Just as customers can influence the profitability of an industry by exerting pressure for higher quality products or lower prices, suppliers can also influence profitability by exerting pressure for higher prices.

3.5   The bargaining power of suppliers

The ability of suppliers to get higher prices is influenced by the following factors:

(a)   There being just one or two dominant suppliers to the industry, able to charge monopoly or oligopoly prices

(b)   Suppliers being threatened by new entrants to the market, or by substitute products

(c)   Whether or not the suppliers have other customers outside the industry and do not rely on the industry for the majority of their sales

(d)   The importance of the suppliers' products to the customers' business

(e)   The supplier having a unique product that buyers need to obtain but that cannot be found elsewhere

(f)   The existence of high switching costs for buyers

EXAMPLE

Until the advent of personal computers (PCs), the computer industry was dominated by a small number of suppliers, led by IBM and followed by companies like Burroughs, Sperry and Data General. The equipment supplied by a manufacturer was generally incompatible with that made by a competitor, nor were software applications easily transportable across ranges and makes of machines. The computer firms were able to 'lock in' their customers, as switching costs were so high, and could charge high prices for upgrades. Customers could not mix and match, and so competition as to price was largely irrelevant when it came to system upgrades.

Recently, however, user organisations, supported sometimes by government agencies (the DTI in the UK, and also the EU), have banded together in support of open systems so that machines can be connected, through the use of a common set of standards. This process has been aided by other changes in competitive conditions (eg the reduction in the cost of microchip technology). Customers now have more bargaining power. Furthermore, the adoption of MS-DOS, Windows and so on as *de facto* operating systems for PCs has meant a great deal more competition in that market.

> **Activity 5**   **(15 minutes)**
>
> Assess the relative bargaining power of customers and suppliers in the following industries:
>
> (a)   The manufacture of fighter aircraft
> (b)   The production of computer hardware to business users
> (c)   Fresh fruit and vegetables

The intensity of competitive rivalry within an industry affects the profitability of the industry as a whole.

3.6 Intensity of competition

Competition can do one of two things.

(a) It can help the industry as a whole to expand, stimulating demand with new products and advertising.

(b) It can leave demand unchanged, in which case individual competitors simply spend more money, charge lower prices and so make lower profits, without getting any benefits except maintaining or increasing market share.

The intensity of competition depends on the following factors, some of which may be more important than others.

(a) Industries with a large number of firms are likely to be very competitive; but when the industry is dominated by a small number of large firms, competition is likely to be less intense, or is restricted.

(b) When firms are all benefiting from growth in total demand, their rivalry is less intense.

(c) In the short run, any revenue from sales is better than none at all, if the firm incurs costs it cannot avoid. This encourages competition just to bring in cash.

(d) *Ease of switching* will encourage suppliers to compete (eg between Coke and Pepsi).

(e) When an industry is characterised by economies of scale from substantial increases in capacity, the industry may face recurring periods of over-capacity and price cutting. People invest too much, produce too much, flood the market, and prices fall.

(f) When one firm is not sure what another is up to, there is a tendency to respond to the uncertainty by formulating a more competitive strategy that assumes the worst.

(g) If a firm in the industry has put a lot of capital and effort into achieving certain targets, it will be likely to act very competitively in order to ensure that its targets are achieved.

(h) *Exit barriers* make it difficult for an existing supplier to leave the industry.

Activity 6   **(10 minutes)**

What types of barrier exist to prevent a car manufacturer from closing down a plant producing small family cars?

---

4 WAYS OF COMPETING

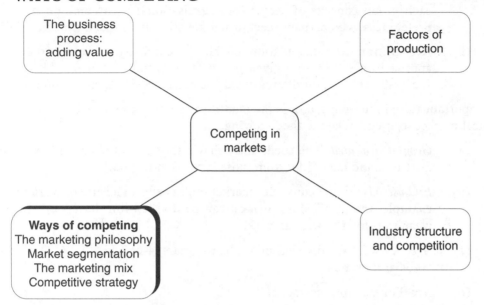

4.1 The marketing philosophy

Marketing has been defined by the Chartered Institute of Marketing as follows.

Definition

> '*Marketing* is the management process which identifies, anticipates and supplies customer requirements efficiently and profitably.'

Marketing is thus more than selling. It starts with the customer: what does the customer want? Once this has been discerned, then a product or service can be designed to satisfy these wants. It can then be promoted to those customers.

Earlier sections have suggested that firms compete in a single market, mainly on price. This model helps us to understand how prices are set, but the real world is more complex. A market is not a single entity, but is composed of many individuals with different needs and aspirations. The segmentation approach, described below, recognises this fact.

4.2 Market segmentation

Definition

> *Market segment*: a group of customers with certain things in common whose needs can be met with a distinct marketing mix.

A market is not a mass homogeneous group of customers, each wanting an identical product. Instead it can be analysed into segments.

(a) Although the total market consists of widely different groups of consumers, each group consists of people (or organisations) with common needs and preferences, who perhaps react to 'market stimuli' in much the same way.

(b) Recognition of segmentation enables a company to adopt the proper approach to selling to a given group of potential customers. This is more successful than an undifferentiated market approach to all customers.

An important initial marketing task is the identification of segments within the market. Typical market segments relate to the following.

(a) *Geographical area*. The needs and behaviour of potential customers in South East England may differ from those in Scotland or Italy.

(b) *End use*. Use in the consumer market might refer to leisure or work use. For example, the men's shirts market can be divided into leisure wear, formal wear and shirts to wear at work.

(c) *Age*. A useful age division might be 0-3 years, 4-6, 7-11, 12-19, 20-34, 35-49, 50-64 and over 64.

(d) *Sex*. For example, cosmetics.

(e) *Family size or family life cycle*. For example, young and single, young and married with no children, with one, two or more children, older and single, older and married with one, two or more children.

(f) *Income*. For example, the market for luxury goods.

(g) *Occupation*. For example, the market for men's suits might be segmented according to occupation.

(h) *Education*. For example, segment by education may be relevant to the marketing of newspapers.

(i) *Religion or religious sect*. For example, this form of segmentation may be important for marketing by charities.

(j) *Ethnic background*. For example, the market for music, records and tapes.

(k) *Nationality*. For example, the market for food.

(l) *Social class*. Socio-economic groupings appear to provide reliable indicators of different consumer attitudes and needs for a wide range of products.

(m) *Life style*. Differences in personality, activities, interests and opinions etc may be condensed into a few categories of life style.

(n) *Buyer behaviour*. For example, the usage rate of the product by the buyer, whether purchase will be on impulse, customer loyalty, the sensitivity of the consumer to marketing mix factors (described later in this chapter).

FOR DISCUSSION

Consider your own college. How might the market for its services be segmented? Suggest some segments that would be worth considering when deciding which types of course are to be offered.

Marketing research

While segmentation can give a basis for marketing, any marketing decision is inevitably made under conditions of uncertainty and risk. The information system for marketing is referred to as marketing research.

Definitions

1	*Marketing research*: the objective gathering, recording and analysing of all facts about problems relating to the transfer and sales of goods and services from producer to consumer or user.
2	*Market research*: finding out information about a particular product or service.

You may have been stopped in the street by a market researcher with a clipboard and a number of questions. Many organisations use market-research techniques. For example, London Underground employ researchers to assess customer satisfaction with train cleanliness.

Having established what customers want we can now decide on how they can be satisfied. The marketing mix does this job.

4.3 The marketing mix

The last word of the Chartered Institute of Marketing's definition of marketing is *profitably*. After all, many customers would be absolutely delighted if you were to satisfy all their needs for exotic holidays, caviar, champagne, private jets and so forth, for nothing. The marketing orientation is a business orientation that seeks to provide satisfaction of customer wants at a profit.

There is thus a balance to be struck between organisational capacity and customer requirements. This balance is expressed in the *marketing mix*, which is the framework in which the customer and the business deal with each other.

Product	Promotion
Place	Price

Figure 7.3 The marketing mix

These are known as the 4 'P's: product, place, promotion, price.

Product

The product element of the marketing mix is what is being sold, whether it be 'widgets', power stations, haircuts, holidays or financial services. Product issues in the marketing mix include such factors as:

   (a)   Design (size, shape)

   (b)   Features

   (c)   Quality and reliability

   (d)   After-sales service (if necessary)

   (e)   Packaging

Some issues related to products are as follows.

   (a)   *Core and augmented products*. The core product is a product's essential features. As a simple example, the core product of a credit card is the ability to borrow up to a certain limit and pay off in varied instalments. Augmentations are extra features. A common augmentation to credit cards is free travel insurance.

   (b)   Marketing managers make the following distinctions.

       (i)   *Product class*: a broad category of product, such as 'cars'. This corresponds to the core product identified above.

       (ii)   *Product form*: the different types of product within a product class. The product form 'cars' may have several classes, including five-door hatchbacks, four-wheel drive vehicles, hearses and so forth.

       (iii)   *Brand or make*: refers to the particular brand or make of the product form. For example, the Nissan Micra, Vauxhall Corsa and Rover 100 are, broadly speaking, examples of the same product form.

Place

The place element of the marketing mix deals with how the product is distributed - how it reaches its customers. Examples of issues relating to place are as follows.

   (a)   Where are products sold? In supermarkets or corner shops? Which sales outlets will be chosen?

   (b)   Will products be sold by mail order? (This might generate cost savings.)

   (c)   The location of warehouses and efficiency of the distribution system. (A customer might have to wait a long time if the warehouse is far away.) Arguably the *speed of delivery* is an important issue in place.

Promotion

Promotion in the marketing mix includes all marketing communications that let the public know of the product or service. Promotion includes the following.

   (a)   Advertising (newspapers, billboards, TV, radio)

   (b)   Direct mail (or 'junk mail')

   (c)   Sales promotion (eg special displays in particular stores, coupons, special offers)

(d)   Direct selling by sales personnel (a more common feature of industrial markets than consumer markets, with the exception of certain products such as financial services)

Price

The price element of the marketing mix is the only one that deals with revenue. Factors affecting price include the following.

(a)   Competitors' prices. High price is often taken as being synonymous with quality, so pricing will reflect part of a product's image. (Stella Artois has been marketed as 'reassuringly expensive'.)

(b)   Discounts.

(c)   Payment terms (eg offering a period of interest-free credit).

(d)   Trade-in allowances.

(e)   The need to make a profit.

Activity 7   **(20 minutes)**

Identify the marketing mix for the following two products and say why you think that the manufacturer of each product chose the mix you have identified:

(a)   Teletubby figures

(b)   A Ferrari car

There is little point in simply copying competitors, and many firms develop a distinct marketing mix of their own. Now we can integrate what we have discussed in the earlier sections of this chapter and identify ways in which businesses compete with each other.

4.4   Competitive strategies

Competitive advantage is anything that gives one organisation an edge over its rivals in the products it sells or the services it offers. Much of the competitive advantage that an organisation might hope to achieve is provided by the nature/quality/price of its products.

(a)   One company's product may have a definite edge over its rivals because it is better in quality, or cheaper in price.

(b)   Where rival products are much alike (eg petrol, many processed foods etc), competitive advantage may be sought by making the product seem different and more desirable than a rival producer's similar product, or by augmenting it in particular ways. For example, J Sainsbury plc have developed 'City Diesel' for sale in their petrol outlets. This is more 'environmentally friendly' than normal diesel. It also costs slightly more.

The type of competitive strategy that a firm adopts depends on the competitive strategies adopted by rivals and has implications for product design and quality, pricing and advertising.

(a)   A *cost leadership strategy* seeks to achieve the position of lowest-cost producer in the industry as a whole. By producing at the lowest cost, the manufacturer can compete on price with every other producer in the industry, and earn the highest unit profits.

(b) A *differentiation strategy* is based on the assumption that competitive advantage can be gained through particular characteristics of a firm's products or brands. These differences might be real (for example, design differences) or largely imaginary, created mainly by advertising and brand image (for example, 'designer label' clothing and washing powders). The customer is prepared to pay more for this distinguishing characteristic. Types of characteristic that may be relevant include:

(i) Colour differences

(ii) Size differences

(iii) Different wrappings or containers

(iv) Variants of the product for different market segments (eg children, adults etc)

(v) Small changes in the products' formulations to maintain their novelty value

(vi) Different technical specifications

(c) A focus strategy is a strategy based on *segmenting* the market and focusing on particular market segments. The firm will not sell its products industry-wide (in contrast to a differentiation strategy), but will focus on a particular type of buyer or geographical area.

(i) A *cost-focus strategy* involves selecting a segment of the market and specialising in a product (or products) for that segment. The firm, by specialising in a limited number of products, or by concentrating on a small geographical area, can keep costs to a minimum. This type of strategy is often found in the printing, clothes manufacture and car repairs industries, for example.

(ii) A *differentiation-focus strategy* involves selecting a segment of the market and competing on the basis of product differentiation for that segment. Luxury goods are the prime example of such a strategy.

Activity 8   **(10 minutes)**

What strategy is being used by the holiday firm described below?

Club 18-30: Targeted at a specific age group, this company promises 'fun' or 'activity' holidays in or around beach resorts. A poster advertising campaign in 1994/5 had to be suspended as a result of complaints that it was too 'raunchy'. Holidays are fairly cheap.

Economists identify a number of industry structures that act as models to explain the characteristics of markets and the behaviour of firms within these markets.

Chapter roundup

- A firm obtains inputs from the environment in order to transform them into outputs that customers will buy.

- The inputs a firm uses are: land (including natural resources), labour, capital (including equipment) and entrepreneurship. These are called the factors of production. The demand for many of these factors is derived from the demand for goods and services.

- For many goods, the quantity demanded by customers increases as the price becomes lower. As far as the supplier is concerned, the supplier wishes to maximise the price available and, if the price gets too low, it will not be worth the supplier's while to produce at all. The price mechanism balances the respective needs of suppliers and consumers.

- The competitive environment consists of five forces: the threat of new entrants, the threat of substitute products, the bargaining power of customers, the bargaining power of suppliers and the competitive rivalry within the industry.

- A key to success in an industry is to adopt strategies that are superior to, or different from, those of competitors. Generic strategies include cost leadership, differentiation and focus. The marketing mix is a key element in all these strategies.

Quick quiz

1 Give a definition of the term *demand*.

2 Give a definition of the term *supply*.

3 What is the equilibrium price?

4 List the factors of production.

5 Describe barriers to entry.

6 List the components of the marketing mix.

7 What is a segment?

8 List three competitive strategies.

9 What is the relationship between a focus strategy and market segmentation?

Answers to quick quiz

1 *Demand* is the number of products that people are willing and able to buy at a certain price.

2 *Supply* refers to the quantity of a product or service that suppliers would want to produce for a given price.

3 The *equilibrium* price for a good is the price at which the volume demanded by customers and the volume that firms would be willing to buy are the same.

4 Land, labour, capital, entrepreneurship.

5   Barriers to entry are the factors that make it difficult for a new entrant to gain a foothold in an industry.

6   Product, place, promotion, price.

7   A market segment is a group of customers with certain things in common whose needs can be met with a distinct marketing mix.

8   A cost leadership strategy, a differentiation strategy, a focus strategy.

9   A focus strategy is a strategy based on segmenting the market and focusing on particular market segments.

Answers to activities

1   You could have listed any of the following factors that make it hard for people to change jobs.

   (a)   Union barriers (for example a closed shop, whereby all workers carrying out certain jobs in an industry must belong to a given trade union).

   (b)   Professional barriers, where professional associations restrict entry by means of competitive examinations.

   (c)   Ignorance of employment opportunities in other parts of the country.

   (d)   A housing system that makes moving between regions difficult; for example, where there are high costs of housing in regions with better job opportunities.

   (e)   Non-monetary considerations (for example friends and social life outside work) that make individuals reluctant to move to a different region.

   (f)   High natural ability required for certain jobs barring people without the necessary ability (eg airline pilots, athletes).

   (g)   Linguistic and cultural differences, making some jobs more socially acceptable than others for some people.

   (h)   Discrimination in the allocation of jobs, such as illegal discrimination on the basis of sex or race.

   (i)   New technology may render old skills redundant, and new skills may be needed

   (j)   People may not have the right training for the job.

2   *Advantages*: green belt land prevents wholesale destruction of the countryside, allows a minimum amount of green space amongst the built up areas, preserves natural wildlife habitats, prevents cities and towns from becoming too large, preserves smaller villages and hamlets.

   Disadvantages: green belt land can sometimes be seen as being too restrictive, may prevent the building of very necessary housing, can be enforced very rigidly by local authorities (there is little flexibility in the use of green belt land), can be overridden by central government (for example to build a road bypass).

3   You have seen that the total use of the factors of production is a derived demand. However, a business may choose whether, for example, it uses machines or labour. If labour is very expensive, capital equipment might be cheaper in relative terms.

4   Jaspal needs to consider the following issues:

(a)   How many other new entrants are trying to join the industry?

(b)   What substitute products may compete (for example traditional Indian restaurants)?

(c)   Will customers expect low prices/high quality?

(d)   Will suppliers be keen to supply him or will he find it difficult to obtain his raw materials?

(e)   Who are the main competitors? How many of them are there? Where are they situated?

5   *Fighter aircraft*: the customer will be quite influential. They are most likely to be contracts from state governments who wield considerable power in terms of the amount of money they can spend. Manufacturers will rely on orders from them - there are no other customers. In addition, the national government where the factory is situated will have considerable influence over which customers the factory is allowed to sell to - there may be sanctions or trade embargoes against certain countries. A declaration of war would affect sales, as would disarmament or scaling down of military operations in any of the states that are customers.

Computer hardware for business users: here the customer is fairly powerful in terms of the likely sales - there will probably be big orders worth a lot of money. Business customers will have high expectations and will expect good service and reliability. Failure to provide this will lead to custom being taken elsewhere. However, the producer has some influence in the transaction too - they will engage in after-sales services, the supply of components or up-dating items and will be heavily involved in developing new and improved machinery. The majority of business customers will rely heavily on their advice as to the best systems to purchase.

Fresh fruit and vegetables: the customer has relatively little bargaining power here. Prices tend to be determined according to demand and supply. The growers decide how much to plant and harvest of each item. They will not know the price until the crop is ready, as it may be affected by factors such as the weather, distribution problems or Delia Smith's latest recommendation for a recipe! Excess demand will push the price up. Excess supply will push the price down.

6   (a)   Equipment, factory etc that are hard to sell (eg there may be no other use for them, or they may be old)

(b)   The cost of redundancy payments to employees, or the cost of relocating and retraining them

(c)   If the business is part of a larger enterprise, its withdrawal from the industry may affect other parts of the group

(d)   The reluctance of managers to admit defeat, their loyalty to employees and their fear for their own jobs

(e)   Government pressures on major employers not to shut down operations.

7   ***Teletubbies***

Product: merchandise linked to a TV series. Product class is toy. Form is various.

Place: variety of outlets including multiple toy shops, newsagents, catalogues, discount stores. All places that children and parents frequent.

Promotion: linked to a TV series. Almost promotes itself. Promoted via TV adverts, children's comics, catalogues.

Price: product is likely to have a limited lifespan so the producer needs to recoup costs quickly. Premium price likely to be charged with considerable reductions at the end of the product's 'saleable' life.

Ferrari

Product: top of the range car.

Place: limited number of outlets. Specialist retail garages.

Promotion: none. Not really necessary. Cars sell on their reputation/image. Promoted generally via car programmes and car racing; also product placement in films and television.

Price: very expensive. Price reflects image and perceived quality.

8   Club 18-30 is using a differentiation focus.

Assignment 7 (4 hours)

You will work in a small group to analyse the information given in the scenario in the light of what you have learned about marketing. You will then prepare and deliver a presentation.

Scenario

You are employed as a marketing trainee with Bosun, Bugle, Bottle and Butt, a large advertising agency. You are a member of a team looking at the latest product range from your client, NHN Leisure PLC. This product range combines, on a single CD, music, movies and interactive games themed around popular bands.

NHN Leisure PLC want an approach that provides the best and most efficient promotional activity for each of the individual product types that are combined in this enterprise. They also want a generic name for the new product, given that existing product names do not provide an accurate description.

Task

Working in small groups prepare a presentation that:

(a) Summarises the existing types of promotion used for each of the individual product types (ie music, video and games)

(b) Identifies the commonalities of approach in each of the three products

(c) Suggests how the new product might be promoted

(d) Identifies a name for the new product

Be prepared to justify your choices.

Chapter 8:
RESPONSIBLE BUSINESS

Introduction

Companies are coming under increasing pressure from many quarters for better environmental performance. Recent surveys have demonstrated that around three-quarters of the population now apply environmental criteria in many purchase considerations. For example, a survey by *Which?* magazine found that 90% of their sample had considered 'green' issues in relation to their consumption on at least one occasion within the past year. This group also claimed to be prepared to pay a premium for green products.

Green pressure groups increased their influence dramatically during the late 1980s. Membership of the largest 13 green groups in the UK grew to over 5 million, and they have a staff of over 1,500. Environmental concerns are more wide ranging than simply a desire for more conservation: the green movement embraces a wide spectrum of beliefs, from those who accept the value of economic development, on the one hand, to those who shun the material successes of the industrial world entirely.

Businesses are also being called to account for their actions towards the community as a whole. People expect a good example to be set.

Your objectives

In this chapter you will learn about:

(a)   Social responsibility of organisations

(b)   The aims of green pressure groups

(c)   The economic arguments

(d)   Key marketing issues

1   GREEN CONCERNS

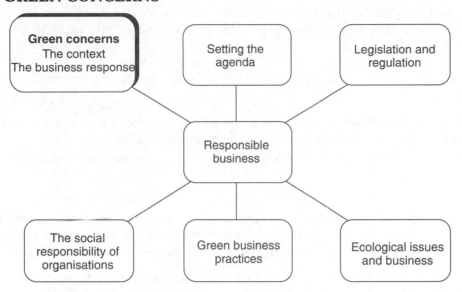

In recent years, the environment has moved up the political agenda. We start by describing some of the issues.

1.1   The context

The modern green movement, although arising from concerns over pollution and overpopulation that are centuries old, was given major impetus by studies carried out in the 1970s into the effects of massive growth on the finite resources of the Earth. The outcomes of these studies were underlined by disruptions in the supply of oil and other raw materials during that decade, caused by wars and economic conflicts. However, initial predictions of impending disaster failed to produce a significant change in public opinion, and policy making on green issues was largely stalled.

From the mid-1980s onwards, a series of ecological disasters (the emission at the Union Carbide plant at Bhopal, India, the Chernobyl nuclear reactor in the USSR, the Exxon-Valdez oil spill in Alaska, and the torching of the Kuwaiti oil fields at the end of the Iraqi invasion) reawakened public concerns and sparked general public fears about environmental dangers. Other factors that prompted increased 'green consciousness' included scientific reports about the state of the North Sea, the forests of Central Europe, and the droughts that afflicted several regions. All these were linked to environmental damage caused by modern industry. A decision by Shell UK to sink an old oil platform in the North Sea drew massive protests in Germany and other states (and was subsequently revoked by Shell).

It is also possible that the end of the Cold War led to a search, on the part of the media and the public at large, for a substitute threat to the safety of the world in place of nuclear war.

Scientific progress enabled us to gain more information about threats that had long been suspected. For example, scientists can now measure the hole in the ozone layer. Pressure groups, agencies and prominent individuals began to play a part in bringing these issues to the public attention.

Saturation coverage of environmentally linked catastrophes, such as the fires in Indonesia and floods in Bangladesh, and the opening up of countries in Eastern Europe, South America and Asia, have highlighted general concerns about the common dangers and conflicts that threaten our environment.

NOTES

Closer to home, there are increasing concerns about water purity and air pollution. Consumers are aware of the importance of green issues. Products and services, and the ways in which they are marketed, are changing to reflect this growing consumer awareness.

Activity 1   **(5 minutes)**

In recent years 'green' issues have come into considerable prominence. How have they affected the way in which products are marketed?

Concerns about the consequences of competition focus on potential damage to the Earth caused by depletion of natural resources. Only a short time ago many people would have dismissed these concerns out of hand as being merely the obsession of a few zealots.

In 1996 a survey was carried out by the Department of the Environment, Transport and the Regions. The results showed that 88% of adults in England and Wales were either 'fairly concerned' or 'very concerned' about the environment.

The issue is also a European one. The Eurobarometer Survey carried out by the European Commission in 1995 showed that 8 out of 10 Europeans considered that protecting the environment and fighting pollution was an immediate and urgent problem

1.2 The business response

(a) *'Green products'*. Companies like Body Shop have cleverly exploited ecological friendliness as a marketing tool. Supermarkets now stock bleaches or cleansing products which are supposed to be kind to 'nature'.

(b) *Changed practices*. Bad publicity has led to improvements. A consumer campaign to boycott tuna from companies whose methods of fishing endangered the lives of dolphins has led to changed fishing techniques.

(c) *Limits*. There is a limit to which consumers are prepared to alter their lifestyles for the sake of ecological correctness.

(d) *Education and confusion*. Consumers may be imperfectly educated about environmental issues. For example, much recycled paper has simply replaced paper produced from trees from properly managed (ie sustainably developed) forests. There is widespread confusion as to green labelling. In short, some companies may have to 'educate' consumers.

(e) *Environmental impact assessments*. Companies review not just the finished product but their production processes too.

FOR DISCUSSION

The green movement is concerned with humankind's relationship to the environment. A major focus of this is concern about the damage to nature and living things that has come about as a consequence of exploitation of natural resources and modern ways of living. This is expressed through philosophical ideas such as:

(a)   Stewardship and paternalism

PUBLISHING

(b)　　Humanism

(c)　　Conservationism

(d)　　Environmentalism

(e)　　Animal rights and welfare

(f)　　Pacifism

Are these ideas mutually exclusive or do some of them overlap?

Activity 2　　　　　　　　　　　　　　　　　　　　**(2 hours)**

Select an interest or pressure group that promotes some of the philosophical ideas above. Prepare a short presentation to introduce the group and its ideas to the rest of your class.

One problem is that it is very hard to incorporate green concerns into the economic analyses described in earlier chapters.

2　SETTING THE AGENDA

2.1　The green agenda

Conventional economics, according to green thinkers, has failed to deal with the problems of our modern environment. Concentration on labour and capital, rather than land has resulted in a devaluing of the land resource. Economists have not, in the past, placed any price on natural resources such as land or the ozone layer. These were seen as 'free' or worthless, since they play no apparent role in economic activity. Pricing mechanisms undervalue these resources in favour of manufactured goods, which have a clear derivation from factors such as labour and raw materials availability. Also, markets do not inhibit pollution, which is only limited by statute.

FOR DISCUSSION

The 'production orientation' of traditional economics focuses on products rather than people and so omits notions such as 'quality of life' and 'consumer satisfaction'. GDP ignores factors such as pollution and environmental degradation. Is this a shortcoming of traditional economics?

As far as *pollution* goes, there has been a longish history on environmental legislation. This is still mainly a problem of the industrialised West. It is likely that government will take an increased interest in this area. Companies might have to face a variety of measures designed to deal with the pollution. Some examples are given below.

(a) *Government fees*. UK firms must pay a Landfill Tax on hazardous waste.

(b) *Government regulations*. Fines might be imposed for persistent breach of pollution guidelines, and pollution might be monitored by government inspectors. The government is currently focusing on how to discourage car usage and on the desirability of environmentally friendly transport.

(c) *Government targets*. The UK government has outlined targets for recycling and carbon dioxide emissions.

(d) *Tradeable permits*. A means of regulating pollution is to charge for it, raising the price over a period.

(e) *Commercial opportunities*. Companies might benefit from the commercial opportunities proposed by environmentalism, but this is no certainty.

(f) *Relocation*. Firms might relocate the business to a country where environmental standards are less strict, or have a lower priority in relation to other economic and social objectives, such as economic growth.

According to green critics, standard economics assumes that consumers have endlessly expandable and insatiable desires, which provide the assurance of constantly expanding markets.

Activity 3	**(10 minutes)**

How can business organisations support pressure groups or public authorities in developing schemes to improve use of resources or reduction of pollution?

A very important green concept is that of sustainability. Some projections in the 1960s predicted that the Earth would have run out of key resources by now - but these projections ignored technological developments and changes in resource use.

2.2   Sustainability

The Brundtland Report

Sustainability involves developing strategies so that a company only uses resources at a rate that allows them to be replenished. This ensures that the resources continue to be available. Similarly, emissions of waste are confined to levels that do not exceed the capacity of the environment to absorb them.

The 1987 Brundtland Report (named after Mrs Brundtland, the Prime Minister of Norway who chaired the Committee) embodied significant advances in green business policies. It presented a convincing blueprint for 'sustainable development', including aspects such as ecosystem preservation, resource conservation, population growth, food supplies and urban development programmes. It stresses the need for:

(a)   *Production systems* that respect the ecological base for development

(b)   *Political systems* that involve citizens in making decisions in these matters

(c)   *Economic systems* that can generate surpluses, and technical knowledge that is appropriate for self-reliance and sustainability

(d)   Sustainable *international relations*

(e)   Flexible, self-correcting *administrative systems*

Sustainability is a general aim rather than a truly practical proposition for business managers. However, new standards have been developed that are beginning to have a significant impact on business practices.

2.3   Environmental pressure groups

Environmental pressure groups have typically exerted pressure through three main types of activity.

(a)   *Information-based activity* - gathering and providing information, mounting political lobbies and publicity campaigns.

(b)   *Direct action* - varying from peaceful protests and the semi-legal activities of organisations such as Greenpeace and Friends of the Earth through to the environmental terrorism of more extreme organisations.

(c)   *Partnership and consultancy* - groups here aim to work with businesses to pool resources and to help them to improve environmental performance.

Employees are increasing pressure on the businesses in which they work partly for their own safety, and partly in order to improve the public image of the company.

Legislation is increasing almost by the day. Growing pressure from the green or green-influenced vote has led to mainstream political parties taking these issues into their programmes. Most countries now have laws to cover land-use planning, smoke emissions, water pollution and the destruction of animals and natural habitats.

Media pressure focuses on large-scale disasters and more technical issues, such as global warming. Newspaper and television reports have generated very widespread public awareness of the issues concerned.

Activity 4   **(30 minutes)**

You are a member of a local group interested in promoting the recommendations of the Brundtland Report of 1987. Prepare an action plan for your group that gives clear proposals for promoting your views to the local community.

We will now look at the legislation and regulation that relate to green issues.

3 LEGISLATION AND REGULATION

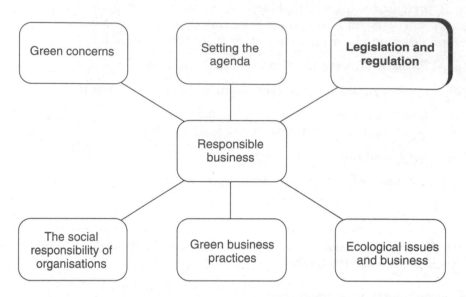

Public concern with environmental pollution has resulted in government action.

(a) Some of this takes the form of tax incentives. For example, the UK government has encouraged the use of lead-free petrol by levying a lower tax than on leaded petrol. The government has also proposed taxing waste.

(b) The UK government has made a public commitment to cut carbon dioxide omissions.

The law on environmental protection is covered mainly in the *Environmental Protection Act 1990* (EPA) and the *Water Resources Act 1991*.

The EPA features the concept of integrated pollution control (IPC). Its aims are:

(a) To prevent pollution happening, rather than to clear it up afterwards

(b) To ensure that business activities are conducted at minimal risk to human health and the environment

(c) To encourage the adoption of the most advanced technical solutions, offering the best practicable option for the environment as a whole

(d) To assess how much pollution the environment can sustain without damage

(e) To ensure that the polluter pays

The objectives of IPC are:

(a) To minimise the release of pollutants and to neutralise the harmful effects of those that are released

(b) To develop an approach to pollution control that considers the environment as a whole

IPC, in part, overlaps with existing planning regulations. Under IPC, the chief regulatory bodies are:

(a) Her Majesty's Inspectorate of Pollution (HMIP) for air, water and land pollution by the most polluting *industrial* processes

(b) For pollution from other sources, the National Rivers Authority and local authorities

Note that the Act identifies certain *processes* as being polluting, and these are subject to control. Polluters must 'curb the creation and discharge of wastes by applying the best available techniques which do not entail excessive costs'. Hopefully, as technology improves, the standards will increase.

IPC is separate from the other aspects of planning. In practice, the government (in the person of the Secretary of State for the Environment) will:

(a)   Identify those processes that require authorisation

(b)   Set emission standards

(c)   Allocate responsibilities between pollution inspectorate and other regulatory bodies

For certain processes, authorisation is required, and it is a criminal offence to carry out certain processes without authorisation. Enforcement is by means of an enforcement notice, supported by court injunctions.

Other air pollution act includes the Clean Air Act 1993, which consolidates earlier legislation (introduced after some spectacular London smogs of the 1950s).

Waste

The handling and disposal of waste has come under a number of EU directives, now incorporated in English Law *(Waste Management and Licensing Regulations 1994)*.

Waste regulation is now organised separately from waste disposal. Waste management plans are meant to encourage firms:

(a)   To prevent or reduce waste production

(b)   To develop products that do not harm the environment

(c)   To develop appropriate techniques for disposing of dangerous substances

(d)   To consider recycling

(e)   To use waste as a source of energy

The overarching principle is that waste must not be treated, disposed of, or kept in a manner likely to pollute the environment or harm human health. This is enforced through a licensing system. Furthermore, to prevent toxic waste from being simply 'dumped' on poorer countries, there are controls over the import or export of waste.

Activity 5   **(30 minutes)**

Imagine that you work for a firm of chartered accountants that up until now has not really had a coherent waste management plan. Prepare a memorandum for the managing director outlining the benefits of recycling where possible. List some common items in daily use that could be used more than once. Also, mention some items that could be utilised that are made from recycled materials

---

Water

The Water Resources Act 1991 and the Water Industry Act 1991 were brought in when the UK water industry was privatised. There are a number of offences relating to discharges into 'controlled waters'.

Different ecological issues have varied impacts on different types of business.

4   ECOLOGICAL ISSUES AND BUSINESS

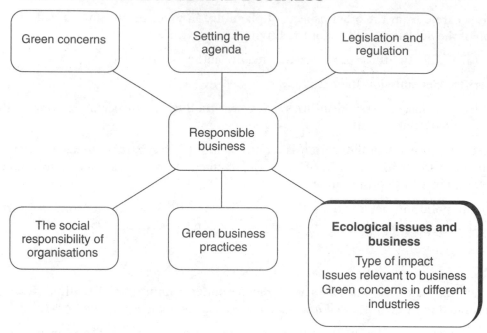

The effects of ecological concerns on businesses can be either direct or indirect.

4.1   Type of impact

Direct impacts

Ecological impacts may be direct.

(a)   They can affect costs or the availability of resources. For example, companies may be prohibited from mining in areas of natural beauty or special scientific interest.

(b)   They can effect consumer demand. Shell became concerned by a consumer boycott in Germany over its plans to sink a disused oil platform in the North Sea.

(c)   They affect power balances between competitors in a market. Environmental damage may place some competitors at a disadvantage because of the additional operating costs required to clean up the product or processes.

(d)   Legislative change may affect the framework within which businesses operate, as we have seen.

Indirect impacts

Indirect impacts may manifest themselves in, for example, pressure from customers or staff as a consequence of concern over ecological problems.

We now look at some examples of how various environmental issues are relevant to business.

4.2 Issues relevant to business

Among the ecological issues that are likely to be seen as relevant to businesses are the following.

Resource depletion

Resource depletion may influence business operations through impacts on the availability of raw materials through damage to soil, water, trees, plant-life, energy availability, mineral wealth, animal and marine species.

Genetic diversity

Genetic diversity is relevant to pharmaceutical firms, firms in biotechnology and the agriculture and food industries. The development of many new strains of plants, new breeds of animals, and new types of medicines can depend on the availability of wild species from which genetic resources can be drawn. In developing high-yield and disease-resistant plants, for example, wild species are a critical resource. Opposition to genetically modified food is growing, because of uncertainties about its long-term effect on people and animals. Production of organically-produced foods is thus becoming more profitable and consumers are willing to pay a premium price.

Pollution concerns

Pollution concerns are at the centre of most worries about the environment.

(a) Businesses are under pressure to curtail the impacts of their activities on the *water table*, the seas and the oceans. Concern over the quality of drinking water has generated a massive increase in the size of the bottled water market in the UK. In the late 1980s, growth rates were around 20% per annum. However, some commentators have argued that the success of bottled water in the UK is simply a triumph of 'marketing'.

(b) The *quality of air* has been much discussed, as a result of the effect of motor car exhausts, and the general impact of road vehicles. This issue may well have a bearing upon distribution policies.

(c) Concerns about the *pollution of land*, through landfill policies and the long-term damage wrought by industry upon the land it occupies, are all likely to require some policy changes over the next few years.

(d) *Noise pollution* is also likely to become more important, and this can have far reaching impacts on the operation of all manner of businesses.

In order to take action to remedy these problems, the *polluter pays principle* was adopted by the OECD in the early 1970s, and it now bas broad acceptance.

Definition

> *Polluter pays principle:* aims to relate the damage done by pollution involved in the production of goods and services to the prices of those goods. The intention is to deter potential polluters by making it uneconomic to produce goods and services that also create pollution. This principle has been broadly accepted and has been a major factor in reaction to major pollution incidents, such as large-scale oil and chemical spills.

NOTES

FOR DISCUSSION

How practical is the proposal to make the polluter pay?

Acid rain

Acid rain is linked to damage to forests throughout northern Europe, and acidification of water supplies and fish-bearing lakes and rivers. It has generated massive bills, but it is not always possible to establish direct culpability, so the polluter pays principle has not enabled Swedish foresters to claim from British industrialists, or Russian power stations. So large are the bills involved, and so clear are the impacts on the natural environment and agri-systems, that political pressures to constrain the effects of industrial production have increased enormously.

Ozone depletion

Similar alarms have been expressed about ozone depletion. Alternatives to CFCs have been developed to act as solvents in the electronics industry and coolants in refrigerators. The use of CFCs for blowing polystyrene foam used as insulation by the building industry has been banned in some countries and is being phased out in many others.

Waste

Waste is causing just as much alarm, whether it is nuclear waste from power stations or industrial or domestic waste in landfill sites. The handling of waste is increasingly becoming the target of legislation by national governments. It is also the subject of new international agreements, arrived at by governments concerned, for example, about the effects of waste dumping on the marine life and on the beaches of many different countries. The new waste management regulations were discussed earlier.

Activity 6   **(20 minutes)**

What issues are raised by the following information?

There is growing pressure on local authorities to pay recycling credits to third parties involved in local recycling schemes. A few years ago, a report by MEL Research for the Department of the Environment found that many waste disposal authorities are not paying voluntary groups for collecting paper, cans and glass for recycling, even though they have the power to do so. The then environment minister Robert Atkins hinted that he might make the payment mandatory if the authorities did not catch up. 'At present, in addition to some authorities not paying at all, others delay payment for months or impose an administration fee that virtually cancels any payment out,' said Ray Georgeso, for Waste Watch. Only a small amendment to the Environmental Protection Act 1990 would be required to make the scheme mandatory, and lobbyists hope that proposed legislation for an Environment Agency will be able to carry through the alteration.

Climatic change

Climatic change, involving the effects of excess carbon dioxide in the atmosphere, is still debatable in terms of its actual effects in producing 'unnatural' weather. Potentially, the consequences could be profound, with average world temperatures increasing and sea levels rising. If this happened there would be disastrous effects on agriculture and flooding of low lying areas. Great changes would be necessary, including, for example, new types of agricultural practices and different areas of tourism, as well as modification to the production processes and consumption patterns that have been identified as contributory factors. Laws would have to be enacted in a wide range of business and marketing-related areas to enforce such restrictions as were thought appropriate.

The Kyoto Treaty of 1997 was an attempt to control pollution of the environment by emission of the 'greenhouse gases' such as chloroflourocarbons (CFCs) which could cause potentially damaging climate change.

The Treaty implements the United Nations Framework Convention for Climate Change and legally binds industrialised nations to reduce emissions by an average of 5.2% below 1990 levels over the next decade. The USA withdrew from the Treaty in March 2001. Although, four months later, nearly 180 nations signed a scaled-down version of the treaty, President Bush has stated that the USA will never sign it.

The Kyoto Treaty assign 'carbon credits' to countries based on existing economic and environmental factors, which countries can then exchange with other countries. Some countries might end up increasing overall emissions, and the system is open to abuse.

Some (such as Sarewitz, in *'Breaking the Global-Warming Gridlock'*) argue that there should be greater emphasis on improvements to infrastructure and land use patterns rather than carbon emissions. Such improvements would make us better prepared for future climatic changes.

Energy resources

Concerns about energy resources and about the environmental impacts of energy usage at the moment are related to the concern over climatic change. Some of the energy sources currently used are yielding far less of their potential than seems possible - coal, for example, typically gives up only 40% of its potential into electricity. Energy-saving programmes are underway in most of the countries of the developed world, involving the development of more efficient plant and projects such as combined heat and power systems serving neighbourhoods or industrial plants. New energy efficient products are also being developed. Possible legislation that would penalise the use of certain scarce, potentially wasteful or dangerous materials - for instance, a 'carbon tax' - may well discourage the demand for such products. This may also lead to changes in the ways in which buildings, cars and electrical devices are designed.

Green issues have varying impacts on the different sectors of industry.

4.3   Green concerns in different industries

The primary sector

Many industries in the primary sector of the economy, such as mining, are involved directly with the physical environment. Primary industries are under constant scrutiny with regard to environmental legislation, and are the target of international concerns about the destruction of natural ecosystems and wildlife habitats. Concerns here relate to the following.

   (a)   Deforestation

   (b)   Threats to wild creatures

   (c)   Replacing a natural habitat containing a diversity of species with a monoculture where only one strain is bred

(d)   Pollution

(e)   Health and safety of produce

(f)   Poor working conditions and wages

Green policies here would aim to promote efficient and effective use of finite resources by diversification of supply and recycling where appropriate, and developing alternatives to the materials that are being used up.

The secondary sector

In the secondary sector of the economy, building and construction are relevant. Recently there has been significant opposition to the building of new roads.

Consumer goods

Manufacturers here may be seen as:

(a)   Damaging the environment or social institutions to meet consumer demand
(b)   Producing 'dirty' products
(c)   Using 'dirty' processes
(d)   Using up scarce raw materials (eg rare woods)

Some manufacturers already make products that contribute to environmental improvements (biodegradable packaging, for example), while larger manufacturers are under pressure to act in a socially responsible manner.

- Manufacturers of washing machines and dishwashers have brought out models that use less water

- Car manufacturers are producing models that have a high degree of recyclability and durability

- Detergent manufacturers are making products that are kinder to animal species, or that perform more effectively with smaller amounts

Industrial and business-to-business marketers

Industrial and business-to-business marketers are finding themselves having to fit in with the policies of customers who are producing green products.

The tertiary sector

Retailing

In retailing the green consumer is dealing directly with the enterprise. The enterprise acts as a 'filter', deciding which products will actually reach the customer.

Service providers

Service providers have traditionally thought that green issues are less relevant to them than to other types of business enterprise. Although service enterprises typically do have less environmental impact than other types of business, they still consume resources and generate waste. Such businesses still face the same decisions in their choice of suppliers, their investments and their contribution to the welfare of staff and customers. In fact, the very proliferation of green marketing practices is creating a growing demand for business services such as environmental auditing, green training, waste management and pollution control specialists.

Small businesses

Small businesses face a different scale of environmental challenge than large-scale enterprises. The latter produce much larger environmental impacts by consuming large amounts of raw materials and producing large volumes of waste.

Despite this difference, green issues are becoming more significant for small businesses for the following reasons.

(a)   Small companies may be able to develop products for green 'niches' more effectively than large enterprises, and can take advantage of flexibility to create green processes and systems.

(b)   Many small businesses are using traditional methods of manufacture, which are often greener than more modern processes, using less energy and fewer non-renewable resources. Demand for such products is increasing.

However, in areas where the demand for green products is increasing, it may be difficult for small companies to compete with larger companies (with their greater command of power and resources).

FOR DISCUSSION

In the West, 'big business' is often blamed for environmental malpractice. The state is seen as the only protector of the environment.

However, Russia and other countries of the former Soviet Union have seen environmental pollution on a catastrophic scale, even though all the industries were owned by the state.

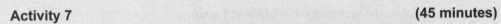

Activity 7	**(45 minutes)**
Assuming the role of press officer of a local chamber of commerce, draft a 200 word statement about environmental concerns in your home district.	

We will now discuss the impact of environmental concerns on specific industries.

5 GREEN BUSINESS PRACTICES

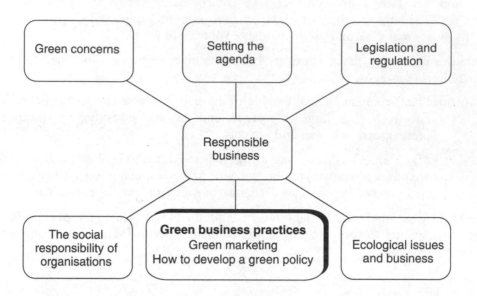

Green marketing begins from the premise that marketing as such is not environmentally unfriendly, and that the products and services with which it deals will necessarily become greener to reflect customers' needs for less waste. Green marketing recognises the dynamics of green consumerism.

5.1 Green marketing

FOR DISCUSSION

How are we to resolve the seeming contradiction between:

(a) Getting more people to buy and consume a product or getting people to try more of the product, and

(b) Getting people to consume fewer of the world's resources?

Energy companies, such as electricity, are increasingly affected.

Definition

> *Green consumption:* the decisions directly or indirectly related to consume choice and usage that involve environmentally related beliefs, values, attitudes, behaviour or choice criteria.
>
> That this is important is evident from:
>
> (a) Surveys that indicate increased levels of environmental awareness and concern
>
> (b) Increasing demand for, and availability of, information on environmental issues
>
> (c) Green product concepts and green substitute products
>
> (d) Value shifts from consumption to conservation
>
> (e) Effective PR and marketing campaigns by environmental charities and causes

A number of barriers have to be overcome.

(a) *Costs* are likely to be incurred by the need to develop new products and services.

(b) *Technical and organisational barriers* have to be overcome in developing, for instance, practical applications of green energy sources, and in reshaping organisations and their workforces into new ways of carrying out their work roles and promoting new attitudes to their jobs.

(c) At the moment, many of the problems that will need to be addressed are highly *complex*, and there seem to be *conflicts* between the various alternatives available. How do we choose between fuels that create acid rain, and those that produce atomic waste? What about the human consequences of dismantling environmentally unfriendly industries in areas where there are no alternative sources of employment?

(d) Many of the policies pursued by a particular enterprise will have implications for the environment in countries beyond national *boundaries.*

(e) Changes that promote beneficial effects, for example on the ozone layer, may well have no visible effects and may be resisted as a consequence.

(f) The fact that problems are generally created, and have to be treated, over a relatively *long timescale* also creates difficulties in promoting policies and mobilising groups to implement them.

FOR DISCUSSION

How do you think companies should respond to these problems?

We will now examine how environmental concerns can be introduced to a business's activities.

NOTES

Activity 8 **(20 minutes)**

The Environment Select Committee of the House of Commons has come out in overwhelming support for waste reduction at source, with re-use and recycling as the next best options. Actual disposal, says the Committee's second report on recycling, 'should be an option of last resort'. With more than 45 specific recommendations, the report demands a coherent waste reduction policy from government and warns against rushing into incineration schemes. Central and local government is also advised to 'lead industry by example, in the use of recycled products'. But sadly, the report itself was not printed on recycled paper.

How could industry 'give a lead'?

5.2   How to develop a green policy

Analysing the process

A company that wants to develop a green policy should attend to the following 'internal green Ps'.

(a)   *Products*. A green audit needs to look at how safe products are in use, how safe they are when disposed of, how long they last, and what the environmental consequences are of materials used in manufacturing and packaging the product.

(b)   *Promotion*. This can involve using green messages in advertising and establishing standards of accuracy and reliability.

(c)   *Price*. Prices set for green products must reflect differences in demand; price sensitivity is also an important issue.

(d)   *Place*. The company must look at how green the means of distribution are.

(e)   *Providing information*. This needs to be related to internal and external issues bearing on environmental performance.

(f)   *Processes*. The company must consider how much energy is consumed and waste is produced.

(g)   *Policies*. These need to motivate the work force, and to monitor and react to environmental performance.

(h)   *People*. Employees need to understand environmental issues, and how the company performs in relation to these issues.

Outside the company, a different set of factors needs to be addressed. These might be referred to as 'external green Ps'.

(a)   *Paying customers*. What are their needs in relation to green products and services? What information are they receiving about green products?

(b)   *Providers*. How green are suppliers of services and materials to the company?

(c)   *Politicians*. Public awareness and concern over green issues is beginning to have a strong influence on the legislation that appears, and this directly impacts on the conduct of business. A modern organisation must make this part of its concerns.

(d) *Pressure groups*. What are the main issues of concern? Which groups are involved and what new issues are likely to concern them?

(e) *Problems*. Which environmental issues have been a problem for the company, or part of the area in which it works, in the past?

(f) *Predictions*. What environmental problems loom in the future? Awareness of scientific research can be strategically vital.

(g) *Partners*. How green are any allies? How are business partners perceived? Will this pose problems?

FOR DISCUSSION

Debate the points concerning the 'internal' and 'external' green Ps set out above.

Being able to predict problems can produce great strategic advantages, but also generate some odd results. For example, the problem of CFCs from aerosols and their effects on the ozone layer was known about from the early 1970s, and Johnson & Johnson abandoned the use of them in their products back in 1975. Consumer reactions to the problem began in the late 1980s, and of course the firm was well prepared, but found themselves in the strange position of having to attach 'ozone friendly' labels to products that had, in fact, been modified more than ten years before!

6 THE SOCIAL RESPONSIBILITY OF ORGANISATIONS

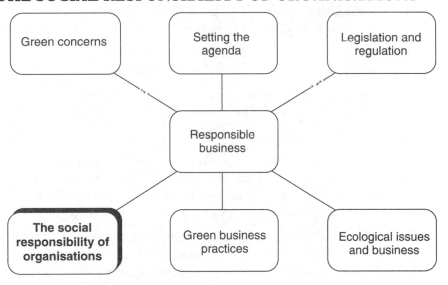

Social responsibility is expected from all types of organisation, be they businesses, governments, universities and colleges, churches or charities.

(a) Local government is expected to provide services to the local community, and to preserve or improve the character of that community, but at an acceptable cost to the rate payers.

(b) Universities and schools are expected to produce students whose abilities and qualifications will prove beneficial to society. A currently popular view of education is that greater emphasis should be placed on vocational training for students.

Arguably, institutions such as hospitals and schools exist because health care and education are seen to be desirable social objectives by government at large, if they can be afforded.

However, where does this leave businesses? How far is it reasonable, or even appropriate, for businesses to exercise 'social responsibility' by giving to charities, voluntarily imposing strict environmental objectives on themselves and so on?

Activity 9	(10 minutes)

What actions might businesses take to show 'responsibility'?

One school of thought would argue that the management of a business has only one social responsibility, which is to maximise wealth for its shareholders. There are two reasons to support this argument.

(a) If the business is owned by the shareholders the assets of the company are, ultimately, the shareholders' property. Management has no moral right to dispose of business assets (such as cash) on non-business objectives, as this has the effect of reducing the return available to shareholders. The shareholders might, for example, disagree with management's choice of beneficiary.

(b) A second justification for this view is that management's job is to maximise wealth, as this is the best way that society can benefit from a business's activities.

    (i) Maximising wealth has the effect of increasing the tax revenues available to the state to disburse on socially desirable objectives.

    (ii) Maximising wealth for the few is sometimes held to have a 'trickle down' effect on the disadvantaged members of society.

    (iii) Many company shares are owned by pension funds, whose ultimate beneficiaries may not be wealthy anyway.

This argument rests on certain assumptions.

(a) The first assumption is, in effect, the opposite of the stakeholder view. In other words, it is held that the rights of legal ownership are paramount over all other interests in a business: while other stakeholders have an interest, they have few legal or moral rights over the wealth created.

(b) The second assumption is that a business's only relationship with the wider social environment is an economic one. After all, that is what businesses exist for, and any other activities are the role of the state.

FOR DISCUSSION

How can shareholders be given real power and control over boards of directors?

This view might be regarded as an oversimplification, however, for the following reasons.

(a) In practice, organisations are rarely controlled effectively by shareholders. Most shareholders are passive investors.

(b)   Large corporations can manipulate markets. Social responsibility, forced or voluntary, is a way of recognising this.

(c)   Moreover, businesses do receive a lot of government support. The public pays for roads, infrastructure, education and health, all of which benefit businesses. Although businesses pay tax, the public ultimately pays, perhaps through higher prices.

(d)   Strategic decisions by businesses always have wider social consequences. In other words, the firm produces two outputs:

    (i)   Its goods and services

    (ii)   The social consequences of its activities (eg increased traffic, pollution, stress) which are inflicted on the wider population

---

Activity 10   **(10 minutes)**

Think about the balance of consideration between the protection of the rights of employees and the rights of shareholders and former employees who become pensioners. Make a list of the possible conflict of interests.

'Social responsibility' would argue that business's responsibilities then do not rest with paying taxes.

FOR DISCUSSION

Is there any justification for 'social responsibility' outside remedying the effects of a business's direct activities?

For example, should businesses give to charity or sponsor the arts? There are several reasons why they might - but what reasons are there why they *should*?

The arguments for and against social responsibility of business are complex ones. However, ultimately they can be traced to different assumptions about 'society' and the relationships between the individuals and organisations within it.

(a)   If the stakeholder concept of a business is held, then 'the public' is the stakeholder in the business. A business only succeeds because it is part of a wider society. Giving to charity is one way of encouraging a relationship.

(b)   Charitable donations and artistic sponsorship are a useful medium of *public relations* and can reflect well on the business. It can be regarded, then, as another form of promotion, which, like advertising, serves to enhance consumer awareness of the business, while not encouraging the sale of a particular brand.

Activity 11   **(10 minutes)**

Recent examples of conflict of interest have arisen between medical specialists and health service managers regarding different opinions about the ethical implications of certain administrative actions. For example, there have been stories in the press about non-urgent operations being cancelled in order to save money. How can professionals maintain their integrity and maintain the disciplinary requirements in their contract of employment?

Market failure

Profit maximisation may be a prime corporate objective. However a strong argument for social responsibility is *market failure*, and the fact the profits are made by incurring costs borne by society, not the organisation. This issue is now explored in more detail. In a perfect world, all companies and individuals would compensate those parties who suffered as a result of their actions. Unfortunately, this is not always the case.

(a) Factories causing pollution do not have to compensate nearby residents for the cost of cleaning their buildings.

(b) Employers do not normally have to pay for work practices which leave their workers feeling unfulfilled, stressed and pressured to put their job before their family.

(c) Car manufacturers do not have to pay for the costs of road congestion which results from the sale of more cars.

Social responsibility can be seen as a way of making up for market failure where government legislation alone is insufficient.

Market failure refers to a situation in which a free market mechanism fails to produce the most efficient (the 'optimum') allocation of resources. Market failure is caused by a number of factors, which might be listed as:

(a) Imperfections in a market
(b) Divergence between private costs and social costs (externalities)
(c) The existence of public goods
(d) The need to consider non-market goals, such as 'social justice'

The principal causes of market failure are considered below.

Social costs and private costs

In a free market, suppliers and households make their output and buying decisions for their own private benefit, and these decisions determine how the economy's scarce resources will be allocated to production and consumption. Private costs and private benefits therefore determine what goods are made and bought in a free market.

(a) *Private cost* measures the cost *to the firm* of the resources it uses to produce a good.

(b) *Social cost* measures the cost *to society as a whole* of the resources that a firm uses.

(c) *Private benefit* measures the benefit obtained directly by a supplier or by a consumer.

(d) *Social benefit* measures the total benefit obtained, both directly by a supplier or a consumer, and indirectly (at no extra cost), to other suppliers or consumers.

When private benefit is not the same as social benefit, or when private cost is not the same as social cost, an allocation of resources which reflects private costs and benefits only may not be socially acceptable.

Here are some examples of situations where private cost and social cost differ.

(a) A firm produces a good, and during the production process, pollution is discharged into the air. The private cost to the firm is the cost of the resources needed to make the good. The social cost consists of the private cost plus the additional 'costs' incurred by other members of society, who suffer from the pollution.

(b)   The private cost of transporting goods by road is the cost to the haulage firm of the resources to provide the transport. The social cost of road haulage would consist of the private cost plus the social cost of environmental damage, including the extra cost of repairs and maintenance of the road system, which sustains serious damage from heavy goods vehicles.

Here are some examples of situations where private benefit and social benefit differ.

(a)   Customers at a café in a piazza benefit from the entertainment provided by professional musicians, who are hired by the café. The customers of the café are paying for the service, in the prices they pay, and they obtain a private benefit from it. At the same time, other people in the piazza, who are not customers of the café, might stop and listen to the music. They will obtain a benefit, but at no extra cost to themselves. They are free riders, taking advantage of the service without contributing to its cost. The social benefit from the musicians' service is greater than the private benefit to the café's customers.

(b)   Suppose that a large firm pays for the training of employees as accountants, expecting a certain proportion of these employees to leave the firm in search of a better job once they have qualified. The private benefits to the firm are the benefits of the training of those employees who continue to work for it. The total social benefit includes the benefit of the training of those employees who go to work for other firms. These other firms benefit, but at no extra cost to themselves.

Externalities

'Externality' is the name given to a difference between the private and the social costs, or benefits, arising from an activity. Less formally, an 'externality' is a cost or benefit which the market mechanism fails to take into account because the market responds to purely private signals. One activity might produce both harmful and beneficial externalities.

Activity 12   **(10 minutes)**

Much Wapping is a small town where a municipal swimming pool and sports centre has just been built by a private firm. Which of the following is an external benefit of the project?

(a)   The increased trade for local shops
(b)   The increased traffic in the neighbourhood
(c)   The increased profits for the sports firm
(d)   The increased building on previously open land

We can use demand and supply analysis to illustrate the consequences of externalities. If an adverse externality exists, so that the social cost of supplying a good is greater than the private cost to the supplier firm, then a supply curve which reflects total social costs will be to the left of the (private cost) market supply curve.

In the figure below:

(a)   If a free market exists, the amount of the good produced will be determined by the interaction of demand (curve D) and supply curve S. Here, output would be Y, at price P_y

(b)   If social costs were taken into account, and the market operated successfully, the amount of the good produced should be X, at price P_x

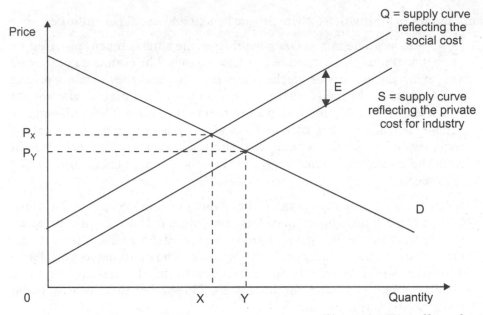

Figure 8.1 The effect of externalities

Given a free market, output of the good will exceed what it ideally should be, and so resources will have been over-allocated to production of this particular good.

Public goods

Some goods, by their very nature, involve so much 'spillover' of externalities that they are difficult to provide except as *public goods* whose production is organised by the government.

In the case of public goods, the consumption of the good by one individual or group does not significantly reduce the amount available for others. And if one individual makes use of the good, it does not reduce the availability of the good and its benefits to other individuals. Furthermore, it is often difficult or impossible to exclude anyone from its benefits, once the good has been provided. As a result, in a free market individuals benefiting from the good would have no economic incentive to pay for them, since they might as well be 'free riders' if they can, enjoying the good while others pay for it.

Defence and policing are perhaps the most obvious examples of public goods. It is not practicable for individuals to buy their own defence systems or policing arrangements.

Merit goods and demerit goods

The existence of market failure and of externalities suggests the need for intervention in markets by the government, in order to improve the allocation of resources. Another possible reason for intervention is to increase the consumption of what are termed *merit goods*. Such goods are considered to be worth providing in greater volume than would be purchased in a free market, because higher consumption is in the long-term public interest. Education is one of the chief examples of a merit good.

On the other hand, many governments want to see less consumption of certain *demerit goods*, such as tobacco.

Chapter roundup

- There is increasing public concern about potential danger to the environment. This can be seen by growing membership of voluntary organisations.

- Marketing strategy is influenced by green issues, as customers prefer, all other things being equal, goods that are friendlier to the environment than others.

- Green economics tries to incorporate green measures into conventional economics.

- Companies have social responsibilities towards those they affect, either directly or indirectly.

Quick quiz

1 Name three leading environmental organisations.

2 What is the central aim of green economics?

3 What barriers have to be overcome in improving green marketing practices?

4 Explain the concept of 'sustainability'.

5 List the main types of pressure utilised by environmental groups in their campaigns.

6 Where is environmental legislation likely to focus in the coming decade?

7 What is the Brundtland Report and what did it recommend?

8 List three types of direct ecological impact on a business.

9 Give examples of indirect pressure that a business could experience.

10 What is the basic idea behind the 'polluter pays' principle?

11 List some of the environmental concerns most relevant to the primary sector of industry.

12 List some of the environmental concerns most relevant to the secondary sector.

13 List some of the environmental concerns most relevant to the tertiary sector.

14 Define 'green consumption'.

15 What do the four Ss stand for?

Answers to quick quiz

1 Greenpeace, Friends of the Earth, National Trust.

2 Monetary valuation of environmental sources, quality of life, mutual aid.

3   Costs, technical and organisational, conflicts, national boundaries, non-visible, effects, timescale.

4   Sustainability involves developing strategies so that a company only uses resources at a rate that allows them to be replenished in order to ensure that they will continue to be available in the future.

5   Information, direct action, partnership and consultancy.

6   Land use, planning, smoke emissions, water pollution and destruction of wildlife natural habitats.

7   See Section 2.2 for explanation. The main issue is full 'sustainability'.

8   Costs, availability of resources, consumer demand, competition, legislation.

9   Customer pressure, staff pressure.

10   The intention is to deter potential polluters by making it uneconomic to produce goods and services that also create pollution.

11   The physical environment is the main concern.

12   Here, building and construction have been particularly contentious issues - for example the protests over the Newbury Bypass.

13   Consumption of resources, production of waste, choice of suppliers, investments, welfare of staff and customers.

14   'Green consumption' - the decisions directly or indirectly related to consumer choice and usage that involve environmentally-related beliefs and attitudes.

15   Satisfaction of customer needs. Safety of products and production for consumers, workers, society and the environment. Social acceptability of products, their production and the other activities of the company. Sustainability of the products, their production and the other activities of the company.

Answers to activities

1   A number of companies have changed their marketing practices or strategies to take green issues into account. For example, prominent 'CFC free' labelling (even by companies whose products never contained CFCs in the first place!), minimal packaging, use of recyled products, encouragement for customers to recycle (for example, The Body Shop encourages customers to take bottles back to get them refilled with the relevant product).

2   Groups you could investigate include Greenpeace, Friends of the Earth, The National Trust, CND, Lynx (anti fur-trade), RSPCA, The Humanist Society.

3   Businesses could set up local consultation groups or send people to sit on committees already in existence. They could sponsor activities. They could 'loan' experts to assist in planning.

4   The action plan could include the following aspects - providing information to both the community and businesses. This could be done by way of a regular newsletter or information sheet, local radio or TV appearances. The group could offer to give talks in schools or other venues.

5   Benefits of recycling: savings on refuse collection, expenditure on office stationery and equipment, environmental 'knock on' effects e.g. less paper used, fewer trees felled.

Items that could easily be recycled include: paper clips (can be used several times), envelopes (can be re-used), spare copies of documents (can be cut up and used for rough memo paper), card dividers (can be re-labelled and used again).

Items that could be made from re-cycled materials: paper for printing/photocopying, files, dividers, office equipment can be made from recycled plastics, wooden furniture can be made from easily renewable sources (eg pine instead of mahogany).

6   Firstly, there is a market for old newspapers. In fact, there have been reports of old newspapers being stolen. This is because there is currently undercapacity in the paper-making industry, and demand for paper is strong. Secondly, government policy is moving towards compulsory recycling (as is the case in Germany). Finally we note the role of lobbyists.

7   You should have considered the following factors.

(a)   Is yours a rural or urban area?
(b)   What industries are important: manufacturing, service, extraction?
(c)   How is public health?

8   For industry to lead by example in the use of recycled products could include:

(a)   Firms buying steel from scrap merchants

(b)   Firms requesting their suppliers to use recycled goods

(c)   Firms using recycled paper in documentation

(d)   Firms offering 'reward' systems to customers who recycle (for example J Sainsbury plc has a system to encourage customers to re-use carrier bags)

Sadly, industry in the past has been the led rather than the leader - as demonstrated by the oil industry's ignoring reports in the early 1970s that indicated the dangers of leaded petrol.

9   To assist you we can give you some examples. Should the company support the Prince's Trust? This helps young people to start up enterprises. Co-operative Retail Services publishes a social report to its shareholding members who number over a million. A number of firms publish reports for their employees. Some companies set aside a percentage of their profits for selected charities.

10   Conflicts of interest largely relate to distributing the profits of the firm, the size of the pension fund and shareholders' returns.

11   There is a need for an agreed procedure so that professionals can invoke an ethical code in their own defence, eg patient confidentiality, drug prescriptions etc.

12   Item (b) is an external cost of the project, since increased volumes of traffic are harmful to the environment. Item (c) is a private benefit for the firm. Item (d) would only be an external benefit if a building is better for society than the use of open land, which is unlikely. Item (a) is correct because the benefits to local shops are additional to the private benefits of the sports firm and as such are external benefits.

Assignment 8 (3 hour)

Task

Pick a product from the list below:

- Bleach
- Biological soap powder
- Disposable nappies
- Diesel cars
- Mahogany furniture
- Beefburgers
- Eggs
- Mobile telephones
- Cable television
- Pesticides

1 Identify the environmental concerns associated with the product.

2 Investigate the way in which companies have responded to these concerns.

3 How did the firms concerned deal with the unfavourable publicity generated about the product?

4 Produce a product information sheet for issue to consumers who have concerns about this particular product. Try to make your leaflet as 'user friendly' as possible and give a balanced view on the product.

Chapter 9:
CONSUMER PROTECTION

Introduction

This chapter concentrates on the ways in which the law protects individual citizens and consumers from unfair trading practice. It explains the types of independent advice available to those seeking redress against unfair practices. It also examines remedies for faulty or defective goods.

Your objectives

In this chapter you will learn about:

(a) The arguments for consumer protection

(b) The role of the Office of Fair Trading

(c) What is meant by 'false trade description' and 'misleading prices'

(d) The remedies available against retailers for defective goods

(e) Manufacturers' liability for defective products

1 THE COMPETITIVE GAME PLAN

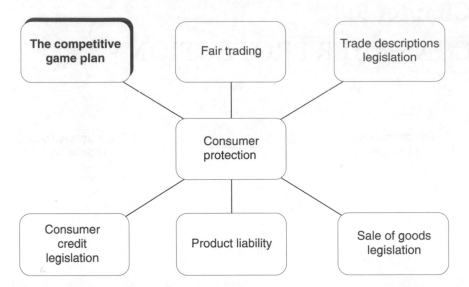

Individuals with complaints against businesses mainly rely upon legislation, voluntary undertakings such as the *codes of practice* published by banks and building societies, or *charters* (guaranteeing standards of service) in public transport, health and local government services.

Official institutions financed by government exist to act as 'watchdogs' on behalf of consumers. Examples are the Users Consultative Committees appointed to represent the public and act as informed judges of the performance of utilities such as gas and electricity. Community Health Councils perform a similar role for the NHS.

In addition to the official complaints agencies, the voluntary sector provides advisory assistance for individuals. Examples are the Citizens Advice Bureaux, and local law centres with a network of branches throughout the country. Both may be staffed by solicitors or other legally trained staff.

Individuals can also help themselves by subscribing to membership of the Consumer's Association to receive regular reports evaluating and comparing the whole range of products and services on offer to the public. There are also regular TV and radio programmes and press features devoted to consumer protection.

In a complex mixed economy, individuals need basic protection against unfair business practice. This is provided through legislation such as the Trades Descriptions Act. But it is not always necessary to resort to legal action - particular individual complaints may best be handled by agreed voluntary methods such as the Ombudsman services provided by banks. The essential point is that unscrupulous behaviour by organisations, public or private, large or small, can be challenged by individuals through legal action or by using voluntary procedures.

Activity 1   **(15 minutes)**

It is Monday morning. You have had the most horrendous weekend. Your neighbour had a party on Saturday night that went on until midday Sunday. The music was blasting out and people parked cars all over your front lawn. When you went round to complain no-one heard your knocking and the door remained firmly shut. Finally, the party guests left and peace and quiet restored. You decided to put a Brahms concerto on to play. You had been desperate to try your new CD player all weekend! You insert the disc only to hear a terrible grinding noise and see a lot of blue sparks coming from the back of the CD player. You give up in disgust. To cap it all you have just opened your morning post. Amongst the circulars and a letter from your Aunty Agatha you discover your bank statement. You appear to be overdrawn by £499, yet you paid in a cheque for £1,000 a week ago. The bank does not appear to have credited it to your account!

In your opinion, what would be the best way to deal with all the problems you have had over the weekend? Do you need to hire a solicitor or can you manage on your own?

The Fair Trading Act 1973 (FTA) is a good starting point in any discussion of consumer protection.

2 FAIR TRADING

2.1 The Office of Fair Trading

The legal powers of the Office of Fair Trading (OFT) derive from The Fair Trading Act 1973. The OFT promotes Codes of Practice.

Definition

The Office of Fair Trading: a government department staffed by over 300 people and financed by the Department of Trade and Industry. It is headed by *the Director General of Fair Trading (DGFT)*, supported by a Deputy Director General. It does not usually deal with complaints received directly from members of the general public, but acts on information from the following sources:

(a)   Its own investigations
(b)   Information provided by local authority trading standards departments
(c)   The courts (who inform the DGFT of material convictions)
(d)   News media

The functions of the OFT are as follows.

(a)   Various activities in relation to monopolies, mergers, restrictive practices and uncompetitive practices (we have already discussed these in Chapter 6)

(b)   Review of the carrying on of the commercial supply to consumers of goods and services

(c)   Collation of evidence of harmful practices that may adversely affect the interests of consumers

(d)   Taking action against persons who persist in conduct detrimental to the consumer

(e)   Encouraging relevant associations to prepare codes of practice (see below)

(f)   Supervision of consumer credit activity

(g)   Supervision of the working and enforcement of the Estate Agents Act 1979

(h)   Powers under the Control of Misleading Advertisements Regulations 1988

The UK's approach is to encourage industries to regulate themselves.

2.2   Codes of practice

Definitions

1   *Code of practice*: lays out a set of procedures and policies that a firm will follow. For example: 'we will always give you two weeks notice of withdrawal of overdraft facilities'. Adherence to the code is sometimes necessary for membership of certain trade associations.

2   *Ombudsman*: used to describe the provision of a final independent appeal that a dissatisfied customer may make against what he or she believes to be unfair or incompetent treatment. (The term is Swedish and does not have a satisfactory English translation.) Some Ombudsmen are provided with government support. In the private sector, banks, building societies and insurance companies may support Ombudsmen on a voluntary basis.

Many codes of practice exist, including the Code of Banking Practice. Some provide for the existence of an Ombudsman. Codes of practice can be classified into four groups:

(a) Codes carrying the DGFT's endorsement
(b) Enforceable codes
(c) Statutory codes
(d) Other codes of practice with limited status

These are described briefly below.

Codes of practice carrying the DGFT's endorsement

The DGFT is responsible under the FTA for promoting codes of practice amongst traders. After negotiations between the DGFT and the relevant trade association a list of rules of conduct is drawn up, in order:

(a) To promote a high standard of trade practice, and
(b) To protect the consumer's interests

Activity 2   **(4 hours)**

Carry out an investigation to find out what codes of practice exist to fulfil the functions identified above. You could work in groups, with each group looking at a different trade or industry.

The weakness inherent in any system of voluntary codes is that they do not bind traders who are not members of an appropriate association. Even disciplinary action by a trade association may be of questionable value since there is the obvious question of bias towards its members. However, the existence of codes can help the consumer to derive reasonable expectations as to acceptable levels of service and facilities.

Enforceable codes of practice

Definition

Enforceable code of practice: a code of practice that is enforceable by means of sanctions falling short of legal proceedings. It will set down codes of conduct that can be enforced against people engaged in a certain trade or business, even though they are not members of the relevant trade body.

EXAMPLE: BRITISH CODE OF ADVERTISING PRACTICE

The British Code of Advertising Practice is an enforceable code of practice. It was developed and promoted by the Advertising Standards Authority (ASA), an independent body. Under the code, advertisements must be 'legal, decent, honest and truthful'. It contains provisions relating to specific products, for example tobacco and mail order advertisements. Complaints are invited from members of the public, and the ASA will carry out investigations and publish the results, issuing warnings to offenders where appropriate.

> ### Activity 3 (20 minutes)
>
> What do you think is meant by 'legal, decent, honest and truthful'? Do you think all advertisements satisfy this requirement? What are the difficulties in enforcing this?

Statutory codes of practice

Codes that are drawn up with the involvement of government departments and the approval of the relevant minister may be given full or partial legal status. Such codes are increasingly common if people feel that other types of code of practice are ineffective. Examples includes the Highway Code (which may be relied upon in legal proceedings to establish liability), the Sex Discrimination Code of Practice (which may be taken into account by Industrial Tribunals) and the Code of Practice on Picketing in the case of strikes.

Other codes of practice

Because of the aura of respectability imparted to a trade that has an association and a code of practice, many commercial areas have acquired codes of practice that have no legal status at all and afford neither legal nor practical assistance.

The Banking Code

An example of a code of practice is the Banking Code, which became effective from March 1992 and which was revised in 1997. It was prepared by the British Bankers' Association, the Building Societies Association and the Association for Payment Clearing Services. It is a voluntary code and sets out the standards of good banking practice to be observed by UK banks and building societies in their dealings with personal customers. These are the key commitments to personal customers (note - not business customers):

(a) To act *fairly and reasonably* in all dealings with customers

(b) To ensure that all services and products *comply with the Code*, even if they have their own terms and conditions

(c) To give *information* on services and products in *plain language*, and offer help if there is any aspect which customers do not understand

(d) To help customers to choose a service or product to *fit their needs*

(e) To help customers understand the *financial implications* of a mortgage, other borrowing, savings and investment products, and card products

(f) To help customers to understand *how their accounts work*

(g) To have *safe, secure and reliable* banking and payment systems'

(h) To ensure that the *procedures* followed by staff reflect the commitments set out in the Code

(i) To correct *errors* and *handle complaints* speedily

(j) To consider cases of *financial difficulty* and *mortgage arrears* sympathetically and positively

(k)   To ensure that all services and products comply with relevant *laws and regulations*

FOR DISCUSSION

Do you think the Banking Code is too general? Why is it general? As a customer of a bank or building society, what would you like to see included in the Banking Code?

We now look at legislation relating to trade descriptions.

3   TRADE DESCRIPTIONS LEGISLATION

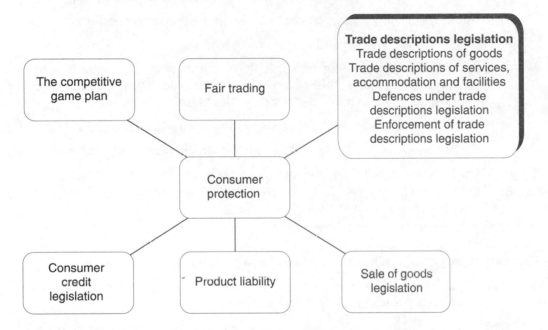

Trade descriptions legislation
Trade descriptions of goods
Trade descriptions of services, accommodation and facilities
Defences under trade descriptions legislation
Enforcement of trade descriptions legislation

The competitive game plan

Fair trading

Consumer protection

Consumer credit legislation

Product liability

Sale of goods legislation

The law relating to trade descriptions is contained in the Trade Descriptions Act 1968 (TDA) and in the Consumer Protection Act 1987 (CPA).

3.1 Trade descriptions of goods

Definition

> *Trade description*: any indication, direct or indirect, of any of the following:
>
> (a) Quantity, size or gauge of goods
>
> (b) Method of manufacture, production, processing or reconditioning
>
> (c) Composition (in the case of British Gas Corpn v Lubbock 1974 a gas board brochure giving details of cookers stated that 'ignition is by hand-held battery torch supplied with the cooker'. A cooker was sold without a torch. The court held that this was a trade description relating to composition of goods
>
> (d) Fitness for purpose, strength, performance, behaviour or accuracy
>
> (e) Any physical characteristics not included in the preceding paragraphs
>
> (f) Testing by any person and the results of testing
>
> (g) Approval by any person or conformity with a type approved by any person. For example, this would cover a statement that the item had qualified for the 'kite mark' of the British Standards Institute
>
> (h) Place or date of manufacture, production, processing or reconditioning
>
> (i) Person by whom manufactured, produced, processed or reconditioned
>
> (j) Other history, including previous ownership or use. For example, this would cover the kind of claim often made by car dealers, 'only one previous owner' or 'one lady owner'

There are three principal offences created by the trade description legislation:

(a) Applying a false trade description to goods and supplying or offering to supply any such goods (a strict liability offence)

(b) Making false statements relating to services, accommodation or facilities

(c) Making misleading statements as to the price of goods

Private individuals are not within the scope of the Act; these activities only constitute an offence if they occur *in the course of a trade or business*.

False trade descriptions need not necessarily be made by the seller: a buyer can commit the offence.

EXAMPLE: FALSE TRADE DESCRIPTION

Fletcher v Budgen 1974

A car dealer bought an old car from a private seller, stating that it was only fit to be scrapped. The dealer paid the seller £2 for the car. Later the seller saw the car on the garage forecourt - it had been repaired and was for sale for £135. The court held that the dealer was guilty of an offence.

A false statement might be made deliberately, recklessly or entirely innocently - the offence is the same. Furthermore, a statement that is misleading - that is, not false to a material degree - may still be caught by the TDA.

EXAMPLE: MISLEADING STATEMENT

Dixons Ltd v Barnett 1988

Dixons correctly described a telescope for sale as having a magnification of 455 times, but did not add that at that level of magnification the image was simply a blur.

The court held that an offence had been committed under s1 TDA.

Odometer readings

The motor trade has featured in a number of cases under the TDA, particularly in respect of the mileage and condition of used cars.

EXAMPLE: USE OF DISCLAIMER

Norman v Bennett 1974

A purchaser looked at a second-hand car in a salesroom. The odometer reading was 23,000 miles, although the car had covered 68,000 miles. The purchaser agreed to buy the car, accepting a salesman's explanation that it was a director's car (regarded as a sufficient explanation for a low recorded mileage). He signed an agreement that included the words 'speedometer reading not guaranteed'.

The court held that a disclaimer as to the accuracy of the clock (mileometer or odometer) given equal prominence as the figure on the clock is a valid defence. But the disclaimer must be reasonable under the Unfair Contract Terms Act 1977 and its terms must be as 'bold, precise and compelling' as the claim itself.

A supplier who has *deliberately* made a false statement cannot issue a disclaimer in relation to it.

As the service sector of the economy grows, descriptions of services will become increasingly relevant.

3.2 Trade descriptions of services, accommodation and facilities

With regard to *services, accommodation or facilities*, it is an offence to make false statements deliberately or recklessly. The statement in question must be false 'to a material degree'. An element of knowledge or recklessness is required. Knowledge requires proof that the defendant knew his or her statement to be false (usually ascertained by their admission or by documentary evidence). Recklessness covers statements made regardless of whether they are true or false. The situation here differs from the situation with regard to goods: false statements with regard to goods are normally an offence whether or not they were made deliberately and/or recklessly.

Statements include such things as information in a travel brochure, wherever communicated to a reader.

EXAMPLE: WHEN IS A STATEMENT FALSE?

Wings Ltd v Ellis 1985

The appellant, a tour operator, had distributed a travel brochure for the 1981/82 winter season. The tour operator then discovered that the brochure contained a statement (which concerned air conditioning in a hotel in Sri Lanka) that was false to a material degree. The mistake was discovered and steps taken to rectify it in May 1981. W had booked a holiday from an unamended brochure; at the time of booking the tour operators were aware that the statement was false.

The court held: 'the brochure was inaccurate, the respondent knew that it was inaccurate and W was misled'.

Activity 4 (10 minutes)

Examine the following situations. For each, decide whether or not a false trade description has been applied.

(a) Mr and Mrs Gullible have booked a weekend break in the Salty Towers hotel. The brochure describes it as 'A friendly beachside hotel with large and comfortable rooms. All rooms with sea view. Swimming facilities and sauna available.' When they arrive they find that the receptionist is aloof and curt, the hotel is indeed next to the beach but the sand itself is at the bottom of a 100 foot cliff, the bed in the room is so soft it is like sleeping on a marshmallow and it turns out that the swimming pool and sauna are not in the hotel but are available at the leisure centre across the road.

(b) A lager pump in the student's union bar is labelled 'probably the best lager in the world'.

(c) A car is described as in 'immaculate' condition. It is in fact very clean and well polished. Mrs Dim buys it but then finds out that although it looks fantastic it does not drive more than 10 miles without overheating.

Falsity is judged as at the time the statement was made, as where a holiday brochure indicates a hotel is fully built when in fact the picture of it is just an artist's impression: *Yugotours Ltd v Wadsley 1988*. But if the statement was true when it was made, subsequent events do not then render it false.

EXAMPLE: WHEN IS A FALSE STATEMENT TRUE?

Sunair Holidays v Dodd 1970

Travel agents described accommodation in a resort as 'all twin-bedded rooms with private bath, shower, WC and terrace'. Two couples booked holidays with them on this basis, but on arrival were given rooms without terraces.

The court held that no offence had been committed. The accommodation existed when the statement was made and the statement was true. Nothing that occurred subsequently affected the accuracy of the statement when made.

Recklessness will be established even though the falsity was due to lack of thought rather than actual dishonesty.

EXAMPLE: RECKLESSNESS

MFI Warehouses Ltd v Natrass 1973

A mail order company advertised goods as 'on 14 days free approval' and 'carriage free'. The offer was intended to cover only certain goods in an advertisement but appeared to cover them all.

The court held that the company had been reckless; the chairman had given insufficient care to the advertisement.

The TDA also covers 'services, accommodation and facilities' and includes when they are provided, how they are provided and who provides them. Furthermore, the Act also covers whether the amenities have been inspected.

Services include professional services such as those of an architect: R v Breeze 1973. However, a description as to the nature of a sale (for instance, advertising a seasonal sale as a 'Closing Down Sale') is not applied to 'facilities' and hence is not covered.

Activity 5   **(5 minutes)**

Sid Gasman tells Mr Swallow that he will give his gas central heating boiler 'a complete going over'.

Cal Gasman's invoice to Mr Zapp states that the fee charged is in respect of 'a complete service' of his gas central heating boiler.

In both cases, only a filter is changed. Has either Sid or Cal committed an offence?

Misleading prices

With regard to the *price* of goods, services, accommodation or facilities, the Consumer Protection Act 1987 Part III makes it an offence to make misleading statements to consumers in the course of business. This covers the provision of goods, services, accommodation or facilities. Such misleading indications might be that the price:

(a)   Is less than it really is

(b)   Depends on facts that are not in fact the case

(c)   Covers matters for which an additional charge will actually be made

(d)   Is expected to rise, fall or stay the same, when in fact the trader has no such expectation

There are other ways in which a price description may be misleading. For example, it may be an offence to indicate a price that fails to state that VAT will be added.

It is not only the person offering goods or services to the public who may commit the offence: it also extends to agents, advertisers and publishers who have not shown due diligence.

The prices code

A code of practice has been issued giving practical advice to retailers as to what exactly constitutes a misleading price indication. It mainly deals with some difficult issues such as price comparisons and seasonal sales. It is not automatically a criminal offence to contravene the code.

Anybody accused has a right to defend themselves.

3.3 Defences under trade descriptions legislation

A person or firm accused of breaching the TDA can put forward the following defences.

    (a)   That the commission of the offence was due to:

        (i)   A mistake, or

        (ii)   Reliance on information supplied to the defendant, or

        (iii)   The act or default of another person, or

        (iv)   An accident or some other cause beyond his or her control, and

    (b)   That he or she took all reasonable *precautions* and exercised all due diligence to avoid the commission of such an offence by him or herself (or any person under his or her control). Such precautions must be more than a token gesture.

The defence will fail unless *both* points in the previous paragraph can be proved.

FOR DISCUSSION

Do you think the defences are fair to the customer, or give the supplier an easy let-out?

The person supplying the goods (the retailer) has a defence if they can show that they did not know and could not reasonably have found out:

    (a)   That the goods did not conform to the description, or

    (b)   That the description had been applied to the goods

Enforcement is often a problem.

3.4 Enforcement of trade descriptions legislation

It is the duty of local weights and measures authorities to enforce the law on trade descriptions; most authorities have appointed *trading standards officers* at district and borough council level to do so. It is not easy for the consumer to get any compensation, as offences are criminal offences. However, it is still possible to ask the court to award a criminal compensation order.

The Sale of Goods Act 1979 gives an alternative route to victims who may wish to sue for damages.

4 SALE OF GOODS LEGISLATION

4.1 Sale of goods to consumers

A sale of goods is a transaction whereby a customer obtains ownership of goods in return for the price. Any sale like this is governed by the *Sale of Goods Act 1979* (SGA) (as amended by the *Sale and Supply of Goods Act 1994*). This act is contained within civil law, which means that a customer could use it to assist them in a case if they had to sue.

The SGA gives a customer certain rights against a business who is selling them goods.

4.2 Implied terms of the Sale of Goods Act

Definitions

> 1 *Implied terms:* terms that are automatically part of a contract whether the parties mention them or not. The implied terms of the SGA cannot be removed from a consumer contract.
>
> 2 *Caveat emptor:* let the buyer beware. There is a duty on customers to be careful in their purchases.

The SGA implies certain terms into any contract of sale between a consumer and a business. They give the consumer the right to expect certain things from the seller and the goods.

There is an implied term that the seller has the right to sell the customer the goods; ie that the goods are not stolen or do not belong to anyone else who would object to the sale. There is also an expectation that the goods are not being sold in breach of anyone else's copyright or trademark.

Goods must be as described. The Trade Descriptions Act already creates *criminal* offences in this area. The SGA gives the customer the right to sue for damages (usually the return of the purchase price) if goods are not as described.

EXAMPLE: GOODS NOT AS DESCRIBED

Beale v Taylor 1967

A car was advertised as a '1961 Triumph Herald 1200'. The buyer purchased the car but later found that in fact only the front half was a Triumph Herald 1200. This had been welded to the back half of a Triumph Herald 948. The car was in fact unroadworthy. The buyer sued for damages.

The buyer got his money back because the car was not as described.

It is important to note, however, that customers are expected to use some 'common sense' when making purchases. They should check anything they are unsure of and ask questions if necessary. If goods are also to be used for a specific purpose it would be sensible to check with the seller that they are suitable for this. The law uses a rule of *caveat emptor*, which gives the customer some responsibility for their own purchases.

FOR DISCUSSION

There is a suggestion often made that 'the customer is always right'. Do you think that this is always the case?

Satisfactory quality

Any goods supplied must be of 'satisfactory' quality. 'Satisfactory' could take into account the following factors:

(a)   Fitness for the purpose for which goods of the kind are commonly supplied
(b)   Appearance and finish
(c)   Freedom from minor defects
(d)   Safety
(e)   durability

Generally, 'satisfactory' means that the goods meet the standard that a reasonable person would expect, taking into account descriptions of the goods, the price and anything else relevant in the circumstances.

You cannot return something simply because you do not like it after all, the colour is not as nice as you thought or it does not fit. You should have checked these things out yourself before buying - *caveat emptor*. However, some shops will exchange or refund for the above reasons. This is done as a goodwill gesture on their part - they are not *obliged* to do so.

EXAMPLES: PURPOSE AND QUALITY

Grant v Australian Knitting Mills 1936

Dr Grant purchased some long woollen underpants. After wearing them he contracted dermatitis and had to spend some considerable time in hospital for treatment. He sued the retailer claiming the goods were not fit for their purpose. It emerged during the course of the trial that some chemicals used in the production process had not been properly removed from the pants and that it was this that caused the dermatitis.

The court held that the pants were clearly not fit for their purpose (ie wearing next to the skin). Dr Grant was awarded damages.

Wren v Holt 1903

Some beer was sold to a customer that contained arsenic.

The court held that the beer was clearly not of merchantable quality.

Priest v Last 1903

A customer purchased a rubber hot water bottle and specifically asked if it would withstand boiling water. He was told by the seller that it would not, but that it would take very hot water. When the water bottle was used it burst and caused injury to the customer's wife. The customer sued.

The court held that the hot water bottle was not fit for the purpose. The customer had specifically stated what he wanted and had relied on the advice given by the shop assistant. He was awarded damages.

Activity 6	**(15 minutes)**
(a)	What could the customer expect from goods labelled 'shop soiled', 'second' or 'special purchase'?
(b)	What can the customer expect if he or she buys second-hand goods?

Finally, the SGA states that where goods are sold by looking at a sample, when the actual purchase arrives it should be the same as the sample looked at when ordering.

We now look at how a customer can act when goods are unsatisfactory.

4.3 Action when goods are not 'satisfactory'

Usually, the easiest thing for the customer to do is to return the goods to the seller. The implied terms give rights against the seller of the goods directly. Customers are under no obligation to accept an offer to have goods returned to the manufacturer, or to have them repaired.

Breach of the implied terms gives the customer the right to reject the goods and claim compensation. This compensation would usually take the form of the return of the purchase price, but if a customer suffered other losses as a result of the goods or was injured by them they might want to claim more.

225

For a normal type of complaint, eg the heel drops off your new shoes after one day's wear, you should go back to the seller and ask for your money back. It is always a wise precaution to keep receipts or other proof of payment so that you can show when and where you purchased goods. State your case calmly and clearly and say what you would like to be done.

If the shop refuses to help you, and your case is justified, then you may wish to enlist the help of your local Trading Standards Officer. Often, a call from them can do the trick.

If your case is potentially more serious, or the shop refuses to co-operate, you may have to sue in the County Court. For most transactions you would use the small claims procedure, which is simple and quick. Your local court will instruct you on the procedure for this.

Activity 7   **(20 minutes)**

Working in pairs, perform a role play of the following situation adopting the roles of Mr Bloggs and the shop assistant.

Mr Bloggs has purchased a pair of shoes from 'Super Shoes'. He had asked for a pair of work boots, telling the assistant he worked on a building site. When the assistant brought him out a pair he was concerned at their lightweight appearance but was told 'Don't worry - these are a new design. They have been developed using new technology and have been made to withstand all sorts of tough conditions.' Mr Bloggs purchased the shoes.

Mr Bloggs wore the shoes for one week. The sole has dropped off one of them. He has taken them back to the shop and wants a refund. The shop does not want to refund the money.

We now look at product liability legislation.

Supply of Goods and Services Act 1982

The Supply of Goods and Services Act 1982 applies to certain contracts which do not fall within the definition of sale of goods even though they do involve a transfer of ownership. The types of transaction which are covered by the Act include the following.

(a) *Contracts of exchange or barter*. These are not contracts of sale of goods because there is no money consideration involved.

(b) *Contracts of repair*. Although some goods are supplied (eg spare parts) the substance of the contract is the provision of services (see below).

(c) *Contracts of hire*. These are not contracts for sale of goods because they contain no provision for ownership to pass to the hirer;

(d) *Collateral contracts to the sale of goods*. For example, where a person buys a car and receives a free set of seat-covers as part of a special deal, the purchase of the car is governed by the Sale of Goods Act 1979 but the seat-covers, for which consideration was given by buying the car, are part of a collateral contract governed by the Supply of Goods and Services Act 1982.

If the main purpose of a contract is, for example, the provision of skilled labour, whilst an ancillary object is the transfer of ownership of goods, the contract is one governed by the 1982 Act. This means that an accountant's contract to prepare a report or an artist's commission to paint a portrait, for example, are covered by the 1982 Act.

We now look at product liability legislation.

5 PRODUCT LIABILITY

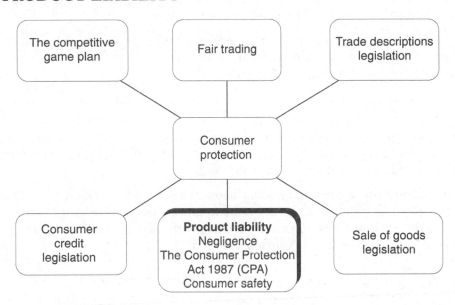

5.1 Negligence

In the past, if you bought a product and there was something wrong with it which caused you harm of some sort, you had to prove that the manufacturer was negligent in some way, and that the manufacturer owed you a duty of care.

Definition

> *Negligence:* to succeed in an action for negligence, the plaintiff (the person taking the matter to court) must show three things:
>
> (a) The existence of a duty of care by the defendant
>
> (b) A breach of that duty by the defendant
>
> (c) Injury or damage (or in some cases financial loss) suffered by the plaintiff as a foreseeable consequence of the breach of the duty of care

Duty of care

A manufacturer's liability for physical damage or injury to users of his or her products has been well established since the case of *Donoghue v Stevenson 1932*. In this celebrated case, the House of Lords ruled that a person might owe a duty of care to another with whom he had no contractual relationship at all.

EXAMPLE: DUTY OF CARE

Donoghue v Stevenson 1932

A purchased from a retailer a bottle of ginger beer for consumption by A's companion B. The bottle was opaque, so that its contents were not visible. As B poured the ginger beer, the remains of a decomposed snail fell into her glass from the bottle. B became seriously ill. She sued C, the manufacturer, who argued that, as there was no contract between B and him, he owed her no duty of care and so was not liable.

The court held that C was liable to B. Every person owes a duty of care to his 'neighbour', to 'persons so closely and directly affected by any act that I ought reasonably to have them in contemplation as being so affected'.

In other words, normally there would be two contracts: one between the manufacturer and the retailer and one between the retailer and the consumer. The case suggested that despite the absence of a contract between the manufacturer and the consumer, the manufacturer had responsibilities to the consumer.

The law of negligence applies in product liability cases such as *Donoghue v Stevenson* itself where physical injury or damage results from a failure to take proper precautions. However, if the consumer/user has a reasonable opportunity of avoiding the injury by or by taking routine precautions, the consumer should take it.

Breach of duty of care

The standard of care when a duty of care exists is that which is reasonable. This requires that the person concerned should do what a reasonable person 'guided upon those considerations that ordinarily regulate the conduct of human affairs' would do, and abstain from doing what a reasonable person would not.

Activity 8   **(30 minutes)**

Investigate the case of Bolton v Stone. Were the defendants held to have acted in a reasonable manner or not?

Consequential harm

In deciding whether a claim should be allowed, the court will consider whether:

    (a)   The breach of duty of care gave rise to the harm (fact), and

    (b)   The harm was not too remote from the breach (law)

Economic loss

The cases above relate to instances of damage to person or property. The question of liability for purely economic loss is still uncertain in its scope. Economic loss usually arises in the form of profits that a business would have generated had it not been for the act complained of. Generally, if financial loss is attached in some way to physical damage it can be claimed, but loss of pure profits is rarely recoverable.

> **Activity 9**   **(5 minutes)**
>
> I am at a car boot sale and I have various items for sale. You knock an ornament off my table that is priced at £1. It smashes into a thousand pieces. You say it was an accident. I say you were careless and should not have touched it and insist on taking your name and address when you refuse to pay me.
>
> You have now been served with a writ in which I am claiming damages of £5.3 m. The basis of my case is that had I sold the ornament and made the £1 profit I would have bought a lottery ticket. I would have used my normal weekly numbers, which this week happened to come up. I am now claiming the winnings I would have collected had I been able to buy that ticket. What are my chances of success against you?

One of the consequences of the law is that consumers are protected even further. EU law is incorporated in the Consumer Protection Act.

5.2 Consumer Protection Act 1987 (CPA)

Under the Consumer Protection Act 1987 (CPA) the consumer no longer has to prove negligence. In other words the Act imposes what is called *strict civil liability*, and this liability cannot be excluded by any disclaimer.

Strict product liability

The consumer can bring claims for losses caused by defects in a product against any of the following:

    (a)   The manufacturer of the end-product

    (b)   The manufacturer of a defective component (unless the instructions or design specifications supplied by the manufacturer of the end-product were to blame)

    (c)   The *importer* of the product into the EU (anybody responsible outside the EU may be much more difficult to find)

    (d)   An 'own-brander'

    (e)   A supplier, who is usually a retailer

In practice, a supplier or retailer only become liable if they will not disclose the identity of the importer or manufacturer.

The *consumer* has to prove that:

    (a)   The product contained a defect
    (b)   He or she suffered damage
    (c)   The damage resulted from the defect, and
    (d)   It was the fault of the producer or some other person listed above

Product

This legislation covers all products, including component parts and raw materials. 'Product' is defined as 'any goods or electricity'; goods include substances (natural or artificial in solid, liquid or gaseous form), growing crops, things comprised in land by virtue of being attached to it, ships, aircraft and vehicles. It does not include primary (non-processed) agricultural products.

'Defective' product

A product will be found to be unsafe where it is not as safe as it is reasonable to expect it to be. This standard of relative safety requires a court to take into account all circumstances surrounding the product - the way it is advertised, the time at which it was supplied, its anticipated normal use, the provision of instructions for use, even its likely misuse - in establishing the standard required. The court should also consider the benefit to society and the cost of making the product safer.

Scope of the Act

Consumers and other users (such as the recipient of an electric iron received as a gift), but not business users, can claim compensation for *death, personal injury or damage to other property* (not to the product itself, nor for economic loss caused by the product not working). There is unlimited liability, but the following limitations apply.

    (a)   A claim must be brought within three years of the fault becoming apparent.

    (b)   No claim may be brought more than ten years after the original supply.

    (c)   Where the claim is for damage to property, it must not be business property that is damaged and the amount of the damage must be more than £275.

Defences

The defendant in a case under this Act has six possible defences.

    (a)   The product complied with mandatory statutory or EU standards.

    (b)   The product was not at any time supplied to another.

    (c)   The product was not supplied in the course of a business.

    (d)   The defect did not exist in the product when originally supplied.

    (e)   'Development risk' - the state of knowledge at the time of manufacture and supply was such that no manufacturer could have been expected to detect the fault. The inclusion of this defence in the Act means that many victims of drugs that had damaging side-effects may be left without a remedy. The defence was kept so as not to discourage medical research. As the Act is new, it is not certain how far reaching this might be.

    (f)   The defect was wholly attributable to the design of a *subsequent* product into which the product in question was incorporated.

The Act is a significant step towards protection against unsafe goods. Producers and other distributors now have to ensure that they are protected by insurance in their business contracts; careful record-keeping is also required so that the other people in the distribution chain are adequately identified.

> **Activity 10**   **(5 minutes)**
>
> What you think is the significance of the development risk defence?

Strict civil liability is a separate issue from that of consumer safety, and adherence of products to safety regulations.

5.3 Consumer safety

It is a criminal offence to supply consumer goods that fail to comply with a *general safety requirement* under Part II of the Consumer Safety Act. This requires that goods must be reasonably safe, bearing in mind the manner in which, and the purposes for which, they are marketed, any instructions or warnings provided with them, any published safety standards and the existence of any means by which it would have been reasonable to make the product safer.

The general safety requirement applies to all consumer goods, except for a defined list of items, each of which is either covered by its own more specific legislation (thus food falls under the Food Safety Act 1990) or falls into a special category (eg tobacco, which 'could raise particular problems').

The Department of Trade and Industry is empowered to make safety regulations under the Act. Contravention of such regulations is a criminal offence. Examples include the following.

(a) Cooking Utensils (Safety) Regulations 1972/1957. These govern the proportion of lead permitted in kitchen utensils used for cooking food.

(b) Electrical Equipment (Safety) Regulations 1975/1366. These require that various items of electrical equipment shall comply with appropriate British Standards.

(c) Pencil and Graphic Instruments Safety Regulations 1974/226. These control the maximum amounts of arsenic, cadmium, chromium, mercury, antimony, lead and barium permitted in pencils, pens, brushes, crayons and chalk.

The general safety requirement and the safety regulations are again enforced by trading standards officers, who have a system of notices that are served on offenders.

Product Safety Regulations 1994 impose additional safety requirements. They are relevant to all suppliers of consumer products, and impose a general safety requirement on all products to be placed on the market by producers or to be sold, offered for sale or possessed by distributors. The two safety requirements (ie the new regulations and Part II CPA 1987) are not identical. The key provision of the 1994 regulations states that no products should be placed on the market unless it is a 'safe product'. This is a product which, under normal or reasonably foreseeable conditions of use, presents no, or minimal, risk. This must be consistent with a high degree of protection for user's health and safety. Four factors will be taken into account.

(a) The characteristics of the product, eg packaging and instructions for assembly

(b) The effect of the product on other products

(c) The presentation of the product, eg labelling and instructions for use

(d) The categories of consumer (eg children) at serious risk

FOR DISCUSSION

Why is it necessary to enforce such a strict regulatory framework on business?

6 CONSUMER CREDIT LEGISLATION

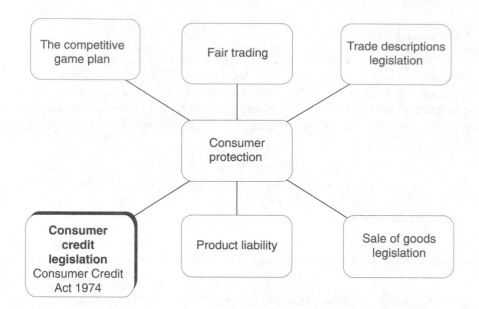

6.1 Consumer Credit Act 1974

The Consumer Credit Act 1974 (as amended) was passed to protect consumers by introducing a new concept - that of 'truth in lending'. The Act applies to loans or other forms of credit offered to individuals, not to companies, and its main provisions govern lending up to and including £25,000. As an example of its scope, the lender must inform the borrower of all charges connected with the loan, and the rate of interest must be calculated and quoted in a similar way. (These are the two requirements for the quotation of the Total Charge for Credit and the Annual Percentage Rate).

The Act was meant to deal with the problems of inaccurate advertising, canvassing and the charging of extortionate rates of interest by lenders. The Act is a complex piece of legislation and seeks to regulate various types of transaction, including:

(a) Hire purchase agreements
(b) Conditional sale transactions
(c) Credit sales, and
(d) Personal loans

The main provisions of the Act address the following areas:

(a) Licensing of businesses that provide credit, lend money or hire out goods

(b) Advertising for credit and the provision of quotations

(c) Canvassing, involving attempts to persuade an individual to sign an agreement for credit facilities when not previously requested to do so in writing or away from the canvasser's trade premises

(d) Regulated agreements - the form and contents of credit agreements is prescribed by the Act, and there are rules as to provision of copies

(e) Debtor-credit-supplier agreements, for example credit card schemes

(f) Charges for credit, which must be advised to the borrower

Activity 11   (15 minutes)

Examine some credit advertisements in newspapers. You will see that some offer 'secured' loans and some offer 'unsecured' loans. What is the difference?

Chapter roundup

- As well as controlling monopolies, the OFT is involved in consumer protection, in monitoring business practices and enforcing the law.

- Many industries have drawn up codes of practice to improve their standing and procedures. Not all are enforceable at law.

- The law on product liability has changed. A consumer who suffers from a product no longer has to prove that the manufacturer was negligent.

- Trade descriptions legislation controls the claims that may be made about goods and services.

- The Sale of Goods Act gives consumers the right to redress when goods do not meet normal expectations.

Quick quiz

1   What is the Office of Fair Trading?

2   Outline what an 'ombudsman' does.

3   What are codes of practice designed to achieve?

4   What is the problem with a voluntary code of practice?

5   List the three principal offences created by trades descriptions legislation.

6   Explain the term 'false description'.

7   Give some examples of false descriptions.

8   What defences are available to an accusation of false description?

9   Does the Sale of Goods Act l979 involve civil or criminal law?

10   What are the four main areas covered in respect to goods?

11   What does caveat emptor mean?

12   What is product liability?

13   What three things must be proved in order to prove negligence?

14   How does the Consumer Protection Act l987 make claiming damages easier?

15   What does the term 'defective' mean?

16   Can business users of a product claim under the CPA?

17   List the six defences to an action taken under the CPA.

18   What is the development risk defence?

19   List some goods covered by safety regulations.

BPP PUBLISHING

20   Who enforces safety requirements and regulations?

21   What legislation seeks to protect and individual who is taking out a personal loan?

Answers to quick quiz

1   The OFT is a government department that generally monitors commercial activities affecting consumers and makes proposals and regulations to control unfair practices.

2   An Ombudsman is the person who provides an avenue of appeal for dissatisfied customers who have not obtained satisfaction from a particular business. Some are supported by government and some are provided voluntarily by organisations.

3   Codes of practice are designed to promote a high standard of trade practice and to protect the consumer's interests.

4   It is not enforceable, merely voluntary.

5   Applying a false trade description to goods, making false statements as to services, being misleading as to price.

6   A false trade description is a description made of goods or services that is untrue or misleading.

7   Some examples of false trade descriptions could be; stating a price without saying that VAT has to be added, stating that certain facilities will be available when they are not, stating that a particular product is 'endorsed' by a celebrity when they have never heard of it.

8   Mistake; reliance on information supplied; act or default of another person; accident or cause beyond their control.

9   Civil law.

10   Title, description, satisfactory quality, bulk corresponds to sample.

11   Buyer beware.

12   The manufacturer's responsibility to a consumer injured by their product.

13   Duty of care, breach of duty, damage resulting.

14   There is no need to prove negligence.

15   Defective means not as safe as it is reasonable to expect.

16   No. The Act only covers consumers.

17   Product complied with EU standards, product was not supplied to another, not supplied in the course of business, no defect when product supplied, development risk defence.

18   The state of knowledge at the time of manufacture would not have allowed for detection of the fault.

19   Cooking utensils, electrical equipment, pencils.

20   Trading Standards Officers.

21   Consumer Credit Act 1974.

Answers to activities

1   You can probably sort out the majority of your problems yourself. If you do decide that you need help there are other potentially more useful sources available than solicitors and courts.

Noisy neighbours: try a diplomatic complaint. Most people are reasonable and will not want to have an argument. However, if problems persist you could contact your local council, who have environmental officers responsible for enforcing laws on noise pollution. They could approach the neighbours for you and prosecute if necessary. As a last resort, you could sue your neighbours for private nuisance, but this will cost you a lot of time, money and effort. It may not be worth it. In a recent case where a neighbour sued over a pig being kept in a residential area the costs of the case amounted to some £20,000 and the loser had to pay these plus £15,000 damages.

Faulty CD player: take it back to the shop and ask for a refund. The Sale of Goods Act 1979 says that the player should be fit for its purpose. It clearly is not, so you are entitled to a refund. Take your receipt with you.

Bank statement: something has obviously gone wrong. Telephone the bank and query the missing money. If they deny receiving the cheques, take your paying-in slip in to prove it. If you still get no help, contact the Banking Ombudsman for assistance.

2   There are codes of practice for many different trades and industries, including the motor trade, shoes, funeral services, dry cleaning, and estate and travel agents. There are about 20 in all. These codes are purely voluntary in that they are not enforced by the courts, but the OFT monitors their operation and the trade associations themselves try to ensure that the standards are adhered to by their members. Common features in these codes would be an agreement not to limit legal liability except in special, stated circumstances (and obviously within the limits of the Unfair Contract Terms Act 1977), a set standard of care, a disciplinary procedure for members and agreed procedures for the settlement of disputes, such as arbitration.

3   Adverts are not always legal, decent, honest and truthful. There are many complaints made each year about advertisements that have given offence. Recently, there have been a number of complaints made about Bennetton adverts that showed graphic scenes of war, people dying of aids and new-born babies. Some people found them offensive. A newspaper advertisement showing three political party leaders hanging from a noose was also the subject of complaints. The problem with enforcement is that people have different interpretations of what is 'legal, decent, honest and truthful'.

4   (a)   Whilst the advert may have been misleading it cannot really be said to be untrue. Also, some of the statements made would depend on an individual's view of what is 'friendly' or 'comfortable'. The swimming pool and sauna are available - the advert did not say they were on the premises. However, if there was an implication that they were available as part of the price then this should be the case.

    (b)   The notice says that the lager is 'probably' the best in the world. It doesn't say it is. The statement is meaningless and again would depend on the opinion of the drinker. Merely an advertising gimmick that would not mislead most people.

NOTES

(c)   This would be a false trade description. A reasonable person would take the statement to include the mechanics of the car as well as its appearance. See the case of *Robertson v Dicicco 1972* where the description of a 'beautiful car' was taken to include the mechanics and the appearance.

5   In Sid's case, it is debatable whether the statement could be said to have been made 'in the course of service'. It is a statement of intent or a promise; it would be difficult to prove it was made 'deliberately or recklessly'. Cal, on the other hand, made the false statement of fact after the work had (or rather, had not) been done; the invoice words are hence capable of being construed as 'being made in the course of service' and, provided they were made carelessly or deliberately, knowing them to be false, an offence has been committed.

'The section specifically refers to the reckless making of a statement that is false. That means that if at the end of the contract a person giving the service recklessly makes a false statement as to what he or she has done, the matter may well fall within s14, but if, before the contract has been worked out, the person who provides the service makes a promise as to what he or she will do, and that promise does not relate to an existing fact, nobody can say at the date when that statement is made that it is either true or false': *Becket v Cohen 1973.*

6   (a)   Goods labelled 'shop soiled' should still be of satisfactory quality, although the customer would not be entitled to complain about any faults that were pointed out at the time of sale. For example, a refrigerator could be labelled 'shop soiled' because it has a scratched door. The customer could not complain about the scratches but they could complain if the refrigerator does not keep food cold. The same would apply to goods marked 'seconds'. They are clearly not going to be as good as perfect goods. 'Special Purchase' goods should be perfect, but they are obviously not as expensive as some goods so the quality may not be as good. They should still be both 'satisfactory' and 'fit for their normal purpose'.

        (b)   The customer knows that they are not likely to get perfection. However, the goods must be reasonably adequate bearing in mind all the circumstances.

7   In your role play, Mr Bloggs should state his case clearly and calmly. He will probably want to argue that the goods are not fit for their purpose. He relied on the assistant's advice, and it was wrong. He should ask for a full refund. When the assistant refuses this he should re-state his case and explain why the law backs him up. He should not get involved in a slanging match with the assistant. If he cannot talk the assistant round he should state that he is going to refer the matter to the local Trading Standards Office and also write to the shop's head office to complain. It often works wonders if you ask to speak to the manager of the shop!

8   In this case Mrs Bolton was hit on the head by a cricket ball that was hit out of a cricket ground. She sued, claiming that the cricket club were negligent in allowing balls to fly out of the ground. The club were able to prove that this type of incident had only happened 6-10 times during the past 35 years and nobody had previously been injured. They had a high fence and had taken every precaution to avoid accidents. The court held that they were not negligent and had acted reasonably in the circumstances. Mrs Bolton's injuries had been caused by a 'freak' accident.

9   It is extremely unlikely that I would win my claim. I may get back the £1 that is attached to physical damage to the ornament. The difficulty in claiming the £5.3 million is that of proof. How can I prove that I would have bought a ticket, that I would have used those numbers etc? Also, the damage is too remote - it is not closely connected enough to the incident to flow from it. You could not have known my intentions.

10   This 'state of the art' or 'development risk' defence challenges directly the concept of strict liability for defective products. Because the Act is relatively new, it is not clear what attitudes the courts will adopt towards the state of the art defence. A practical approach might look to a producer to make his or her product as safe as possible, taking into account reasonable constraints on cost, an assessment of market expectations and the existence of safe alternatives to the product. A stricter approach might assume that the producer should be aware of all available information relating to the product, regardless of cost and circumstances.

11   A 'secured loan' attaches to an asset which the borrower already has. For example, a house. If the loan is not repaid as agreed then the lender can take possession of the specified property. An unsecured loan only gives the lender the remedy of suing for the outstanding payments. They cannot take possession of any property automatically.

Assignment 9 (1 hour)

Scenario

You are an adviser in the Trading Standards Department of Borchester City Council. You have come into work this morning to find the following notes in your in-tray. The Chief Trading Standards Officer (CTSO) has left them for you and would like you to summarise the legal issues concerning each person and recommend suitable courses of action.

Mr Bland

Mr Bland is on a gluten-free diet. He needs to consult the list of ingredients on everything he buys. He went to his local health store and asked for gluten free biscuits. He was given a packet of biscuits by the assistant who said "these are just what you want". Later, having eaten some of the biscuits he suffered a severe attack of stomach trouble. Your department has had the biscuits tested and they are not gluten free. The label on the packet makes no mention of it.

Ms Spark

Ms Spark went to her local department store and purchased a new toaster. It had a label on it that stated 'BSI approved'. The first time she used it it gave her a nasty electric shock. She is very angry as she contacted the British Standards Institute who told her they did not approve this particular toaster. She has since discovered that BSI stood for Bill Suggs Incorporated.

Mr V Gullible

Mr Gullible bought a watch from a stall on his local market. The watch was labelled 'ROLEX' and cost £2.99. Later the same week he over-wound the watch by accident and took it to a jewellers for repair. The jeweller laughed and told him it wasn't worth repairing. Vic is very disappointed to find out that he bought a fake. He had thought it was an incredible bargain.

Mrs T Hick

Mrs Hick went to buy a car from her local car dealer. She offered her old car in part exchange and was a bit disappointed when the dealer seemed reluctant to take it. In the end he said he would 'do her a favour' and give her £50 off the price of her new car. He then says he will get rid of it at the breakers' yard.

Later that same day Mrs Hick is astonished to see her car on the garage forecourt with a big poster stuck to it stating:

'TODAY'S MEGA BARGAIN! IMMACULATE CAR. ONE LADY OWNER. REAL SNIP AT £500'

Task

Read the notes given for each person. Produce a memorandum for the CTSO that outlines the nature of each problem, whether civil or criminal law (or both) is involved and what you would advise each of the people to do.

Chapter 10:
PEOPLE IN THE WORKPLACE

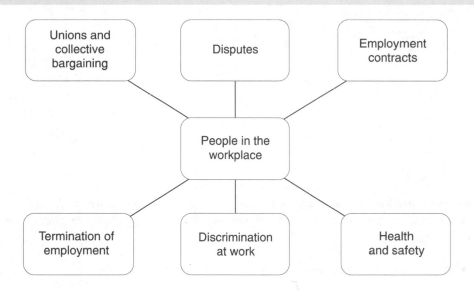

Introduction

The management of people is a crucial factor in the success of any business. Investment in selection and training increases and improves the skills of employees and enhances their value to the organisation. There are a number of matters that are common to all organisations - namely, the statutory rights of employees. Evidence from cases heard by Industrial Tribunals reveal that many firms are not familiar with the concept and law of employee rights, and their failure to understand this has proved costly in terms of financial compensation, legal defence and damaging publicity. Instances of sexual and racial discrimination are regularly reported.

Employee relations can prove one of the most potentially dangerous areas of the operating environment. Everyone responsible for staff should know that employees have rights that are incorporated in legal or other procedures.

Your objectives

In this chapter you will learn about:

(a)   The importance of contracts of employment

(b)   The basis of collective bargaining

(c)   The concept of unfair treatment of the employee and the role of industrial tribunals

(d)   Discrimination law

(e)   Redundancy procedures

1 UNIONS AND COLLECTIVE BARGAINING

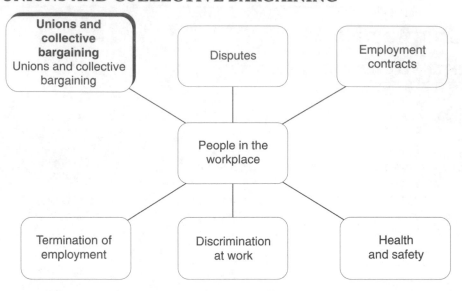

We can now proceed to identify the principles and the institutions through which employee relations are conducted. The issues outlined in the following pages relate to collective bargaining.

1.1 Unions and collective bargaining

A trade union's purpose and activities are centred around the requirements of its members. Its first objective is to promote their interests and improve their pay and conditions of employment, and to represent them in negotiations with employers and government. Most unions also provide personal services to members, such as representing and advising in cases involving grievances, discipline, accidents, dismissal and redundancy. Some even provide financial services, by using their large membership as a means of getting good deals from financial service firms.

Most trade unions have other and wider social objectives and feel that they have responsibilities for promoting what they consider to be a more equitable society. They therefore have subsidiary political objectives and seek to influence governments on matters such as employment and the welfare of workers.

Some of the functions carried out by a trade union are directly related to its objectives of improving pay, conditions and job security for its members by representation of employees in formal discussions with management (for example disciplinary procedures), negotiation and consultation. Other functions which are not *directly* connected to the achievement of its goals, but which might indirectly be effective, are the following.

(a) *Lobbying* politicians to obtain legislation to improve conditions of work (for example, a statutory minimum wage and hours of work)

(b) Developing *political affiliations* with other trade unions, to create a power base for achieving political influence

(c) Providing finance for a *sympathetic political party*

(d) Attempting to *become involved in management's planning functions and executive decisions*. This might be achieved by means of joint consultative committees. Greater involvement in planning will promote the extensions of 'industrial democracy'.

(e) *Help for individual members* who need support. This help may arise from a particular incident or dispute at work but, on a more general level, a union might wish to provide financial support for members or their dependants in distress.

In many large UK organisations, employee's wages and conditions are the outcome of a process called *collective bargaining.*

Definition

Collective bargaining: the terms and conditions under which employees work may be the result of agreements reached between employers and trade unions through the process of collective bargaining between employees, represented by a union, and management. It is dependent on the willingness of both parties to enter negotiations and to establish machinery and mutually acceptable rules. Collective bargaining is traditionally practised in the public sector, and manufacturing industries in the private sector. During the past twenty years there has been a trend away from this method of determining employee conditions of service, towards individual or personal contracts of employment. The Trade Union Reform and Employment Rights Act 1993 enables management to offer separate personal contracts to people prepared to give up these collective bargaining rights. Management can give financial inducements to do so.

Trade unions recruit their members in the work place. There are about 7 million members in more than 70 different unions who each belong to the Trade Unions Congress (TUC). There are nearly 200 trade unions that do not belong to the TUC, but they form a small proportion of the total membership.

Over the years there has been a general decline in union membership. Union membership now tends to be concentrated amongst 'professional' occupations, perhaps indicating the high unionisation in the teaching profession.

The process of negotiating conditions of employment is conducted between the trade unions representing the employees of enterprises and the management of the organisation, usually represented by the Director of Personnel acting on behalf of the employer.

The Nissan company's agreement with the AUEW is an example whereby the union reaches agreement with the company. Many firms have tried with some success to institute single-union agreements at various business sites. This is to save on administration.

EXAMPLE: NISSAN AND AUEW

General principles of the agreement

The objectives of this agreement are:

- To develop and maintain the prosperity of the company and its employees and to promote and maintain mutual trust and co-operation between the company, its employees and the union

- To establish procedures by which matters affecting these relationships can be dealt with effectively and speedily

BPP PUBLISHING

- To recognise that all employees, at whatever level, have a valued part to play in the success of the company

- To this end both parties are agreed on the need:

- To establish an enterprise committed to the highest levels of quality, productivity and competitiveness using modern technology and working practices and to make such changes to this technology and working practices as will maintain this position

- To avoid any action that interrupts the continuity of production

- To seek actively the contributions of all employees in the furtherance of these goals

- To respond flexibly and quickly to changes in demand for the company's products

- To maintain open and direct communication with all employees on matters of mutual interest and concern

The Union recognises the right of the company to plan, organise, manage and decide finally upon the operations of the company.

The company recognises the right of its employees to belong to the union and of the union to represent its members.

The company and the union recognise the overriding nature of the principles covered in this paragraph and are agreed that it is their joint responsibility to endeavour to ensure that these principles are put into effect and maintained. If other paragraphs of this agreement are considered to conflict with paragraph one, then paragraph one will take precedence.

Activity 1   **(5 minutes)**

People are often attracted to work in personnel as they believe it only involves dealing with people. What other skills are required from personnel staff besides getting on well with people?

The framework below outlines an approach to dealing with disputes.

2 DISPUTES

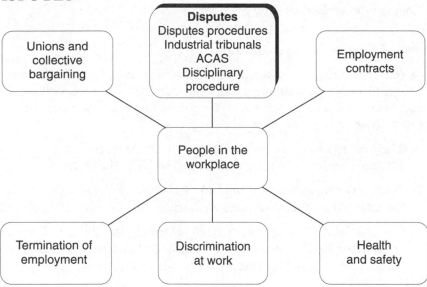

2.1 Disputes procedures

The legal framework surrounding disputes between employers and employees includes contracts of employment, the Employment Rights Act 1996, and various other matters to do with health and safety.

The procedures are outlined in Figure 10.1.

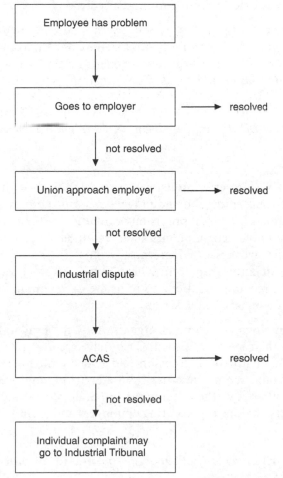

Figure 10.1 Disputes procedures

NOTES

The institutions involved include trade unions, employers' associations, and ACAS (the Advisory Conciliation and Arbitration Service).

What does third party involvement mean?

Where it is felt appropriate for a third party to be involved in an individual appeals procedure, some form of arbitration is usually sought. This is a process where the parties put the issue to an independent arbitrator for determination. Normally the parties put their cases in writing and later orally at a hearing.

(a) The arbitrator then makes a decision that the parties will have agreed in advance to accept as a means of finally resolving the matter.

(b) Alternatively, instead of a binding decision, the mediator produces one or more formal recommendations for further consideration by the parties.

(c) Conciliation, is an attempt, through informal discussion, to help the parties reach their own agreement. (This is a particularly flexible process used primarily in collective issues.)

If a dispute proceeds to a strike or other industrial actions by the employees, the following is necessary.

(a) Notification of action by trade unions must be given to the employer.

(b) The trade union must carry out a ballot of members, sending the voting paper to the member's home.

(c) There must be specific parties to disputes, and outside action such as picketing is strictly limited to those involved.

(d) Settlement of disputes is usually by mutual consent, but a company may dismiss employees who remain on strike after the company has withdrawn recognition. The main legislation governing this is the consolidating Trade Union and Labour Relations (Consolidation) Act 1992.

We are also interested in third party involvement, as an environmental influence.

2.2 Employment

Employment tribunals (formerly industrial tribunals) deal with a large variety of jurisdictions, mostly concerning the individual rights of employees. The majority of cases arise from the unfair dismissal provisions contained in the employment protection legislation. Other cases involve complaints about redundancy payments, sexual or racial discrimination at the workplace, maternity rights in employment, trade union membership and non-membership rights, health and safety at work, and contractual issues. They may take recommendations to reinstate or re-employ staff who have been dismissed or enforce financial compensation.

There are separate employment tribunal organisations for England and Wales and for Scotland, each with their own President. Tribunals are independent judicial bodies consisting of a legally qualified chairperson and two lay members, one drawn from a panel of employer members, and the other from a panel of employee members. The lay members are appointed by the Secretary of State for Employment, following consultation with organisations representing employers and employees.

Where employment tribunals adjudicate, the parties in dispute often benefit from mediation.

BPP
PUBLISHING

2.3 Advisory, Conciliation and Arbitration Service (ACAS)

ACAS is an independent organisation established under the Employment Protection Act 1975 to help employers, workers and their union representatives improve the conduct of their industrial relations. ACAS was set up to provide a third-party mediator in disputes between employers and employee representatives, on a collective basis.

ACAS provides information, assistance and advice to employers, trade unions and individuals on industrial relations and personnel management.

These services are provided free of charge and are available through trained industrial relations officers in Scotland, Wales and at seven regional offices throughout England.

Sometimes disputes and grievances arise out of disciplinary matters. It helps to specify the procedures involved.

2.4 Disciplinary procedure

Large employers are expected to draw up their own rules and procedure for dealing with breaches of *discipline*, such as misconduct at the place of work. No elaborate formality is required (nor is it appropriate), but any such procedure should give to the employee a right to be informed of what is alleged against them and also to be accompanied by an appropriate adviser, such as a trade union official, while they state their case. It is desirable, but not essential, that a decision to dismiss should be subject to review and confirmation at a higher level before it is implemented. The written particulars given to an employee within the first two months of employment should inform him of any disciplinary procedure. If the employer has a formal procedure, he or she should be scrupulously careful to follow it, though their failure to do so on some technical point may be disregarded if no unfairness follows from it. For employers who do not wish to draw up their own procedure, a model set of rules is provided in the ACAS code on Disciplinary Practices and Procedures.

Activity 2	**(5 minutes)**

Industrial tribunals frequently hear cases concerning discipline and behaviour involving such matters as dress and personal appearance. How might firms take action to avoid such situations arising in the first place?

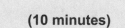

Activity 3	**(10 minutes)**

Suggest factors that need to be included in a written discipline procedure.

The content of discipline procedures should:

    (a)   Be clear and to the point

    (b)   Have regard to the nature of the work

    (c)   Reflect social and attitudinal change

    (d)   Be subject to regular review and update

    (e)   Be understood as part of the contract of employment

    (f)   Follow principles of natural justice

(g)   Give information on employee rights

(i)   Representation
(ii)   Appeal
(iii) Written warnings about unsatisfactory conduct

Ideally, employee training programmes and the staff handbook should spell out any special behavioural requirements and explain what constitutes:

(a)   Misdemeanours - eg unpunctuality, sloppy dress
(b)   Gross misconduct - stealing, violence

Company officers must be informed about industrial tribunals. In the event of a case being brought by an employee all relevant paper work must be presented. Company personnel practice must be explained to third parties and may result in publicity as well as financial loss.

Warnings

Except in the most flagrant cases, it is not reasonable for an employer to dismiss an employee without first warning them that if they continue or repeat what has happened at least once they are likely to be dismissed.

Activity 4   **(30 minutes)**

Find out the difference between gross misconduct and misconduct. Give some examples of conduct that would seem to fit each category.

Employee rights and conciliation

The following employment rights include a provision for individual conciliation, whereby the employee and employer attempt to sort out their differences.

(a)   Unfair dismissal (including the right to return after maternity absence)

(b)   Equal pay

(c)   Sex discrimination

(d)   Racial discrimination

(e)   Guarantee payments

(f)   Suspension on medical grounds

(g)   Time off for ante-natal care

(h)   Time off for public duties

(i)   Time off for trade union activities/duties

(j)   Time off in the event of redundancy to look for work or arrange for training

(k)   Written statement of reasons for dismissal

(l)   Itemised pay statements

(m)   Certain matters concerning redundancy consultation

(n)   Action short of dismissal on grounds of trade union membership and activities or non-membership

(o) Action short of dismissal for carrying out safety representation duties (offshore workers only)

(p) Certain matters relating to the transfer of undertakings

(q) Deductions from pay contrary to the Wages Act 1986

(r) Exclusion or expulsion from trade union membership

(s) Unjustifiable discipline by a trade union

(t) Refusal of employment or the service of an employment agency on the grounds of being, or not being, a union member

3 EMPLOYMENT CONTRACTS

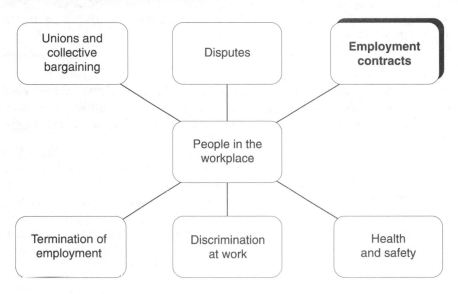

Normally, the *contract of employment* will be a written document, and will contain details of the terms and conditions of the employment and various employment particulars. If the contract was not in writing, or did not contain the pertinent information, an employee is entitled within two months of starting work to receive a written *statement of particulars*. The statement must contain, or refer to, other documents that contain the information below.

(a) The names of *employer* and *employee*

(b) The *date* on which employment began (important if it becomes necessary to decide what period of notice should be given)

(c) Whether any service with a previous employer forms part of the employee's *continuous period* of employment (important if the employee wished to claim for redundancy or unfair dismissal)

(d) *Pay* (scale or rate and intervals at which paid)

(e) *Hours of work* (including any specified 'normal working hours')

(f) Any *holiday* and *holiday pay* entitlement (including any right to accrued holiday pay on termination of employment)

(g) *Sick leave* and *sick pay* entitlement (if any)

(h) *Pensions* and *pension schemes* (unless statutory)

(i)   Length of *notice* of termination to be given on either side (or the expiry date if employed for a fixed term)

(j)   The *title* of the job that the employee is employed to do

Whenever any change is made in any term contained in the written particulars, the employer must, within one month, provide a written statement of the change. If a change is made by collective agreement between the employer and a trade union, the terms of employment of the individual employee are effectively changed without his consent. If such change is possible, the statement must say so.

Activity 5   **(30 minutes)**

Draft a letter of appointment for a new member of staff at your college and include terms and conditions of the appointment. Base the offer on the information in this chapter.

Employment particulars can be given by instalments, during the two months period. A 'principal statement', which must include items (a) to (f) above and the title of the job, must be provided, but other particulars may be given by way of separate documents.

The written particulars must also contain details of disciplinary procedures and grievance procedures, or refer to where they can be found. If they are in a separate booklet, each employee must be given a copy. Employers with fewer than 20 employees do not need to provide particulars of disciplinary procedures, but employees must still be told of grievance procedures. Failure by an employee to initiate an established grievance procedure may, in the event of unfair dismissal, amount to contributory fault leading to a reduction in any award.

A few other facts are of relevance.

(a)   If there is no express agreement in the contract as to how much, the employee is entitled to a 'reasonable' pay, decided on the particular facts by the court. The Government have recently announced the introduction of a statutory minimum wage.

(b)   If the written particulars do not contain terms as to payment during illness, the employee may go to a tribunal to determine whether it was agreed; it is generally presumed to be payable but not necessarily from the employer's own funds.

(c)   An employee is entitled to receive an *itemised pay slip* at or before payment of wages or salary. This will show both gross and net pay. It will also show all deductions (ie tax, national insurance contributions etc) made and the method of calculation of different parts of net pay if these are made in different ways.

4 HEALTH AND SAFETY

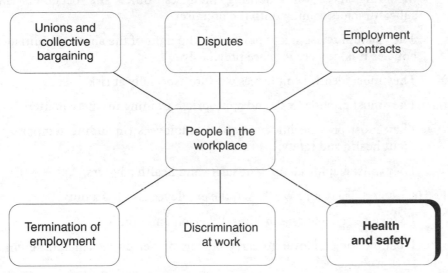

Health and safety was briefly mentioned in Chapter 1. We can now consider it in more detail. Health and safety in the work place is regulated by both UK and EU law. Apart from humanitarian concerns about employee well-being, employers are liable to be sued if unsafe practice leads to injury or worse.

Health and safety is not only relevant to factories with potentially dangerous equipment, or building sites. It is also relevant to the *office*. (Many accidents are caused when people stand on 'swivel chairs'.)

The legal issues on health are governed by:

(a)   The Health and Safety at Work Act 1974

(b)   Regulations issued in 1992 and 1999, relating to the management of health and safety, and health and safety in the workplace (health and safety regulations)

Other specific regulations relate to fire.

In brief, the employer's duties are these.

(a)   All systems (work practices) must be safe.

(b)   The work environment must be safe and healthy (well-lit, warm, ventilated and hygienic).

(c)   All plant and equipment must be kept up to the necessary standard (with guards on machines and so on).

In addition, information, instruction, training and supervision should be directed towards safe working practices, and the safety policy should be clearly communicated to all staff.

Implementation of the *EU directives* as (legally enforceable) regulations means that employers have the following additional general duties (as summarised in the *Administrator*, September 1992).

(a)   They must carry out risk assessment, generally in writing, of all work hazards. Assessment should be continuous.

(b)   They must introduce controls to reduce risks.

(c)   They must assess the risks to anyone else affected by their work activities.

(d) They must share hazard and risk information with other employers, including those on adjoining premises, other site occupiers and all subcontractors coming onto the premises.

(e) They should revise safety policies in the light of the above, or initiate safety policies if none were in place previously.

(f) They must identify employees who are especially at risk.

(g) They must provide fresh and appropriate training in safety matters.

(h) They must provide information to employees (including temporary staff) about health and safety.

(i) They must employ competent safety and health advisers.

Under the Health and Safety and Work Act, the employee also has a duty:

(a) To take reasonable care of himself/herself and others

(b) To allow the employer to carry out his or her duties (including enforcing safety rules)

(c) Not to interfere intentionally or recklessly with any machinery or equipment

Employees must inform their employer of any situation that may be a danger (although this does not reduce the employer's responsibilities in any way because his or her risk assessment programme should have spotted the hazard in any case). Employees must use all equipment properly, in accordance with instructions.

Other more detailed regulations cover areas such as equipment handling and VDUs.

FOR DISCUSSION

Do you think employers should go further than obeying the letter of the law and instead take a more active approach in promoting employee health, for example by prohibiting smoking at work, providing health check-ups or providing counselling?

We now look at workplace health, safety and welfare regulations.

Health and safety regulations

The Workplace (Health, Safety and Welfare) Regulations 1992 implemented the European *Workplace Directive* covering matters that have been statutory requirements for many years in the UK under legislation such as the *Offices, Shops and Railway Premises Act 1963*, although in some cases the requirements have been more clearly defined. The following provisions are made.

(a) *Equipment*. All equipment should be properly maintained.

(b) *Ventilation*. Air should be fresh or purified.

(c) *Temperature*. The temperature must be 'reasonable' inside buildings during working hours. This means not less than 16°C where people are sitting down, or 13°C if they move about to do their work. A thermometer should be provided.

(d) *Lighting* should be suitable and sufficient, and natural, if practicable. Windows should be clean and unobstructed.

(e) *Cleaning and decoration.* Floors, walls, ceilings, furniture, furnishings and fittings must be kept clean. Floors should be cleaned weekly. Rubbish should not be allowed to accumulate.

(f) *Room dimensions and space.* Each person should have at least 11 cubic metres of space, ignoring any parts of rooms more than 3.1 metres above the floor or with a headroom of less than 2.0 metres.

(g) *Floors* must be properly constructed and maintained (without holes, not slippery, properly drained and so on).

(h) *Falls or falling objects.* These should be prevented by erecting effective physical safeguards (fences, safety nets, ground rails and so on).

(i) *Glazing.* Windows should be made of safe materials and if they are openable it should be possible to do this safely.

(j) *Traffic routes.* These should have regard to the safety of pedestrians and vehicles alike.

(k) *Doors and gates.* These should be suitably constructed and fitted with any necessary safety devices (especially sliding doors and powered doors, and doors opening in either direction).

(l) *Escalators and travelators* should function safely and have readily accessible emergency stop devices.

(m) *Sanitary conveniences* and washing facilities must be suitable and sufficient. This means that they should be properly ventilated and lit, properly cleaned and separate for men and women. 'Sufficient' means that undue delay is avoided!

(n) *Drinking water.* An adequate supply should be available with suitable drinking vessels.

(o) *Clothing.* There should be suitable accommodation for outdoor clothing, which should be able to dry out if wet. Facilities for changing clothing should be available where appropriate.

(p) *Rest facilities and eating facilities.* These must be provided unless the employees' workstations are suitable for rest or eating, as is normally the case for offices.

The *Management of Health and Safety at Work Regulations 1999* extend the 1992 regulations in some respects, and covers the following issues.

- *Risk assessments* to be undertaken by employers
- *Health and safety* arrangements
- Health *surveillance*
- Health and safety *assistance*
- Procedures for *danger areas*
- Contacts with *external services*
- *Information* for employees
- *Co-operation* between employers sharing a workplace
- Working in '*host*' premises
- Taking account of *employee capabilities*
- *Employee duties*
- *Temporary workers, expectant mothers* and *young* people

- *Liability* and *exclusion* of civil liability
- Premises and activities *outside Great Britain*

Activity 6   **(1 hour)**

You have recently been appointed as assistant to the Health and Safety Officer for Thermo plc, a manufacturer of thermal underwear. The premises house the production areas of the factory, the office staff and the executive offices. There is a wide variety of different working environments and equipment and this creates quite a health and safety priority.

Lately, your boss has noticed that people seem to have become somewhat careless about health and safety issues. They have adopted an attitude of 'it's not my problem - we have a Heath and Safety Officer to think about it'. People are not taking responsibility for their own well-being and safety.

The occupational nurse also works within your department and she is concerned about the general health and fitness levels of the workforce. A number of workers are heavy smokers and the canteen does a roaring trade in chips and fry-ups. She has also noticed that a number of the executives have very high pressure jobs and she is worried about their stress levels.

You have been asked to outline some ideas on how to introduce effective training for health and safety in the various parts of the firm. You have also been asked to jot down some ideas for a health-promotion campaign that the occupational nurse could run. Your main brief is to make people want to participate in the activities rather than attend because their boss says they must.

---

5 DISCRIMINATION AT WORK

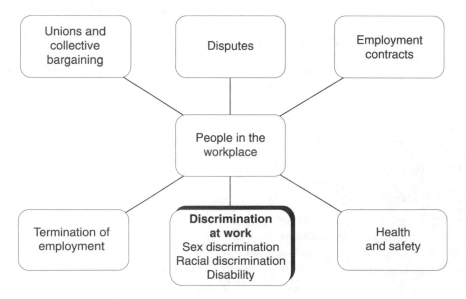

One area of employment law that has given rise to several pieces of legislation in the last twenty-five years is the issue of equal opportunities and discrimination at work. This may be on the grounds of sex, marital status, race or disability. We briefly covered these issues in Chapter 1, and they are explored here in greater depth.

5.1 Sex discrimination

Sex discrimination is governed by the Sex Discrimination Act and Equal Pay Act. These are policed by the Equal Opportunities Commission.

Equal Pay Act 1970

Under this Act, contractual employment terms given to a man or woman should be at least as favourable as those given to an employee of the opposite sex. This has been held to mean that where, say, a woman does work 'of equal value' to a male colleague, she is entitled to equal pay. The Act covers other terms such as sick pay, holiday pay and working hours, and it applies to all forms of full-time and part-time work.

EXAMPLE: EQUAL PAY FOR WORK OF EQUAL VALUE

Hayward v Cammell Laird Shipbuilders 1986

The House of Lords upheld the claim of a canteen cook to equal pay with painters, joiners and thermal insulation engineers employed in the same shipyard on the ground that her work was of equal value. This very important decision was based on a report by an independent expert who compared the jobs under five headings (physical demands, environmental demands, planning and decision-making demands, skill and knowledge demands and responsibility demands). Under each heading the demands were ranked as low, moderate or high.

Overall the applicant was considered to be employed on work of equal value. Hayward's application was the first successful claim for equal pay for work of equal value. It is interesting to note that the claim succeeded even though the applicant had better fringe benefits (eg paid meal breaks, extra holidays) than the workers with whom her work was compared.

The right to equal pay applies:

(a) To employees in the United Kingdom whether or not they are British and regardless of the law governing their employment contract, and

(b) To men as well as to women

FOR DISCUSSION

Should there be any exceptions to sex discrimination legislation? Do you think anti-discrimination legislation should be extended to include sexual orientation?

Under the Act, an equality clause is implied into every person's contract of employment that, where the person is employed on similar or equivalently rated work to that of a person of the opposite sex, or on work of equal value to that of a person in the same employment, the right to equal pay is assumed.

Furthermore, the *employer* has to show that the reason for any difference is a genuine material factor *other* than sex. Examples of differences are these:

(a)   Greater length of service is a material factor.

(b)   Working at different times of day is not a material factor.

(c)   A distinction in hourly pay between workers in London and those based in (the cheaper area of) Nottingham is based on a material factor.

Sex Discrimination Acts 1975 and 1986

This legislation prohibits discrimination on the grounds of sex against any employee, male or female, in the recruitment, promotion, training, benefits or dismissal of employees. A Code of Practice drawn up in April 1985 recommends that:

(a)   Employers should have a clearly stated equal opportunities policy, regularly monitored, and

(b)   Advertisements should be worded to encourage applicants of both sexes.

Companies with a compulsory retirement age must abolish different retirement ages for men and women. The Act does not, however, affect the payment of company or State pensions.

There are two forms of discrimination that can be distinguished.

(a)   *Direct discrimination* occurs where an employer or prospective employer treats an employee or job applicant less favourably than another on grounds of sex.

(b)   *Indirect discrimination* occurs in cases such as the imposition of a qualification for promotion with which fewer people of one sex than the other could comply.

EXAMPLE: INDIRECT DISCRIMINATION

Price v Civil Service Commission 1978

The Civil Service Commission imposed a maximum age limit of 28 for appointment to the civil service grade of Executive Officer. A woman argued that this was indirectly discriminating against women since women in their twenties are often prevented by care of children from taking up employment.

The court held that the imposition of an age limit was indirect discrimination.

In some jobs, however, it is accepted that male or female sex is a 'genuine occupational qualification' (GOQ). An advertisement for a job abroad in a country whose laws and customs might make it difficult for a woman to perform her duties would be acceptable. Decency may require a male attendant in a male lavatory or sports facilities. Some occupations, such as ministers of religion and police and prison officers, are exempt from the statutory rules.

The *Equal Opportunities Commission* (EOC) oversees the working of safeguards for equality of men and women. It promotes test cases in the courts and makes recommendations for changes in the law. It may issue codes of practice and conduct investigations.

Discrimination on the grounds of marital status

The Sex Discrimination Acts make it unlawful to discriminate against married people in any way, for example if an employer believes that a single man will be able to devote more time to a job than a married man. Oddly, however, there is no provision preventing discrimination against single people.

In recent years there have been many developments in Europe to promote equality. The Equal Pay and Equal Treatment Directives have mainly been incorporated into UK legislation. Directives have also addressed the rights of pregnant workers, and the Amsterdam Treaty now addresses issues of sexual orientation.

At a similar time, an Act was passed to prohibit discrimination on grounds of race, colour or ethnic origin.

5.2 Racial discrimination

Discrimination on the grounds of race is prohibited by the *Race Relations Act 1976*, which also set up the *Commission for Racial Equality (CRE)*. It is an offence to discriminate against an employee on account of his or her colour, race, ethnic or national origin. Discrimination consists of treating an employee less favourably than the employer treats other employees. The Act's provisions are similar to the Sex Discrimination Act 1975, although there are fewer grounds to justify discrimination, being:

(a)   Authenticity in entertainment, art or photography: a black man to play Othello for instance

(b)   Personal services: recruiting a Bangladeshi housing officer in a Bangladeshi area, for example

(c)   Maintaining ethnic authenticity in a bar or restaurant: such as Chinese waiters in a Chinese restaurant

The Act covers discrimination in advertising for engaging or dismissing an employee, or in conditions of employment (such as opportunities for training and promotion). The CRE published a code of practice in 1983 that, among other points, advised employers to make periodic analysis of the racial composition of their workforce and of the decisions taken on recruitment, training and promotion. It is argued that only if such matters are kept under systematic and active review will covert racial discrimination be disclosed so that remedial measures may be taken.

An individual employee may apply to an industrial tribunal if he or she considers that his or her rights have been infringed by discrimination. There have been many awards of high compensation in recent years. Many organisations aim to go further than the strict letter of the law by having an equal opportunities policy.

Activity 7   **(10 minutes)**

What value could there be for a firm to maintain records of the ethnic origin of employees? What other information would be useful to help a firm to obtain a good profile of its employee base?

5.3 Disability

The Disability Discrimination Act 1995 came into force in December 1996 in relation to employment.

The Act applies to employers who have 20 or more employees, making it unlawful for them to discriminate against disabled people in terms of recruitment or at the workplace. It is illegal to treat someone less favourably than able-bodied workers, or to fail to make 'reasonable adjustments' to enable a disabled employee to do their job.

We can now examine the specific considerations relating to an individual contract of employment. These relate to some of the issues regarding discipline and so on, which we discussed earlier.

6 TERMINATION OF EMPLOYMENT

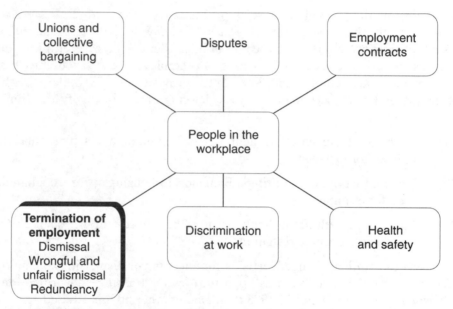

An employment contract is terminated by breach where there is:

- (a) Summary dismissal
- (b) Constructive dismissal
- (c) Inability on the employer's behalf to continue
- (d) Repudiation of the contract by the employee

6.1 Dismissal

Summary dismissal

Summary dismissal occurs where the employer dismisses the employee without notice. This may be done if the employee has committed a serious breach of contract. Summary dismissal in these circumstances does not incur any liability for the employer. If, however, the employer has no sufficient justification for a summary dismissal, the employer is liable for breach of contract and the employee may claim a remedy for wrongful dismissal (see below). Whether the employee's conduct justifies summary dismissal varies according to the circumstances of the case.

Constructive dismissal

Constructive dismissal occurs where the employer, although willing to continue the employment, repudiates some essential term of the contract, (for example by the unilateral imposition of a complete change in the employee's duties) or makes it very difficult for the employee to remain in post, and the employee resigns. The employer is liable for breach of contract. For example, an employer who constantly sexually harassed staff could be accused of constructive dismissal if those staff felt that the only way to resolve the problem was to leave the job.

Employer's inability to continue employment

The employer may become unable to continue to employ the employee, for example if the firm is wound up and ceases trading.

Repudiation of the contract by the employee

If the employee resigns or goes on strike or fails to perform the contract and to observe its conditions, that is breach of contract on their part, and the employer may dismiss them for that reason.

Summary dismissal and constructive dismissal are both examples of dismissal without proper notice. A dismissal with proper notice is generally held to be lawful, unless it is shown to be wrongful or unfair.

6.2   Wrongful and unfair dismissal

(a)   Wrongful dismissal is a common law concept, arising in specific circumstances, which gives the employee an action for breach of contract.

(b)   Unfair dismissal is a concept introduced by employment protection legislation. As a rule, every employee has the right not to be unfairly dismissed.

Wrongful dismissal

Where the employer has summarily dismissed an employee without notice, or with less notice than the period outlined in the contract (as where the employer becomes insolvent), there may be a claim for damages for wrongful dismissal. However, a claim will not succeed where the employer can show justification (eg breach of contract).

Unfair dismissal

Unfair dismissal is a concept that was created by industrial relations legislation about twenty years ago. It is now an extremely important element of employment protection legislation.

Whereas the remedies available following a successful action for wrongful dismissal are limited to damages equivalent to the earnings if proper notice had been given, the unfair dismissal legislation seeks to widen the scope of protection and increase the range of remedies available to an employee who has been unfairly dismissed.

Activity 8   **(10 minutes)**

List some reasons for dismissal that are automatically considered to be unfair.

Remedies for unfair dismissal: application to a tribunal

An employee who alleges *unfair dismissal* must normally present their complaint to an *industrial tribunal* within three months of the effective date of termination.

The industrial tribunal might decide the following remedy for unfair dismissal.

(a) *Reinstatement*. If unfair dismissal is established, the tribunal first considers the possibility of making an order for reinstatement, which is return to the same job without any break of continuity.

(b) *Re-engagement*. The tribunal may alternatively order re-engagement. The employee is given new employment with the employer (or their successor or associate) on terms specified in the order. The new employment must be comparable with the old, or otherwise suitable.

(c) *Compensation*. If the tribunal does not order reinstatement or re-engagement, or if the employer does not comply with such an order, the tribunal may award compensation.

    (i) A basic award is calculated as follows. Those aged 41 and over receive one and a half weeks' pay (up to a maximum of £220 gross per week) for each year of service up to a maximum of 20 years. In other age groups the same provisions apply, except that the 22-40 age group receive one week's pay per year and the under 22 age group receive half a week's pay. If the employee is also entitled to redundancy pay, the lesser is set off against the greater amount.

    (ii) A compensatory award (taking account of the basic award) for any additional loss (earnings, expenses, benefits) on common law principles of damages for breach of contract.

    (iii) If the employer does not comply with an order for reinstatement or re-engagement, and does not show that it was impracticable to do so, a punitive additional award is payable.

    (iv) There is an overall limit on the amount that may be awarded, which is raised from time to time to keep it in line with average earnings. In line with a recent European Court judgement, there is no upper limit on the awards that may be made in sex discrimination or race discrimination cases.

Redundancy is a special case. Here it is the job that is ended, rather than the individual's occupation of the post.

6.3 Redundancy

To qualify for redundancy pay, the following conditions apply.

(a) The employer has ceased, or intends to cease, to carry on the business in which the employee has been employed, or

(b) The employer has ceased to carry out the business in the place where the employee was employed, or

(c) The requirements of the business for employees to carry out work of a particular kind have ceased or diminished (or are expected to)

In order to obtain a redundancy payment:

(a) The employee must be under the normal retirement age for the business, or under 65 if no retirement age is specified, and

(b)   Must have been continuously employed for at least two years, and

(c)   Must have been dismissed (or laid off or put on short time), and

(d)   The reason for dismissal must be redundancy

Redundancy pay is calculated on the same scale as that specified for unfair dismissal compensations. Note that if the employee unreasonably refuses an offer of alternative employment with the employer, they lose their redundancy pay.

Activity 9   **(5 minutes)**

Bert is 45 years old. He has worked for your company for the past 10 years. Unfortunately you have no alternative but to make him redundant. Calculate how many weeks' pay he should get as redundancy pay.

Resignation

An employee is not entitled to redundancy pay if he or she resigns voluntarily.

Misconduct of the employee

An employee who is dismissed for misconduct is not entitled to redundancy pay.

Consultation with trade unions

In the event of planned redundancies, it is the employer's duty to consult any trade union that is independent and recognised (in collective bargaining) by them as representative of employees. The consultation must begin not later than the beginning of the appropriate period, which is:

(a)   90 days before the first dismissal, if 100 or more employees are to be dismissed at any one establishment

(b)   30 days before the first dismissal of 10-99 employees

(c)   At the earliest opportunity before even 1 (but not more than 9) employees are to be dismissed for redundancy

These rules are applied to the total number involved and cannot be evaded by making essential dismissals in small instalments.

Consultation with employees

The ACAS Code of Practice recommends that employees should be consulted where plans are made for their redundancy, even if such consultation will make no difference (as when a company is insolvent).

NOTES

Chapter roundup

- Most employers are required to give employees a statement of prescribed particulars relating to their employment within eight weeks of commencement, unless the employee already has a written contract of employment covering these particulars.

- The employer has an implied duty to take reasonable care of his or her employees; the employer must select proper staff, materials and provide a safe system of working. The employee has a duty to exercise care and skill in performance of his or her duties.

- Breach of the employment contract occurs where there is summary dismissal, constructive dismissal, inability on the employer's side to continue employment, or repudiation of the contract by the employee.

- If an employee is dismissed with shorter notice than the statutory or contractual requirements, or without notice when summary dismissal is unjustified, the employer can be sued by them for damages for wrongful dismissal.

- Dismissal is *automatically unfair* if it is on the grounds of trade union membership or activities, refusal to join a trade union, pregnancy, redundancy when others are retained, a criminal conviction that is 'spent' under the Rehabilitation of Offenders Act 1974, the employee taking steps to avert danger to health and safety at work, race or sex.

- Dismissal is caused by redundancy when the employer has ceased to carry on the business in which the employee has been employed or the business no longer needs employees to carry on that work. Dismissal is presumed by the courts to have been for redundancy unless otherwise demonstrated.

- The only effective remedy available to a wrongfully dismissed employee is a claim for damages based on loss of earnings.

- Remedies for unfair dismissal include reinstatement, re-engagement and compensation.

- To obtain a redundancy payment, the employee must be under retirement age, must have been continuously employed for at least two years, must have been dismissed, laid off or put on short-time and must have been dismissed for redundancy.

- The employer planning redundancies has a duty to consult any independent trade union that is recognised for collective bargaining as the representative of the employees. Certain consultation procedures are laid down.

Quick quiz

1 Why is investment in selection and training important?

2 What is a common method of deciding pay and conditions in the workplace?

3 Where is union membership most concentrated now?

4 Which institutions would be involved in drawing up disputes procedures?

5 What service is provided by Industrial Tribunals?

PUBLISHING

6   What is the function of ACAS?

7   What key points should be included in discipline procedures?

8   Who are the parties to collective bargaining?

9   What are the rights of employees concerning individual conciliation?

10   When should an employee be issued with a written statement of particulars?

11   Do terms and conditions of employment all have to be contained in the same document?

12   Distinguish between wrongful dismissal and unfair dismissal.

13   How is health and safety in the workplace regulated?

14   What are the employer's duties regarding health and safety?

15   What are the employee's duties regarding health and safety?

16   Define 'discrimination'.

17   List two types of dismissal.

18   What remedies may be available for unfair dismissal?

19   What is redundancy?

20   What does the ACAS Code of Practice recommend when redundancies are inevitable?

Answers to quick quiz

1   Investment in selection and training is important as it can increase and improve the skills of employees and enhance their value to the organisation.

2   Collective bargaining.

3   In the professions, teaching is a good example.

4   Trade unions, employer's associations and ACAS.

5   Tribunals are independent judicial bodies who deal with cases mostly concerning the individual rights of employees.

6   ACAS is an independent organisation to help employers, workers and their union representatives improve the conduct of their industrial relations.

7   Employees should be given an indication of behaviour deemed unsuitable and should be told of the procedures to be followed if, and when, disciplinary action is taken.

8   Employers and unions.

9   See Section 2.4.

10   Within two months of commencing work.

11   No. An employee can be referred to a variety of documents.

12   Wrongful dismissal is when the dismissal procedure has been carried out incorrectly e.g. the correct notice has not been given. Unfair dismissal is when the reason for the dismissal is wrong.

13   By UK and EU law.

14   All systems must be safe, the work environment must be safe and healthy, all plant and equipment must be kept up to the necessary standard.

15   The employee should take reasonable care of himself/herself and others, must allow the employer to carry out his or her duties and must not interfere with any machinery or equipment.

16   Discrimination means treating a particular person or group less favourably than another.

17   Summary dismissal, constructive dismissal.

18   Reinstatement, re-engagement, compensation.

19   Redundancy is where a particular job or job function is no longer required.

20   Consultation with employees and/or unions.

Answers to activities

1   A personnel officer comes into contact with all departments in a company. He or she needs to have skills in a number of different areas, including law, finance/payroll, technical knowledge about the types of job available in the organisation and the skills required, creating and implementing policies and decision making.

2   Firms should make sure that rules are clear. A good induction programme can help 'set the scene' when a new employee starts. Disciplinary procedures should be explained and understood at all levels of the organisation. Training and communication are essential.

3   Refer to the ACAS checklist shortly after the activities.

4   Gross misconduct: a fundamental breach of the employment contract so serious as to warrant instant dismissal. Examples could include fighting at work, proven theft, dangerous conduct. Misconduct: a less important breach that may lead to a warning or other disciplinary proceedings, but that is not likely to amount to instant dismissal. Constant misconduct can lead to dismissal if warnings are ignored. Examples could include lateness, failure to perform tasks properly, poor attitude to customers.

5   Try to study examples of contracts of employment from family or friends, or even your tutor. See Section 3 to remind yourself of the required content.

6   You could do the following: establish a health and safety consultative committee. Review communications and training procedures. Start a health and safety campaign - ask all departmental managers to have a meeting with their staff, put up posters everywhere to make people think about the issues. Start a staff suggestion scheme for ways to improve safety. The nurse could also have a health and fitness campaign. Use it as publicity for the firm, eg the accounts department doing a fun run for charity. Get the staff association to suggest some social events that could be sporty or informative. Ask staff to suggest things they would like help with, such as a quit smoking support group, weight watchers. Offer staff a free health MOT. Start some sports teams. Get some celebrity chefs to come and do a healthy lunch session, get the canteen to vary their menu and not offer chips every day. Provide free bowls of fruit in staff rest rooms.

7   Keeping this type of record can allow a firm to see if a particular ethnic group is under-represented bearing in mind the local population patterns. If so, the firm can investigate the cause. Other areas to look at would be the sex distribution of the workforce - are there any particular trends, how many women are managers, do men work part-time? Age is also relevant - is it an ageing workforce or a young one, or is there a good mix?

8   Some examples of dismissal that would automatically be considered unfair include dismissal purely on grounds of pregnancy, dismissal for participating in union activities or for joining a union, dismissal for taking steps to avert dangers to health and safety at work, and dismissal on grounds of racial discrimination.

9   Bert would receive 1.5 weeks pay for each year of service = 15 weeks money.

Assignment 10   (2 hour)

Scenario

Fido Cars PLC is a small British car manufacturer. The firm has seen better times and sales of their current range are disappointing. Yamahoho, the Japanese motor cycle manufacturer, has suggested a pooling of resources to design and build a supermini class car for the millennium. Management at Fido are keen to participate but recognise that their current organisation will need to change significantly in order to work in the flexible and task-oriented way demanded by best Japanese practice. One area they have immediately identified is the number of trade unions with which they have to deal. These includes TGWU (Transport and General Workers' Union) - for most of the shop floor workers, GMB (General, Municipal, Boilermakers union) - for the rest of the shop floor workers and warehouse staff, AUEW (Amalgamated Union of Engineering Workers) - for staff working in the engineering and design department, MSF (Manufacturing, Science, and Finance Union) - for staff working in the administration and sales departments, RMT (National Union of Rail, Maritime, and Transport Workers) - for six staff working in the service section. Each union has representatives (or shop stewards) on a Joint Consultative Committee and the JCC is headed up by a Convenor whose role is to try to bring together all the different interests represented by the six trade unions.

Task

What are the advantages for (a) the employer and (b) the employee for all workers to be represented by a single trade union? Prepare this as a question-and-answer handout that can be issued with the payslips for all employees.

PUBLISHING

Chapter 11:
BUSINESS ETHICS

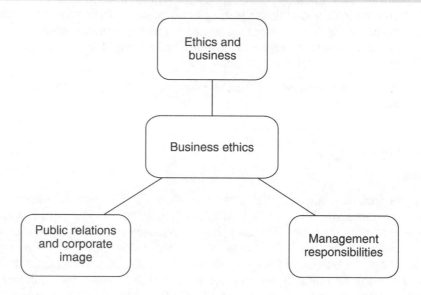

Introduction

Social responsibility and ethical issues relate to many aspects of the firm: its environment; its culture, and management practice. It is one of the firm's objectives or goals. However, it is the nature of ethics to deny easy answers; in the context of business, ethical prescriptions have to be practical to be of any use.

One way of discussing the social responsibility of firms is by using the concept of stakeholder analysis. However, some argue that the purpose of business is business, and nothing else.

Your objectives

In this chapter you will learn about:

(a)   How firms express their ethical codes

(b)   How ethical behaviour can be enforced in organisations

1 ETHICS AND BUSINESS

'Ethics' is about the codes of moral principles that people follow with respect to what is right or wrong. Ethical principles are not necessarily enforced by law, although the law can incorporate moral judgements (murder is 'wrong' ethically, and is also punishable legally).

1.1 Ethics

Ethical codes are rooted in a wider value system, as to what is right or wrong. Is killing always wrong? What about killing in self defence? For example, there are conflicting views and continuing debates about such questions as:

(a) Criteria for distribution of profit

(b) The relative pay and rewards for all employees - from directors to junior staff

(c) Decisions about priorities, for example in respect of public expenditure

(d) Loan charges, ie payment of interest to lenders of money

(e) The sale of harmful products, eg tobacco

People who work for organisations bring their own values into work with them. These can be personal (eg deriving from a person's upbringing, religious or non-religious beliefs, political opinions, personality) and professional (eg code of ethics, medical ethics). The way the organisation behaves also has an ethical dimension.

Some organisation specialists suggest that ethical decisions are becoming more important as penalties (in the US at least) for companies that break the law become tougher. (This might be contrasted with UK, where a fraudster whose deception ran into millions received a sentence of community service.)

(a) A *compliance-based* approach is primarily designed to ensure that the company acts within the letter of the law, and that violations are prevented, detected and punished. Some organisations, faced with the legal consequences of 'unethical behaviour' are attempting to define how the idea of *social responsibility* affects business. This gives a wider approach than mere adherence to the letter of the law, and avoiding problems such as bribery (discussed later).

(b)   This *integrity-based approach* takes a wider view, based on promoting ethical behaviour in the business by building it into the very assumptions with which people go about their work.

Table 11.1 indicates some of the differences between the two approaches.

Area	Compliance	Integrity
Ethos	Knuckle under to external standards	Choose ethical standards
Objective	Keep to the law	Enable legal and responsible conduct
Originators	Lawyers	Management, with lawyers, HR specialists etc.
Methods (both include education, and audits, controls, penalties)	Reduced employee discretion	Leadership, organisation systems
Behavioural assumptions	People are solitary self-interested beings	People are social beings with values
Standards	The law	Company values, aspirations (including law)
Staffing	Lawyers	Managers and lawyers
Education	The law, compliance system	Values, the law, compliance Systems
Activities	Develop standards, train and communicate, handle reports of misconduct, investigate, enforce, oversee compliance	Integrate values into company systems, provide guidance and consultation, identify and resolve problems, oversee compliance

Table 11.1 Compliance v. integrity based approaches to ethics

In other words, an integrity-based approach incorporates issues of ethics in corporate procedure and systems.

Activity 1   **(5 minutes)**

A business may be strictly operated on principles that strive to be:

(a)   Moral and legal
(b)   Immoral and legal
(c)   Moral but illegal
(d)   Immoral and illegal

Try to list one example of current business practice that would fit each heading.

An example of the difference between the legality and ethicality of a practice is the sale in some countries of defective products without appropriate warnings. Companies trading internationally often discover that conduct that infringes recognised standards of human rights and decency is legal in some jurisdictions.

The compliance approach also over-emphasises the threat of detection and punishment in order to channel appropriate behaviour. Arguably, some employers view compliance programmes as an 'insurance policy' for senior management, who can cover the tracks of their arbitrary management practices. After all, some performance targets are impossible to achieve without cutting corners: managers can escape responsibility by blaming the employee for not following the compliance programme, when to do so would have meant a failure to reach target.

Furthermore, mere compliance with the law is no guide to behaviour that sets an example and is above reproach.

Many modern companies are publishing the terms under which they choose to operate as a 'code of ethics', although this may also be published under different titles (such as a code of conduct, principles of conduct, guidelines, operating principles, company objectives or a staff handbook).

Activity 2   **(40 minutes)**

Conduct a brief survey of newspapers or business journals. Try to find some examples of companies who specifically state their code of practice or ethical stance on business issues.

There are differing views about the extent to which external environmental constraints modify business objectives and form boundaries to the exercise of management discretion.

1.2 Stakeholder views

The *stakeholder* view of company objectives is that many groups of people have a stake in what the company does. Shareholders own the business, but there are also suppliers, managers, workers and customers. A business depends on appropriate relationships with these groups. Each of these groups has its own objectives, so that a compromise or balance is required.

The ethical environment refers to justice, respect for the law and a moral code. The conduct of an organisation, its management and employees will be measured against ethical standards by the customers, suppliers and other members of the public with whom they deal.

Below we identify some ethical problems that managers face.

1.3 Ethical problems facing managers

Managers have a duty (in most enterprises) to aim for profit. At the same time, modern ethical standards impose a duty to guard, preserve and enhance the value of the enterprise for the good of all touched by it, including the general public. Large organisations tend to be more often held to account over this than small ones. The types of ethical problem a manager may meet with in practice are very numerous. A few of them are suggested in the following paragraphs.

In the area of products and production, managers have a responsibility to ensure that the public and their own employees are protected from danger. Attempts to increase profitability by cutting costs may lead to dangerous working conditions or to inadequate safety standards in products. In the United States, product liability litigation is so common that this legal threat may be a more effective deterrent than general ethical standards. The Consumer Protection Act 1987 and EU legislation generally is beginning to ensure that ethical standards are similarly 'enforced' in the UK.

EXAMPLE: DEVELOPMENT RISK

The pharmaceutical industry is one where the problem of product liability is particularly acute. On the one hand managers may be influenced by a genuine desire to benefit the community by developing new drugs that at the same time will lead to profits; on the other hand, they must not skimp their research on possible side-effects in rushing to launch the new product. In the UK, the Consumer Protection Act 1987 attempts to recognise this dilemma. Drugs companies are not held liable for side-effects that could not have been foreseen by scientific knowledge, as it existed, at the time the drug was developed - the 'development risk' defence.

Ethical issues also arise in the area of corporate governance and finance. An example is provided by the various allegations made against the Maxwell empire and some accusations that companies are over zealous in their use of creative accounting techniques.

Another ethical problem concerns *payments by companies to officials* (particularly officials in foreign countries) who have power to help or hinder the payers' operations. There are fine distinctions in this area.

(a)   *Extortion*. In some countries officials have been known to threaten companies with the complete closure of their local operations unless suitable payments are made.

(b)   *Bribery*. This refers to payments for services to which a company is not legally entitled. There are some fine distinctions to be drawn; for example, some managers regard political contributions as bribery.

(c)   *Grease money*. Multinational companies are sometimes unable to obtain services to which they are legally entitled because of deliberate stalling by local officials. Cash payments to the right people may then be enough to oil the machinery of bureaucracy.

(d)   *Gifts*. In some cultures (such as Japan) gifts are regarded as an essential part of civilised negotiation, even in circumstances where to Western eyes they might appear ethically dubious. Managers operating in such a culture may feel at liberty to adopt the local customs.

A difficult area for managers concerns the extent to which an organisation's activities may appear to give support to *undesirable political policies*. The boycotting of goods and services from South Africa, when it was run by the apartheid regime, is an example.

Business ethics are also relevant to competitive behaviour. This is because a market can only be 'free' if competition is, in some basic respects, fair. There is a distinction between competing aggressively and competing unethically. The dispute between British Airways and Virgin centred around issues of business ethics, and *allegations* of:

(a)   The theft of information

(b)   The planting of inaccurate and derogatory stories in the press

(c)   The refusal of normal aircraft service to Virgin (when it was offered to other airlines)

(d)   An unfair price war

FOR DISCUSSION

Look at the following scenarios. Which would you say merely involve aggressive competition and which would you say involve unethical practices?

(a)   The Widget Company buy up advertising space so that they can place their advertisements directly opposite those of their main competitor Widgets Incorporated. They intend to match whatever statements are made by Widgets with better ones of their own.

(b)   A company is very worried as it feels that they are losing a competitive battle with a rival. They decide to hire a private detective to follow the Chairman of their rival company in order to gather information about his private life, which they will then use to instigate a smear campaign against him. They hope that the resulting publicity will lead to his resignation and produce turmoil in the management structure.

(c)   The Sweetness Sugar Company engages a team of scientists to discover possible risks associated with the use of artificial sweeteners in place of sugar. A discovery is made that doses of artificial sweetener several thousand times more than any person would be subjected to may cause cancer in rats. The sugar company publish this information and makes it the basis of a major advertising campaign to convert people back to using sugar.

Next we examine some examples of management responsibility.

2   MANAGEMENT RESPONSIBILITIES

The stakeholder view suggests that management is responsible not only to the organisation's owners (shareholders), but also has responsibilities to:

(a) Employees

(b) Customers

(c) Suppliers

(d) Competitors

(e) The local community

(f) The general public (and government)

We start with looking at responsibilities to employees.

2.1 Responsibilities to employees

An organisation's broad responsibilities to its employees may be similar to the following example.

EXAMPLE: UNITED BISCUITS AND ITS EMPLOYEES

The following is drawn from a code used by United Biscuits.

'To achieve the dynamic morale and team spirit based on mutual confidence without which a business cannot be successful, people have to be cared for during their working lives and in retirement. In return we expect, from all our staff, loyalty and commitment to the company. We respect the rights and innate worth of the individual. In addition to being financially rewarding, working life should provide as much job satisfaction as possible. The company encourages all employees to be trained and developed to achieve their full potential.

United Biscuits takes a responsible attitude towards employment legislation requirements and codes of practice, union activities and communications with staff. We place the highest priority on promoting and preserving the health and safety of employees. Employees, for their part, have a clear duty to take every reasonable precaution to avoid injury to themselves, their colleagues and members of the public.'

General principles have to be converted into practice, and should take the form of good pay and working conditions, and good training and development schemes. They should also extend into:

(a) Recruitment policy, and

(b) Redundancy and retirement policies

Recruitment of new staff should be done as carefully as possible, because if an organisation recruits an individual who turns out to be bad at the job, the company has to sack them. Dismissals are inevitable in any large organisation, but careful recruitment methods should manage to keep such demoralising incidents down to a small number.

Staff who are about to retire, after years of service with the organisation, should be provided for in their *retirement*.

(a) The organisation might have a good pension scheme.

(b) One of the problems for retired people is learning what to do with their leisure time. Some organisations provide training courses and discussion groups for employees who are coming up for retirement, to help them to plan their future time constructively.

Dealing with *redundancies* is a more difficult problem. Even for organisations that show an ethical sense of responsibility towards their employees, there may be occasions when parts of the business have to be closed down, and jobs lost. In such a situation, the organisation:

(a) Should try to redeploy as many staff as possible, without making them redundant, and

(b) Where necessary, should provide retraining to give staff the skills to do a new job

For those staff who are made redundant, the organisation should take steps to help them to get a job elsewhere. Measures could include:

(a) Counselling individuals to give them suggestions about what they might try to do

(b) Providing retraining, or funds for training, in other skills that the employees could use in other organisations and industries.

(c) Arranging 'job fairs', by inviting other employers to come and display the jobs that they have on offer, and to discuss job opportunities with redundant employees

(d) Providing good redundancy payments, which employees might be able to use to set up in business themselves, or which at least should tide them over until they find employment again

Next we consider responsibilities towards the customers of a business.

2.2 Responsibilities to customers

Ethical responsibilities towards customers are mainly those of providing a product or service of a quality that customers expect, and of dealing honestly and fairly with customers.

The guidelines of United Biscuits plc again provide a good example of how these responsibilities might be expressed.

EXAMPLE: UNITED BISCUITS AND ITS CUSTOMERS

'UB's reputation for integrity is the foundation on which the mutual trust between the company and its customers is based. That relationship is the key to our trading success.

Both employees and customers need to know that products sold by any of our operating companies will always meet their highest expectations. The integrity of our products is sacrosanct and implicit in the commitment is an absolute and uncompromising dedication to quality. We will never compromise on recipes or specification of products in order to save costs. Quality improvement must always be our goal.

No employee may give money or any gift of significant value to a customer if it could reasonably be viewed as being done to gain a business advantage. Winning an order by violating this policy or by providing free or extra services, or unauthorised contract terms, is contrary to our trading policy.'

Suppliers are another important group towards whom a business may be thought to have responsibilities.

2.3 Responsibilities to suppliers

The responsibilities of an organisation towards its suppliers are expressed mainly in terms of trading relationships.

(a) The organisation's size could give it considerable power as a buyer. One ethical guideline might be that the organisation should not use its power unscrupulously (eg to force the supplier to lower his prices under threat of withdrawing business).

(b) Suppliers might rely on getting prompt payment in accordance with the terms of trade negotiated with its customers. Another ethical guideline is that an organisation should not delay payments to suppliers beyond the agreed credit period.

(c) All information obtained from suppliers and potential suppliers should be kept confidential.

(d) All suppliers should be treated fairly, and this means:

    (i) Giving potential new suppliers a chance to win some business, and also

    (ii) Maintaining long-standing relationships that have been built up over the years with some suppliers. Long-established suppliers should not be replaced unless there is a significant commercial advantage for the organisation from such a move.

Organisations also have some responsibilities towards competitors.

2.4 Responsibilities to competitors

Some ethical responsibilities should exist towards competitors. United Biscuits again provides a good example.

EXAMPLE: UNITED BISCUITS AND ITS COMPETITORS

'We compete vigorously, energetically, untiringly but we also compete ethically and honestly. Our competitive success is founded on excellence - of product and service. We have no need to disparage our competitors either directly or by implication or innuendo....

No-one may attempt improperly to acquire a competitor's trade secrets or other proprietary or confidential information. 'Improper' means are activities such as industrial espionage, hiring competitors' employees to get confidential information, urging competitive personnel or customers to disclose confidential information, or any other approach which is not completely open and above board.'

Responsibilities regarding competition are by no means solely directed by ethics however: there is also a great deal of law surrounding the conduct of fair trading, monopolies, mergers, anti-competitive practices, abuses of a dominant market position and restrictive trade practices.

Finally, we consider responsibilities towards the wider community.

2.5 Responsibilities towards the community

An organisation is a part of the community that it serves, and it should be responsible for:

(a) Upholding the social and ethical values of the community

(b) Contributing towards the well-being of the community, eg by sponsoring local events and charities, or providing facilities for the community to use (eg sports fields)

(c) Responding constructively to complaints from local residents or politicians (eg about problems for local traffic caused by the organisation's delivery vehicles)

EXAMPLE: EMBASSY REGAL

In 1993, it was reported in various UK newspapers that children in a number of towns in the north of England were beginning to use the word 'Reg' as a term of abuse, replacing 'Wally' as a generic term to denote stupidity, grossness etc. This came from advertisements for Embassy Regal cigarettes. ('Reg on train spotting: "There's one!"')

Although the company claimed that the advertisements were not directly aimed at children and, like all cigarette advertising, are supposedly aimed at existing smokers, the company withdrew the campaign after fears were voiced that youngsters were proving susceptible to it.

Activity 3   **(40 minutes)**

The Heritage Carpet Company is a London-based retailer that imports carpets from Turkey, Iran and India. The company was founded by two Europeans who travelled independently through these countries in the 1970s. The company is the sole customer for carpets made in a number of villages in each of the source countries. The carpets are hand woven. Indeed, they are so finely woven that the process requires that children be used to do the weaving, as their small fingers are required for the task. The company believes that it is preserving a 'craft', and the directors believe that this is a justifiable social objective.

Recently a UK television company reported unfavourably on child exploitation in the carpet weaving industry. There were reports of children working twelve hour shifts in poorly lit sheds and cramped conditions, with consequent deterioration in eyesight, muscular disorders and a complete lack of education. The examples cited bear no relation to the Heritage Carpet Company's suppliers, although children are used in the labour force, but there has been a spate of media attention. The regions in which the Heritage Carpet Company's supplier villages are found are soon expected to enjoy rapid economic growth.

Explain the issues that are raised for the Heritage Carpet Company.

---

3 PUBLIC RELATIONS AND CORPORATE IMAGE

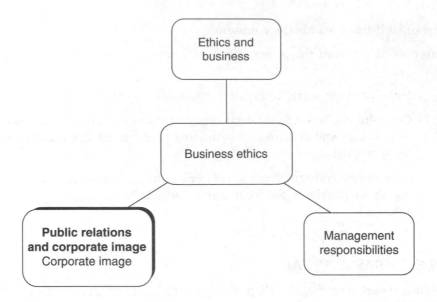

3.1 Corporate image

Corporate image describes the public attitude towards a company, or the image of the company in the mind of the general public and, perhaps more specifically, in the minds of potential customers. It is possible to promote a desired corporate image through a combination of public relations, advertising and the experience and attitudes built up by customers over the years. (For example, the favourable corporate image of Marks and Spencer grew up over many years, without the need for substantial PR or advertising.)

There are various reasons why an organisation might attempt to build up a corporate image.

(a) The organisation may want to strengthen customer loyalty, and so a corporate image of good quality products and services, and concern for the customer's interests, could be fostered.

(b) Rather than strengthen customer loyalty, a corporate image might be developed to create customer awareness. Some companies have faced the problem that customers do not know what they are and have never heard of them. A corporate image is then needed to give the company a public identity (eg Racal plc spent large sums advertising itself as one of the largest companies no one had ever heard of).

(c) Corporate image can strengthen an employee's attachment to the company for which he or she work, because of corporate identity. People may want to work for a company because of its image in the mind of the public ('prestige' jobs) or because the company has a 'get-ahead' image.

(d) Some companies may wish to develop a corporate image of social responsibility, in order to avoid unfavourable legislation, to prevent adverse publicity or to prevent pressure from stakeholder groups. Examples of this motive are:

(i) The attempt by oil companies to establish an image of caring for the environment and for the future needs of society

(ii) The attempt by British Nuclear Fuels to promote an image of deepest concern for the environment

(iii) The attempt by fur traders to counter the adverse publicity built up against them by the efforts of animal rights activists, and

(iv) The efforts of independent TV companies to promote an image of 'quality' programme-makers, to strengthen their chances of winning a bid for franchises

(e) Some companies may wish to have a favourable corporate image that they can subsequently use to win public and political support.

(f) A good corporate image has a variety of benefits for management, in addition to strengthening customer loyalty. An image of a sound, well-established company might encourage investors to put more money into the business, and suppliers to grant longer credit.

Market research by MORI has shown that:

(a) Two out of every three people in the UK believe that a company that has a good reputation would not sell poor quality products (this suggests that customers would be more willing to try a new product if it is promoted by a well-known corporate name than if it is made by an unknown company), and

(b) Nine times out of ten, the better known a company is, the more highly it is regarded

Activity 4 **(15 minutes)**

A company manufacturing baby food, in a very competitive market, has received in private, a disturbing phone call. Some cartons of its product have been tampered with, and contain shards of broken glass. The affected cartons are already for sale in chemists and supermarkets. What would be the most ethical approach to deal with this problem? Which of the following do you think would be in the best interests of the company?

(a) Withdraw all goods from sale?

(b) Take out warning advertisements in newspapers?

(c) Assume a hoax, but offer substantial compensation to people whose children were affected, in return for their silence if the threats turn out to be true?

Give reasons for your answer.

Chapter roundup

- The stakeholder view holds that there are many groups in society with an interest in the organisation's activities. Some firms have objectives for these interests. Some argue, however, that a business's only objective should be to make money: the state, representing the public interest, can levy taxes to spend on socially desirable projects or can regulate organisational activities.

- Firms have to ensure they obey the law: but they also face ethical concerns, because their reputations depend on a good image.

- Inside the organisation, a compliance-based approach highlights conformity with the law. An integrity-based approach suggests a wider remit, incorporating ethics in the organisation's values and culture.

- Organisations sometimes issue codes of conduct to employees. Many employees are bound by professional codes of conduct.

Quick quiz

1 Distinguish between responsibilities and boundaries.

2 What ethical problems face management?

3 To whom might management have responsibilities, and what are some of these responsibilities?

4 Describe two approaches to the management of ethics in an organisation.

5 What responsibilities have managers to persons other than their organisation?

6 What might shareholders argue is the main responsibility of an organisation?

7 Why is it good PR for a business to show it has social responsibility?

8 List some *stakeholders* management is responsible to.

9 List some ways in which a business can demonstrate its responsibility to employees.

10 What factors contribute to a 'good' corporate image?

11 How can government ensure that business contributes to the well being of society?

12 What is the role of the PR department?

Answers to quick quiz

1 Responsibility is something you are likely to be called into account for if you fail to exercise it. A boundary is a limit beyond which you cannot go. In business terms, responsibilities are things you ought to do, boundaries are rules that must not be broken, or limits that you are obliged to remain within. For example, a haulage firm should instruct its drivers to drive carefully and be considerate to other road users, but they are not obliged to do so. However, all lorries must be fitted by law with a tacograph and drivers must only drive within their permitted hours.

2 Management has a duty to aim for profit. They also have a duty to maintain the ethical stance of the company. Sometimes it can appear that the two conflict. The problem then is which comes first, profit or ethics?

3 Management has responsibilities to almost anyone who comes into contact with the business.

For example, responsibilities to employees for their safety and welfare, responsibility to customers under consumer safety legislation, responsibility to shareholders to protect their interests, legal responsibilities of corporate governance and financial dealings, responsibility to the general public - pollution, image, advertising etc.

4 See Section 1.1 for the *compliance-based approach* and the *integrity-based approach*.

5 Customers, suppliers, competitors, the general public, the state.

6 Shareholders might argue that the main responsibility of management is to make a profit.

7   It can enhance the corporate image of the company. This can lead to increased sales, customer loyalty, employee loyalty and desirable shares.

8   Stakeholders could include shareholders, employees, customers, suppliers, competitors, the local community, the general public and government.

9   Good pay and working conditions, good training and advancement opportunities, good retirement packages, social aspects.

10   Factors that could contribute to a 'good' corporate image include, being a responsible employer, dealing fairly with suppliers and customers, good quality products leading to few customer complaints, clear statements of company policy, avoidance of unethical investments or trading practices.

11   Government can legislate to enforce certain types of behaviour, eg product standards legislation, safety rules, consumer law, pollution regulations. It can also tax businesses so that they contribute to the society within which they operate. It can ask the business community to become involved in an advisory capacity or to contribute to debates on employment or education.

12   The role of the public relations department is to maintain the good image of the company at all times. Sometimes, when a company is new or is not well known, an image needs to be created. The role when the company has transgressed is of damage limitation.

Answers to activities

1   (a)   A company that promotes itself as acting morally and legally is the Body Shop.

(b)   An activity that could be classed as immoral and legal could be selling arms to brutal military dictators.

(c)   An activity that could be seen as moral but illegal would be the publishing of stolen, but revelatory, documents about government mismanagement, eg a 'leak' of secret information.

(d)   An activity that could be classed as immoral and illegal would be the drugs trade.

2   Companies that appear to have clear ethical codes and promote these widely include the Body Shop, The Co-operative Bank (advertises the fact that it does not invest in arms dealers etc), Daewoo (which has clear codes about customer care), and Café Direct (which imports coffee from third world countries in order to assist their economic development). There are also a number of insurance and unit trust companies that specialise in ethical investments.

3   Many issues are raised in this situation. This is a case partly about boundary management and partly about enlightened self-interest and business ethics. The adverse publicity, although not about the Heritage Carpet Company's own suppliers, could rebound badly - potential customers might be put off. Economic growth in the area may also mean that parents will soon prefer to send their children to school than to work. The Heritage Carpet Company, as well as promoting itself as preserving a craft, could reinvest some of its profits in the villages (eg by funding a school), or by enforcing limits on the hours children work. It could also pay a decent wage. It could advertise this in a 'code of ethics', so that customers are reassured that the children are not simply being exploited.

Alternatively, it could not import child-made carpets at all. (This policy, however, would be unlikely to help communities in which child labour is an economic necessity.)

4   This is similar to a case in the US. The affected company withdrew all its products for sale, and better security procedures were installed at the factory. An advertising campaign was instituted to reach people who had purchased the product. This draconian approach earned the company public goodwill. You might also find it interesting to compare the actions taken by various businesses over the uncertainties about BSE ('mad cow disease').

Assignment 11   (2 hours)

Scenario

You are employed as a management trainee for a large engineering company, GREG Engineering PLC. You work in the Company Secretary's office. The company secretary is Anthea Topcoat and is newly appointed. Her Grandfather is Gregory Topcoat, the founder of the company, and her father and uncle are, respectively, the chief executive and chairman of the board of Directors. Anthea herself has worked in most departments in the company, has a degree in Engineering and has just completed an MBA at Harvard University where she specialised in Business Ethics.

At a recent board meeting, concern was raised by certain non-executive directors at the apparent level of 'inducements' that were allegedly being accepted by managers at GREG Engineering from suppliers seeking to encourage orders to be placed with their companies. The directors had no firm details about the extent of the problem but felt that it was a matter that ought to raised as an issue of policy. On checking the records, it was noted that there were no guidelines for staff with purchasing powers as to the acceptability of receiving items from suppliers. In fact it was noted that the old man Gregory himself regularly took delivery of a case of single malt scotch from the main supplier of machine tools right up until his retirement at the age of 87.

Following discussion, it was agreed that the issue should be investigated to discover the extent of the problem, and guidelines would be drawn-up to safeguard the interests of both employees and the company.

Information

GREG Engineering PLC has 3500 employees, of whom some 225 have some responsibility of placing orders with suppliers. When questioned, most had in fact been given items from suppliers as a reward for being 'good customers'. Most of these items were of relatively low value, such as calendars, pens, bottles of wine or spirits and were usually given at Christmas. There were a number of examples of more significant gifts, including the case of single malt whisky that was now being given to the Production Manager every year. A couple of items were more substantial: the corporate sales manager was 'loaned' a high-performance sports car for six months just after agreeing to a new purchase of fleet cars, and the office manager was given a Multimedia Pentium PC for use in her home so that she could judge how effective a machine it was when considering the upgrade of 200 PCs in the administration department (in fact the order went to a different company). The company does itself provide gifts for its own customers; last year these were a calendar and a desk diary with the company logo and pictures of products.

Task

The Company Secretary has asked you to prepare a first draft of a company policy on the acceptance of gifts for all employees. While the board has no wish to prevent employees accepting gifts, it does want a system that registers the acceptance of gifts over a certain value and defines a procedure whereby permission for gifts over a certain value are granted by senior managers or the board itself.

ANSWERS TO ASSIGNMENTS

BPP PUBLISHING

Some of these are full answers and some are guidelines only, especially where you have been required to conduct your own research and/or base your assignment on an organisation with which you are familiar.

Answer to Assignment 1

The experience of former Eastern European countries has shown that there is no single recipe for success and the same might be said of this assignment. Dolminia has many advantages not shared by some other former Warsaw Pact countries, but it also has many of the disadvantages. Students should show evidence that they have researched the progress of one or more eastern European countries and have drawn logical conclusions on the possible way forward for Dolminia.

(a)   Dolminia has a number of options for possible privatisation. The most straightforward is likely to be the moped company Hosper, since it is likely already to be organised along industrial lines and may be a likely candidate for a management buy-out. It is likely that the EU 'know-how' fund could be of use for the new management team and students obtaining the best grades are likely to refer to this initiative.

The second most likely area for privatisation is agriculture. Successful experiments even prior to the collapse of the Soviet Union have shown that farms and agricultural enterprises adapt quickly to the market system and can achieve considerable growth of productivity and output given the profit incentive. Wine in particular would seem to be a logical candidate given the increase in demand for wines across Europe and the rest of the world and in light of the early contribution a successful wine industry might make to the country's balance of payments. This has proved to be a success in other ex-communist countries like Romania and Hungary.

The third most likely candidate relates to tourism, as some expertise has already developed (in quality 'tourism' for important customers). However, the difficulty here might be concerned with the structure of the enterprise: balancing the advantage of a large operator able to work with external tour companies against the relative inexperience of scale in such operations. In such circumstances a semi-governmental agency working with independent hotels or groups might be the best option.

(b)   The tertiary sector of the economy is always the last to develop, so for the foreseeable future it might make sense for this to remain within the governmental sphere of operations. The gold mines might make a good candidate for a joint venture with a western company, but the gold produced could support the purchase of know-how and technology from the west rather than be a source of profit for the newly emerging private sector.

The oil reserves represent the biggest asset of Dolminia and potentially the most useful to 'kick start' the economy. This would only be possible with support from more developed nations, but there is a danger that they might channel profits away from the country. An immature private company is unlikely to represent the best option in this case.

(c)   Candidates should indicate that they appreciate the influence that government can have on development. Students should refer to the incentives in the taxation system for both individuals and organisations as well as the broader role that government can have in encouraging an enterprising culture.

Answer to Assignment 2

For this assignment you need to draw up a sensible plan of action. Try to define the 'key players' in the dispute and target those you will need to influence. You will also need to get some influential people on your side who can help with the campaign.

(a) You might decide to make representations to the following people/bodies:

- Minister for Education

- Association of Vice-Chancellors

- The MP local to your university/college

- The MEP

- Most universities have a Chancellor who is an influential person - try to enlist his or her help

- The students at your university

- The Students' Union

- The University lecturers' unions

- Varying media outlets - the *Times Higher Educational Supplement*, any newspapers, local and national TV, local and national radio, journals

In addition you might want to produce a poster campaign or leaflets to hand out.

All this action needs to be co-ordinated. Work out what your priorities would be and who would do what.

(b) With this scenario you would need to be very diplomatic in your approach. First, arm yourself with useful information and use this to assist when presenting your points to management. Remember - people don't want to lose their jobs - they just want to try and change the policy. Strike action or other industrial action should always be a last resort.

Tactics to try are as follows.

- Meeting with Personnel Department to find out the reasons behind the management decision.

- Information gathering - contact organisations such as The Institute of Personnel Development, Health Education Council, drugs awareness organisations to see what the extent of the problem is.

- Try to gather statistics about the number of problems encountered in your workplace over the last 5 years.

- Canvass staff for their opinions - are lots of people concerned or only a few?

- Enlist help - bring the relevant Trade Unions to assist. Organisations like the National Council for Civil Liberties may get involved.

- Present your views to management - be prepared for what they might say eg 'If you've got nothing to hide it shouldn't be a problem.'

In this type of scenario, tact and diplomacy are paramount - the aim should be to reach an amicable solution to the problem, therefore an outside publicity campaign which embarrasses your employer may be counter-productive.

Answer to Assignment 3

Your answers will be specific to the particular company selected. If there is a real problem with finding a company in your locality you may wish to look at a larger company such as Nestle, Muller (yoghurts), Mars or Ford.

You may find that it is a good idea to visit the company selected and perhaps interview a manager who can help you with the questions. But remember not to make a nuisance of yourself by badgering busy business people.

You will find that most UK-based companies that have moved into Europe on a wider basis have had to alter their marketing strategy to take into account language and cultural differences.

Changes in trading practices could involve staff contracts, product specifications, transportation, legislative differences (although this is becoming less of a problem as the process of harmonisation begins to work).

Outline of the company - what does the company do? Which countries does it operate in? Does it have factories or outlets in more than one country? Does it mainly export or import goods/services? How big is the business? Who owns the business - are they British or some other nationality?

Marketing aspects - how does the company conduct its market research? How does it advertise/promote the product/service? Has the company had help from the Government (for example the Department of Trade and Industry) in gaining contacts, knowledge, experience in a particular country? Has the company received help from the EU in getting established in Europe? Did the company have to revise its product, promotions, pricing to compete in different countries? What packaging, labelling and product names had to change. (For example, think about why Marathon bars became Snickers. Why wouldn't the Swedish toilet roll brand called 'Krapp' sell well here?)

What type of people buy the company's products? How does the firm communicate with its customer?

Does the firm only have local competitors, national competitors or is there international competition?

Did the company have to adapt to new laws or working practices? Were there differences in salary structures? Were there differences in Health and Safety rules or product standards? Were there different rules about obtaining premises?

Answer to Assignment 4

Successful groups will have undertaken research into the tele-cottaging movement and given a definition of what a tele-cottage is. They will have identified the reasons why many have been so successful. The presentation will address the main issues identifying the advantages of tele-cottages against other types of working, the difficulties for commercial organisations in this area and some of the considerations that would have to be addressed, as follows.

Advantages of tele-cottages

- Near to workers' homes, fewer transport and commuting problems

- Bring work into rural areas

- Cheap to run

- Save on office maintenance costs

- Better working environment than a city or town

- Provide for social interaction

- Bring together technological expertise

Difficulties for commercial organisations

- Have tended to be run mainly by charities and rural development agencies to date

- Many of the prime sites have already been developed

- There could be some considerable expenditure initially to provide the necessary electronic infrastructure

Considerations

- Is it profitable?

- Are there any sites left?

- Problems involved in moving to a new location very different from the norm.

- Does the company have the expertise to run and service the centre?

Answer to Assignment 5

You will need to demonstrate that you understand how the material in this chapter may be used in practice.

You should look at factors determining demand which may affect your product or service. How will your product or service be affected by others? Consider the implications of consumers' incomes and other social factors. Can you suggest what price and income elasticity might be for your product?

Answer to Assignment 6

You will need to demonstrate that you understand how the material in this chapter may be used in practice.

You should consider: how supply is affected by price and your proposed prices; the implications of prices of other products/services; your costs; changes in technology and other factors which may be beyond your control; your response to any such changes; customers' perceptions of your product or service and your competitors' prices.

Answer to Assignment 7

(a) You should have investigated the marketing for each of the three product groups and identified the main types of promotional activities for each. These are:

Music: mainly reliant on product placement on radio and television by use of 'pluggers' who encourage radio and television producers to include the product on the play list. Will often involve 'below the line' marketing that provides incentives for those able to provide air play. Traditionally groups undertake promotional activities that might include giving interviews, making guest appearances and doing 'newsworthy'

things to heighten their profile. This activity is often supported by some advertising on television and radio as well as in the printed media.

Video: often similar to music promotion with guesting on TV and in the media, some advertising - but usually with far more links with producers of other products. These often take the form of competitions or give aways such as in the case of a Star Trek movie where purchase of a breakfast serial includes a free Klingon face mask plus the chance to enter a prize draw to win the chance to meet a real Tribble in their own home.

Games: these have traditionally been promoted through advertising on television and in the printed media. Changes in the nature of games have resulted in promotional activities that are closer to both music and video, particularly where there has been a tie-in, for example in the 'Waterworld' game, which feeds from the success of the film or video. Increasingly, interactive games have stars appearing as characters in them and often the sound track is produced by famous musicians or groups who then promote their involvement.

(b) You will have to identify considerable commonalties and will identify a number of cross-over products that already exist.

(c) You will use the best and most effective example of each method and should draw out some ideas for an integrated approach to the new product type.

(d) You may come up with suggestions for names based on the characteristics of the new products or on the technology used to deliver the product. Phillips used the title 'Interactive CD', while Microsoft use 'CD-ROM'.

Answer to Assignment 8

Task 1

All the products listed have had some issues of concern.

Bleach: concerns about bleach entering the water system. Concerns about dioxins leaching from the product and poisoning users of bleached articles such as tampons, nappies, tissues etc.

Biological soap powder: damage caused to washing. Concerns about allergic reactions in users. Damage to flora and fauna due to powder not being biodegradable when it enters the water system.

Disposable nappies: difficult to dispose of. Problems with users flushing nappies down the toilet - sewage. Dioxins leaching out of bleached products. Amount of paper consumption in production.

Diesel vehicles: airborne particulates entering the atmosphere. Smog. Originally seen as 'greener' than petrol vehicles, which encouraged sales. Diesel buses - smell. Increase in asthma in population.

Mahogany furniture: depleting resource. Not easily sustainable. Destruction of eco-systems in the third world. Deforestation.

Beefburgers: allegations made re deforestation - logging in rain forests. Use of hormone growth agents in cattle. Concerns about BSE ('mad cow disease').

Eggs: battery farming. Salmonella.

Mobile telephones: noise pollution - irritating. Health risks alleged. Interference with sensitive electronic equipment.

Cable TV: damage to the environment - trees, pavements.

Pesticides: concerns over use of pesticides in fruit and vegetables, particularly apples and root vegetables.

Tasks 2-3

All the companies concerned suffered adverse publicity. They responded in a variety of ways. Some companies initiated wide-ranging publicity campaigns designed to reassure customers, others entered into litigation, others just changed their products. In some cases the response was industry wide and not just managed by one company.

No company did nothing.

Task 4

The leaflet should give customers the facts without scaring them unnecessarily. Where possible, it should give a balanced view of the product and highlight progress made since the scare stories emerged.

Answer to Assignment 9

The memorandum should be in the correct format. It should give clear answers and advice for each customer. Cases should be quoted where relevant and used to back up assertions. The relevant legislation should also be mentioned. You should find other cases to mention - try looking in '*Which?* magazine for up to date consumer disputes.

Mr Bland

Clearly the goods are not 'as described' nor 'fit for the purpose' he had made clear. So there could be some Sale of Goods Act breaches here. He may want to claim compensation. Mr Bland is likely to want more than just a refund since he has been made ill by the product. The cases of *Beale v Taylor* and *Priest v Last* are relevant here. It may be that there are also criminal offences under trades descriptions legislation - the goods may have been falsely described by the assistant.

Ms Spark

The toaster has clearly been labelled in a misleading fashion - the label makes it look as if the toaster has been approved by the BSI. This could amount to a trades description offence. The goods are not as described or of satisfactory quality so the least Ms Spark could expect is a refund. These would be civil matters.

Mr V Gullible

There has probably been a trades descriptions offence here - the goods have been made out to be an expensive designer product when in fact they are not. This was clearly intentional. A prosecution should follow. Mr Gullible is unlikely to have much success with a civil action. The Sale of Goods Act takes into account the circumstances of the purchase and the price paid. If you buy a watch on the market for £2.99 you really cannot be expecting it to be a high quality item. The watch was working until Mr Gullible broke it so he probably has no real complaint in civil law.

Mrs T Hick

The garage has committed a false trade description when buying the car from her - see case of *Fletcher v Budgen*. It should be prosecuted. In civil law Mrs Hick could sue for damages as the garage has made a misrepresentation to her in order to get her to make a contract with it.

Answer to Assignment 10

Fido are caught in a typical British situation where representation for employees has not changed with the times and the company is having to deal with a carryover from earlier days. The key issue for the employers is flexibility and this can only be achieved through a streamlined process of negotiation and consultation. Dealing with a single union will enable the company to incorporate changes into the organisation to enable it survive, and this is also in the long-term interests of the employees. It will also allow them to make considerable savings in administration costs.

For employees, the advantages will relate to the simplicity of a single union arrangement. It will do away with inter-union disputes and will enable the staff representatives to focus on the main issue of getting the best deal for their members.

You should have posed questions that will enable these points to made in a clear and unambiguous way, and couched the answers in appropriate and simple language. The joint declaration from Nissan and AUEW earlier in the chapter make a number of these points in a clear and unambiguous way.

Answer to Assignment 11

The board has recognised that the acceptance of small gifts by employees of the company is acceptable and does not pose any significant risks in terms of good business practice. Employees need to be made aware of what is acceptable and any policy should define three categories of gifts. These might be as follows

(a) Items with a value below £10 that are acceptable on certain occasions such as at Christmas. These would not need to be recorded.

(b) Items with a value of more than £10 but less than £50. Again, these would be acceptable on certain occasions such as Christmas. These would be recorded in a register of gifts held by the personnel department that would be subject to annual review.

(c) Items with a value of more than £50 would be acceptable only in exceptional circumstances and with the prior permission of a senior manager. (In the case of a gift to a senior manager, approval would need to come from the board itself. All such gifts would be recorded in the register of gifts held by the personnel department, which would be subject to annual review.)

The policy should include sanctions for staff who breach the procedures, which would probably link in with the company discipline procedure.

GLOSSARY
AND INDEX

BPP
PUBLISHING

Anti-competitive practice (ACP): a course of conduct that restricts, distorts or prevents competition in the production or acquisition of goods or in the supply of goods and services in the UK.

Barriers to entry: a term used in economics to describe the factors that make it difficult for a new entrant to gain a foothold in an industry.

Capacity: the maximum amount of goods a firm can make. A firm (or industry) with overcapacity is able to produce more than it actually needs to satisfy customers. A firm that is operating at less than full capacity is producing less than it can.

Capital: money used for investing rather than consumption, although in practice the distinction is not hard and fast.

Caveat emptor: let the buyer beware. There is a duty on customers to be careful in their purchases.

Central bank: a bank that acts as banker to the government and other banking institutions; it also acts as the national representative in the international banking community.

Code of practice: lays out a set of procedures and policies that a firm will follow. Adherence to the code is sometimes necessary for membership of certain trade associations.

Collective bargaining: the terms and conditions under which employees work may be the result of agreements reached between employers and trade unions through the process of collective bargaining between employees, represented by a union, and management.

Command economy: sometimes referred to as *state controlled*. In this type of economy, decisions are taken collectively, usually by central planning committees. The government controls what is produced, how much is produced, the price and who the goods are available to.

Commercial rent: rent paid to a landlord who owns capital (for example when renting a house, a car or a television). Commercial rent is not the same as the more specific *economic rent*.

Constitution: the fundamental principles by which a state is governed. This includes the organisation and structure of government.

Consumer credit: borrowing by individuals for domestic consumption (eg food, cars, hi-fi equipment, holidays, cosmetics).

Culture: the sum total of the inherited ideas, belief, values and knowledge that make up the basis of social action.

De-industrialisation: often used to describe the long-term decline in the importance of manufacturing industry and the secondary sector in general.

Demand: the quantity that potential purchasers could buy if the price was set at a certain level; the number of products that people are willing and able to buy at a certain price.

Demography: concerned with the study of population. Demographic information is collected through the national census and is used by many market research organisations to provide a framework for studying how and why consumers buy.

Dependency ratio: the number of children and pensioners for every 100 people of working age.

Disposable income: the amount of money people have to spend. It includes income from all sources, such as salaries and benefits, after tax and rent or mortgage interest are taken into account.

Divestment: a firm gets rid of one of its businesses by closing it down or by selling it to another company. This is often the opposite process to diversification.

Economic rent: a payment made in excess of the payment needed to keep a factor of production, such as land, labour or capital, in current use.

Economies of scale: the reductions in the average cost of producing a commodity in the long run, as the amount of output of the commodity increases. The larger a business is, the more efficiently it can produce.

Embargo on imports: an embargo from one particular country is a total ban, ie effectively a zero quota.

Employers' association: an interest group that is 'an organisation of employers that seeks to assist, influence or control the industrial relations decisions of member firms and/or engage in trade activities on behalf of members'.

Empowerment: a term developed in the US covering the practice of delegating responsibility. Workers are given more control over their own work, with less interference from their supervisors. They also take decisions. In many circumstances it is not so much individuals who are empowered, but teams, which decide collectively how to parcel out the work.

Entrepreneurship: the organising factor in production. An entrepreneur is someone who undertakes the task of organising the other three factors of production in a business enterprise, and who, in doing so, bears the risk of the venture. He or she creates new business ventures. The reward for the entrepreneurship is profit.

Equilibrium price: the price for a good at which the volume demanded by consumers and the volume that firms would be willing to supply are the same.

European Economic Area (EEA): EFTA's link with the EU created a European Economic Area (EEA) with a population of 380 million, so extending the benefits of the EU single market to the EFTA member countries (excluding Switzerland, which stayed out of the EEA).

Exchange rate: the price of one currency in terms of another. If £1 could buy you 8 French francs, that would be the exchange rate.

Executive: implements laws, and perhaps proposes laws to the legislature.

Firm: a wide term for any organisation that carries on a business. In spite of their many differences, we treat firms as single, consistent decision-taking units and, for the purposes of economic analysis, we ignore any differences in decision-making procedures and economic structures between them.

Free enterprise economy: sometimes called capitalism. In this type of economy most decisions are taken through the operation of the *market mechanism*. Supply and demand and the ability to pay influence decision making. There is very little government intervention in business decision making.

Free trade agreements: aim to reduce existing barriers to free trade; to eliminate discrimination in international trade; to prevent the growth of protection by getting member countries to consult with others before taking any protectionist measures.

GDP (gross domestic product): is the result of all economic activity in the economy (even though UK citizens or organisations may receive income from assets abroad, or make payments to foreign individuals or organisations).

Global industry and global competition: imply an industry in which producers in different countries compete with each other, with the emergence of multinational or international companies. A government can put restrictions on global competition by favouring its domestic industries.

GNP (gross national product): is *GDP* inclusive of amounts earned by the UK from overseas assets, but exclusive of amounts paid to overseas holders of UK assets.

Green agenda: within the *natural environment*, this might involve issues such as: destruction of ecosystems, deforestation, ozone depletion, desertification, global warming, threats to water supplies, energy sources, chemical pollution, air pollution, waste management, animal protection and welfare.

Within the *human environment* concerns would relate to: population growth, displacement of indigenous populations, poverty, appropriate development strategies, health, self determination, education, disastrous impacts of human activities, employment, the arms trade, the global division of wealth between 'North and South', cities, working environments, international debt, health problems and food quality.

Green consumption: the decisions directly or indirectly related to consumer choice and usage that involve environmentally related beliefs, values, attitudes, behaviour or choice criteria.

Green economics: a form of economics based on alternative ideas, which include: monetary valuation of environmental resources; promoting the quality of life; self reliance; mutual aid; personal growth and human rights.

High technology: usually used to refer to very complex equipment, for example an airliner.

Household: a person living alone, or a group of people, who have an address as their only or main residence and who either share one meal a day or share the living accommodation. Household size refers to the number of people who normally live there.

BPP
PUBLISHING

Implied terms: terms that are automatically part of a contract whether the parties mention them or not. The implied terms of the SGA cannot be removed from a consumer contract.

Information technology: the result of the combination of computer technology and communications technology.

Insolvency: when a business runs out of cash and cannot pay its debts. The courts may order the business to be closed down and sold off, so that its creditors - people to whom it owes - can be satisfied. Alternatively, the business itself could make the decision to declare itself insolvent before it is forced to do so.

Interest group: a group that represents the wider interests of a particular group of people, such as trades unions. Some groups may be both pressure groups and interest groups, and the terms are often used interchangeably.

Judiciary: arbitrates between citizens, between the state and citizens, and between the legislature and executive branches of the state.

Labour: both the mental and the physical resources of human beings. Labour is rewarded with wages (including 'salaries').

Land: property (the land element only, buildings are capital) and the natural resources that grow on the land or that are extracted from it. Land is rewarded with rent.

Legislation: the act of legislating or the end product of it.

Legislature: the body empowered to make or amend legislation.

Lobbying: a method used to influence political decision making. It involves maintaining regular contact with ministers or members of parliament, to put forward a case.

Market research: finding out information about a particular product or service.

Market segment: a group of customers with certain things in common whose needs can be met with a distinct marketing mix.

Market share: the sales of a good or service by one firm in the industry as a percentage of the sales of the good or service by all companies in the industry.

Marketing research: the objective gathering, recording and analysing of all facts about problems relating to the transfer and sales of goods and services from producer to consumer or user.

Metatechnology: technology that can be used in many different ways.

Mixed economy: in this type of economy there is a balance between market forces and state intervention. The view is taken that certain activities need to be regulated by the state whilst others can be left to the influence of the market. A mixed economy usually comprises a free enterprise sector, public ownership and control of key central industries and a welfare sector to provide a minimum level of medical, social and educational services for all citizens regardless of wealth.

Monopolies: where 25% or more of the goods or services of a particular kind supplied in the UK are supplied either by a single person or to a single person.

Monopsony: a single buyer for a good or service.

Multinational enterprise or **company:** one that owns or controls production facilities or service facilities outside the country in which it is based.

Negligence: to succeed in an action for negligence, the plaintiff (the person taking the matter to court) must show three things: the existence of a duty of care by the defendant; a breach of that duty by the defendant; which results in injury or damage (or in some cases financial loss) suffered by the plaintiff as a foreseeable consequence of the breach of the duty of care.

Office of Fair Trading: a government department which acts on information from the following sources: its own investigations; information provided by local authority trading standards departments; the courts (who inform the DGFT of material convictions); and news media.

Oligopoly: oligopoly may result in a market where there are just a very few large competitors. Competition may be restricted because of this, especially if this is supported by informal agreements between the competitors.

Ombudsman: used to describe the provision of a final independent appeal that a dissatisfied customer may make against what he or she believes to be unfair or incompetent treatment.

Organisation structure: the way in which work is allocated to individuals; how the work is controlled (eg supervisors); the chain of command from the most senior to the most junior person in the organisation; how people and activities are grouped together.

Perfect competition: a state in which there are so many people in the market, and other conditions are such that no-one can influence the price, all other things being equal.

Policy: a way of expressing the broad purposes of government activity in a particular field, with some desired outcome in mind.

Polluter pays principle: aims to relate the damage done by pollution involved in the production of goods and services to the prices of those goods. The intention is to deter potential polluters by making it uneconomic to produce goods and services that also create pollution.

Pressure group: a collection of people promoting some particular course or objective.

Price cartel: also known as a price ring, this is created when a group of oligopoly firms combine to agree on a price at which they will sell their product to the market.

Primary sector: this sector of industry consists of industries that produce raw materials such as crops and minerals.

Privatisation: the transfer of enterprises owned by the state into private hands.

Productivity: a measure of the efficiency with which output has been produced.

Protectionism: occurs where governments try to restrict imports, to protect inefficient domestic producers or to enable domestic firms to grow.

Rationalisation: the reorganisation of a business's operations, often to cut costs and improve efficiency, or to reduce the number of businesses in which the firm operates.

Scenario: an internally consistent view of what the future might turn out to be.

Secondary sector: this sector of industry consists of industries that use the raw material produced by the primary sector.

Shareholder: a person who owns a share of a company. A share entitles the owner to a share in the company's profits. The management of a company is appointed, indirectly, by shareholders and runs the company on the shareholders' behalf.

Society: the collection of all the institutions that make it possible for individuals to share things in common such as work, leisure and family life. It provides protection, security, continuity and an identity for its members.

Stakeholders: the many different groups and individuals whose interests are affected by the activities of a firm.

Subsidiarity: the principle that sets the limits of EU action. Decisions should be taken at the lowest possible level.

Substitute product (or service): a product or service that can stand in for another product or service in satisfying a customer need.

Sunrise industries: rising new industries, such as information technology and genetics. Their importance is increasing worldwide.

Sunset industries: gradually dying industries. In the western economies, they include heavy industries such as steel and shipbuilding, whose prices have been undercut for many years by more efficient producers in Korea and other countries in the Pacific.

Supply: the quantity of a product or service that existing or potential suppliers would want to produce for a given price.

Technical complexity: the extent to which the production process is controllable and its results are predictable.

Technology: equipment, the techniques whereby equipment is used, and the organisation of people, techniques and equipment in work processes.

Tertiary sector: distribution and service industries. Services include activities as diverse as banking, tourism, hairdressing, teaching, office cleaning, tax advice and the media.

Trade deficit: the deficit that occurs when imports are greater than exports.

Trade description: any indication, direct or indirect, of any of the following: quantity, size or gauge of goods; method of manufacture, production, processing or reconditioning; composition of goods fitness for purpose, strength, performance, behaviour or accuracy; any physical characteristics not included in the preceding paragraphs; testing by any person and the results of testing; approval by any person or conformity with a type approved by any person; place or date of manufacture, production, processing or reconditioning; person by whom manufactured, produced, processed or reconditioned; other history, including previous ownership or use.

Trade surplus: an excess of exports over imports.

Trade unions: organised associations of working people in a trade, occupation or industry (or several trades or industries) formed for protection and promotion of their common interests, mainly the regulation and negotiation of pay and conditions.

PUBLISHING

ORDER FORM

Any books from our HNC/HND range can be ordered in one of the following ways:

- Telephone us on **020 8740 2211**

- Send this page to our **Freepost** address

- Fax this page on **020 8740 1184**

- Email us at **publishing@bpp.com**

- Go to our website: **www.bpp.com**

We aim to deliver to all UK addresses inside 5 working days. Orders to all EU addresses should be delivered within 6 working days. All other orders to overseas addresses should be delivered within 8 working days.

BPP Publishing Ltd
Aldine House
Aldine Place
London W12 8AW
Tel: 020 8740 2211
Fax: 020 8740 1184
Email: publishing@bpp.com

Full name: _____

Day-time delivery address: _____

_____

_____ Postcode _____

Day-time telephone (for queries only): _____

Please send me the following books:

		No. of copies	Price	Total
Core				
Unit 1	Marketing (8/00)		£7.95	
Unit 2	Managing Financial Resources (8/02)		£7.95	
Unit 3	Organisations and Behaviour (8/00)		£7.95	
Unit 4	Organisations, Competition and Environment (8/02)		£7.95	
Unit 5	Quantitative Techniques for Business (8/02)		£7.95	
Unit 6	Legal and Regulatory Framework (8/02)		£7.95	
Unit 7	Management Information Systems (8/02)		£7.95	
Unit 8	Business Strategy (8/00)		£7.95	
Option				
Units 9-12	Business & Finance (8/02)		£10.95	
Units 13-16	Business & Management (1/01)		£10.95	
Units 17-20	Business & Marketing (1/01)		£10.95	
Unit 21-24	Business & Personnel (1/01)		£10.95	

Sub Total	£	

Postage & Packaging

UK : Course book £3.00 for first plus £2.00 for each extra	£
Europe : (inc. ROI) Course book £5.00 for first plus £4.00 for each extra	£
Rest of the world : Course book £20.00 for first plus £10.00 for each extra	£

Grand Total	£	

I enclose a cheque for £_____ (cheque to BPP Publishing Ltd) or charge to Access/VISA/Switch

Card number: ☐☐☐☐☐☐☐☐☐☐☐☐☐☐☐☐☐☐☐☐

Issues number (Switch only): _____

Start date: _____ Expiry date: _____

Signature _____

REVIEW FORM & FREE PRIZE DRAW

We are constantly reviewing, updating and improving our Course Books. We would be grateful for any comments or thoughts you have on this Course Book. Cut out and send this page to our Freepost address and you will be automatically entered in a £50 prize draw.

Pippa Riley
HNC/HND Range Manager
BPP Publishing Ltd, FREEPOST, London W12 8BR

Full name: _____

Address: _____

_____

_____ Postcode _____

Where are you studying?

Where did you find out about BPP range books?

Why did you decide to buy this Course Book?

Have you used our texts for the other units in your HNC/HND studies?

What thoughts do you have on our:

- Introductory pages

- Topic coverage

- Summary diagrams, icons, chapter roundups and quick quizzes

- Discussion topics, activities and assignments

The other side of this form is left blank for any further comments you wish to make.

Please give any further comments and suggestions (with page number if necessary) below.

FREE PRIZE DRAW RULES

1   Closing date for 31 January 2003 draw is 31 December 2002. Closing date for 31 July 2003 draw is 30 June 2003.

2   Restricted to entries with UK and Eire addresses only. BPP employees, their families and business associates are excluded.

3   No purchase necessary. Entry forms are available upon request from BPP Publishing. No more than one entry per title, per person. Draw restricted to persons aged 16 and over.

4   Winners will be notified by post and receive their cheques not later than 6 weeks after the relevant draw date.

5   The decision of the promoter in all matters is final and binding. No correspondence will be entered into.